THE KINGDOM AND THE QUR'AN

The Kingdom and the Qur'an

Translating the Holy Book of Islam in Saudi Arabia

Mykhaylo Yakubovych

OpenBook Publishers

https://www.openbookpublishers.com

©2024 Mykhaylo Yakubovych

This work is licensed under a Creative Commons Attribution-NonDerivative International (CC BY-ND 4.0) license. This license enables reusers to copy and distribute the material in any medium or format in unadapted form only, and only so long as attribution is given to the creator. The license allows for commercial use. Attribution should include the following information:

Mykhaylo Yakubovych, *The Kingdom and the Qur'an: Translating the Holy Book of Islam in Saudi Arabia*. Cambridge, UK: Open Book Publishers, 2024, https://doi.org/10.11647/OBP.0381

Further details about CC BY-ND licenses are available at http://creativecommons.org/licenses/by-nd/4.0/

All external links were active at the time of publication unless otherwise stated and have been archived via the Internet Archive Wayback Machine at https://archive.org/web

Any digital material and resources associated with this volume may be available at https://doi.org/10.11647/OBP.0381#resources

Global Qur'an Series Vol. 2.

ISSN (Print): 2753-8036
ISSN (Digital): 2753-8044

ISBN Paperback: 978-1-80511-176-4
ISBN Hardback: 978-1-80511-177-1
ISBN Digital (PDF): 978-1-80511-178-8
ISBN Digital eBook (EPUB): 978-1-80511-179-5
ISBN XML: 978-1-80511-180-1
ISBN HTML: 978-1-80511-181-8

DOI: 10.11647/OBP.0381

Cover image: Photograph by Mykhaylo Yakubovych (2023) of the Qur'an with a commentary published by King Fahd Qur'an Printing Complex (2019) and the Saheeh International Qur'an Translation (Riyadh, 2018).
Cover design: Jeevanjot Kaur Nagpal

Contents

A Note on the Author vii

Acknowledgements ix

Notes on Transliteration and Translation xi

Abbreviations xiii

Introduction 1

1. Twentieth-Century Debates on the Translatability of the Qur'an in the Middle East 9
   - Early Debates on Translatability at al-Azhar University 10
   - The Domestic Salafi Context: Wahhabi Hermeneutical Theory and Translation Activities Prior to the Age of Modernisation 21

2. The Muslim World League: A Forerunner to International Translational *daʿwa Networks* 35
   - The MWL: An Innovative Step in the International Promotion of Islam 35
   - The First Translations 37
   - (Dis)Approved for Publication: The First MWL Translation of the Qur'an into English 42
   - The MWL's Japanese Translation 44
   - The MWL's Turkish Translation 46
   - MWL Translations into African Languages 49
   - The MWL's Bulgarian Translation 51
   - Concluding Remarks 53

3. The Hilālī-Khān Translation: The First Interpretation of the Qur'an in a Foreign Language by Saudi Scholars 55
   - Al-Hilālī and His Legacy 56
   - The Background to the First Edition 58

The First Edition 64
The Second, Revised Edition(s): From Darussalam to the KFGQPC 71
The Third Edition: The KFGQPC Edition 77
The Hilālī-Khān Translation in Contemporary Islamic Discourse 84

4. The King Fahd Complex for the Printing of the Qur'an: A Turning Point in the History of Qur'an Translations 89
The Emergence of the KFGQPC 90
The First KFGQPC Translations 96
The KFGQPC Center for Translations: The Production of New Translations 111
Al-Tafsīr al-muyassar: The First Exegesis Designed for Use in Translation Projects 121
Newly Standardised Editions: Qur'an Translations Published After the Mid-1990s 131
The KFGQPC's Status as the Largest Producer of Qur'an Translations 143

5. Translation for Everyone: Collaborative Saudi Publishing Projects in Foreign Languages 147
The Qur'an in 'Turkistani': The First Foreign-Language Translation Produced in Saudi Arabia 148
The 'Saheeh International' Qur'an: A New 'Saudi' Team Translation into English 152
Private Publishers: Darussalam, the *Tafsīr al-ᶜushr al-akhīr Project*, the Noor International Center, and Others 160
Al-Mukhtaṣar fī tafsīr al-Qurʾān al-karīm: The Arabic Text and its Numerous Translations 172

Conclusion 177

Bibliography 185

Index 203

A Note on the Author

Mykhaylo Yakubovych (born 1986 in Ostroh, Ukraine) obtained his PhD in 2011 from The National University of Ostroh Academy with a study on interreligous relations in medieval Sunni traditionalism. Currently a member of the research team on the ERC-funded project 'GloQur—The Global Qur'an' (University of Freiburg, Germany), he studies Qur'an translations produced by international institutions and publishers, with a focus on Central Asian and Eastern European languages. He is the author of an annotated translation of the Qur'an into Ukrainian (first published in 2013), along with several books and translations from Arabic, and many research articles published in academic journals from the UK, Turkey, Saudi Arabia, and Australia. Yakubovych has conducted several academic projects on the Islamic manuscript heritage, including the post-classical intellectual history of the Crimean Khanate (at the Institute for Advanced Study, Princeton University, USA) and sixteenth-seventeenth century Qur'an interpretations produced by Lithuanian Tatars (at Nicolaus Copernicus University, Poland). His ORCID iD is 0000-0002-8305-1166.

Acknowledgements

This book owes its existence to a research project that received generous funding from the European Research Council (ERC) under the Horizon 2020 research and innovation program of the European Union (grant agreement n° 863650). I am deeply indebted to Professor Johanna Pink for extending her invitation to join the project, providing constant support, conducting meticulous reviews of various drafts of the manuscript of this volume, offering invaluable advice, and providing other forms of academic guidance that have been highly inspirational to me. I must also acknowledge the invaluable contributions of my colleagues on the GloQur team (Elvira Kulieva, Kamran Khan, and Yulianingsih Riswan), who have participated with me in numerous discussions, colloquia, and workshops that have helped shape many of the ideas presented in this book. I am also deeply thankful to the British Academy for organising my research stay at Coventry University, where I discussed some of my preliminary findings related to Muslim-Christian relations in Qur'an translations.

The list of people to whom I owe thanks would also be incomplete without mention of Dr V. Abdul Rahim, the head of the Translation Center at the King Fahd Glorious Qur'an Printing Complex, who not only provided me with a unique academic setting that was highly conducive to working on Qur'an translations but also shared his personal experience as a prolific author, editor, and translator during our meetings in Medina. I would also like to express my gratitude to the various people from Muslim organisations and communities who have helped me with contacts and sources, including those who have sent me specific translations, such as Ayşe Zuhal Sarı (of the Turkish Directorate of Religious Affairs in Ankara), Mehmet Timoshev (of the Sinan-Pasha Medrese in Istanbul), not to mention Abdallah Shisterov,

Musa Medvedev, and Artur Shevchenko (all graduates of the Islamic University of Madinah).

I would like to give special thanks to Dr Helen Blatherwick, the editor who worked with me to transfer the original project into English so as to make it available to a wider readership. Any mistakes or shortcomings that may exist in this work are solely my own responsibility.

Finally, publication of this book would not have been possible without funding from the University of Freiburg in Germany.

Notes on Transliteration and Translation

This book covers the recent history of Islam in Saudi Arabia and beyond. In addition to the Arabic sources quoted (using the transliteration system and standards established by the *International Journal of Middle East Studies*), plenty of material in other languages is cited as well. In an attempt to make the text as reader friendly as possible, words which are already in common usage in English (e.g., 'Qur'an', 'Sunni', 'Hanafi', and 'Salafism') are presented according to conventional spelling. These are only transliterated in the context of Arabic quotations. For all other non-Roman scripts, almost all of the sources quoted, and names of individuals and organisations, are presented using a simplified transcription system. Dates are normally referenced according to the Gregorian calendar (Hijri dates are given only when Gregorian are not stated in the source cited). For those persons and organisations that have an officially recognised English spelling, transliterated forms of their original names are provided only when necessary. All quotations of English translations of the Qur'an are presented verbatim (so, for example, the sometimes 'problematic' wording of the first edition of the Hilālī-Khān translation is replicated exactly), but additional explanations are provided where necessary.

Abbreviations

DITIB: Turkish-Islamic Union for Religious Affairs

IIIT: International Institute of Islamic Thought

IUM: Islamic University of Madinah

KFGQPC: King Fahd Glorious Qur'an Printing Complex

KSA: Kingdom of Saudi Arabia

MOIA: Ministry of Islamic Affairs, Call, and Guidance of the Kingdom of Saudi Arabia

MWL: Muslim World League

PCSRI: Permanent Committee for Scholarly Research and Ifta

TDRA: Turkish Directorate of Religious Affairs

TDV: Turkish Religious Foundation

WAMY: World Assembly of Muslim Youth

WICS: World Islamic Call Society

Introduction

What makes the governments and peoples of Arabic-speaking countries interested in the translation of the Qur'an? One might expect there to be a long tradition of interpreting the Qur'an in foreign languages, especially in non-Arabic speaking areas of the Muslim world (as well as a history of polemical or scholarly interest in interpreting the Qur'an from the West). However, one might reasonably *not* expect to see any significant developments in this field from Saudi Arabia, since the country is part of a region known not only for its cultivation of Arabic identity (so-called *ᶜurūba*) but also as a centre of the kind of religious fundamentalism usually associated with the Wahhabi/Salafi movement in Sunni Islam. Yet, nowadays, Saudi Arabia is the most important global actor in the production and distribution of Qur'an translations. The fact that the present-day approach to translation of the Qur'an involves something more than merely transcribing the Arabic text into another language might lead one to enquire how significant the contribution of these translations is to the modern intellectual history of Islam. The process of *translating* the Holy Book of Islam, which is sometimes and somehow equated to *interpreting* it, raises some important questions: Who reconstructs the meaning of the Qur'an for non-Arabic speakers and how? Why is this so important for modern Muslims? And, finally, who are the readers of these translations? The Qur'an, as the primary living textual source of Islam (which is recited, commented on, and, of course, translated), is one of the most important bases for contemporary Muslim religiosity, and around eighty percent of Muslims are not native speakers of Arabic and, thus, can access its meaning only through their own languages. The significance of such translations is heightened even more in situations where the state is directly involved in the process, becomes visible as both sponsor and interpreter of the text,

©2024 Mykhaylo Yakubovych, CC BY-ND 4.0 https://doi.org/10.11647/OBP.0381.00

and sanctions its publication and distribution via a state-approved or supported network of religious scholars or even institutions created specifically for this purpose.

Saudi Arabia provides perhaps the best example of how a Muslim-majority, Arab country has developed a Qur'an translation publishing industry. By studying the history and evolution of this industry, one can trace how Sunni Muslim perspectives on 'foreignisation' of the Qur'an changed during the twentieth century, including the establishment of specialised institutions to create and authorise Qur'an translations, the building of distribution networks, and the wider development of what could be rightly called a 'translation movement'. Since premodern Islamic scholarship in the Arabian Peninsula had no interest in translating the Qur'an for an internal readership (in contrast to non-Arabic-speaking areas like India, Central Asia, Persia, or Anatolia, with their long history of interlinear interpretations), this 'movement' is a twentieth-century phenomena—one which has become a major point of connection between modern print culture and contemporary Islamic theology.

The term 'translation movement' is used here to describe the complex and persistent efforts of individuals and institutions inside Saudi Arabia to produce translations of the Qur'an and to develop a more or less fixed 'hermeneutical standard' for those translations. That is, it refers to both the initial translation process and the secondary process of revising both new and pre-existing translations to conform to an approved set of standards. Some of the roots of this movement were closely tied to basic features of Salafi theology that generally treated non-Arabic renderings of the Qur'an as the 'translation of the meanings' [*tarjamat al-maᶜānī*]—a concept discussed in Chapter One. Some of the main underlying ideas held in Salafi Islam, such as the focus on returning to the sources, the Qur'an and Sunna and the concept of the re-orientation of Islam in accordance with the supposed righteous creed of the first Muslims who witnessed the revelation, have opened up a big window of opportunities for Saudi translators. Another opportunity came with the expansion of Islamic missionary activity, as this led to the political involvement of the Saudi state in religion, both of which were inextricably intertwined with the development of the Qur'an translation movement. The proactive, positive stance on Qur'an translation that was adopted by the state as part of its political effort to establish religious leadership in the Muslim world effectively closed off any avenue for opposition. In contrast to Egypt, where a powerful anti-translationist movement criticised anything labelled a 'translation' of the Qur'an, religious circles in Saudi Arabia very quickly recognised how useful translation could be as a tool for the promotion of Islam (or, rather, their specific 'Salafi' version of Islam) around the world. A complete understanding of this powerful trend in modern Muslim intellectual history, namely, an analysis of who publishes Qur'an translations in Saudi Arabia and why and how they do so will lead to a better understanding of how the Qur'an figures in the modern Muslim imagination as both a source of belief and a book of guidance for everyday life. On another level, it will also cast light on the role and use of religion as soft power in foreign relations and on how Saudi Arabia has tried, and continues to try, to position itself as the leading power in the Muslim world.

The complexity of the issues involved requires a specific kind of approach, not least due to the number of actors involved (translators, editors, publishers, the government, and non-government institutions). In this context, relevant studies on the bibliography of Qur'an translation include Muhammad Hamidullah's list of Qur'an translations published in European languages,[1] the IRCICA's *World Bibliography of Translations of the Meanings of the Holy Quran*,[2] and, among the more recent studies that relate to translations into individual languages, Kidwai's *Bibliography of the Translations of the Meanings of the Glorious Quran into English*.[3] However, more important to the analysis undertaken in this volume are a number of foundational works that treat the history and theoretical aspects of Qur'an translation, such as the problem of translatability, the visibility of the translator, and related discourses.[4] It is critical to look at

1 See the 'Liste des traductions du Coran en langues européennes', in Muhammad Hamidullah, *Le Saint Coran* (Paris: Club Francais du Livre, 1959), pp. xliii–lxvii.

2 İsmet Binark, Halit Eren, and Ekmeleddin İhsanoğlu, *World Bibliography of Translations of the Meanings of the Holy Qur'ān: Printed Translations, 1515–1980* (Istanbul: Research Centre for Islamic History, Art, and Culture, 1986).

3 Abdur Raheem Kidwai, *Bibliography of The Translations of The Meanings of The Glorious Quran into English: 1649–2002* (Medina: King Fahd Glorious Qur'an Printing Complex, 2007).

4 See, for example, the following studies on approaches to Qur'an translation: Bruce B. Lawrence, *The Koran in English: A Biography* (Princeton: Princeton University Press, 2017), https://doi.org/10.2307/j.ctvc773k4; Hussein Abdul-Raof, *Qur'an*

the translation from this perspective and go beyond simply examining how a given work interprets the Qur'an, to analyse why it was actually produced, why it favours one exegetical choice over another, and, finally, how the readership responds to the exegetical choices within the text. My approach is, thus, not confined to analysis of the linguistic features of the text (although this angle is also important) or the primary historical impetus behind the translation but also includes research into the translator as an agent who determines meaning, not to mention the influence of their sponsor(s), publisher(s), and editor(s). It is also worth mentioning at this point that sometimes Islamic publishers appear to want to render the translator ultimately invisible (often by overriding his or her personal authority by appointing someone else to 'approve' the translator-produced text. As we will see, this kind of subversion is common with translations produced in Saudi Arabia). Such internal discourses and tensions would remain completely opaque if one does not look beyond the surface to explore the driving forces that motivate and shape the translation in a formative way. At the time of writing, Saudi Arabia has produced Qur'an translations and interpretations in over one hundred languages. This fact alone makes it important to seek answers to the question: who translates the Qur'an in Saudi Arabia (or with Saudi support), how, and why? Moreover, what distinguishes these works from translations produced elsewhere, and how influential and extensive has been their impact on modern Islamic thought?

This study takes a three-pronged approach. It addresses the basic literary sources (that is, the translations themselves), explores the broad context of their production by undertaking historical research on specific developments in the field, and, finally, investigates the lives and biographies of some of the translators who have worked within the Saudi framework. This entailed a number of field studies, which I undertook during various research trips to Saudi Arabia between 2010

Translation: Discourse, Texture and Exegesis (London and New York: Routledge, 2001), https://doi.org/10.4324/9780203036990; Johanna Pink, 'Translation', in *The Routledge Companion to the Qur'an*, ed. by George Archer, Maria Dakake, and Daniel Madigan (London: Routledge, 2022), pp. 364–76, https://doi.org/10.4324/9781315885360-36; M. Brett Wilson, *Translating the Qur'an in an Age of Nationalism: Print Culture and Modern Islam in Turkey* (Oxford: Oxford University Press, 2014); Stefan Wild, 'Muslim Translators and Translations of the Qur'an into English', *Journal of Qur'anic Studies*, 17.3 (2015), 158–82, https://doi.org/10.3366/jqs.2015.0215

and 2012, primarily to the King Fahd Glorious Qur'an Printing Complex (KFGQPC) and the Islamic University of Madinah (IUM), which are the main think tanks that produce the translations. Other research has been conducted during visits to Turkey (to the libraries of various religious foundations in Istanbul), Azerbaijan, and the UK. This field work has been extremely helpful in arriving at an understanding of the revision and publishing processes involved in the production of Qur'an translations. In addition, it has allowed me to forge contacts with a wide number of private publishers and religious networks in Saudi Arabia, Turkey, and Iran whose work and output is also relevant to the research presented in the following pages.

Chapter One, 'Twentieth-Century Debates on the Translatability of the Qur'an in the Middle East', covers not only the period of the first debates over the translatability of the Qur'an in the Muslim world (primarily Egypt, Syria, and Iraq) during the early- and mid-twentieth century but also the local development of the 'translation movement' in the Saudi context. It discusses the significance to these debates of a corpus of religious texts by authors ranging from the twelfth-century thinker Ibn Taymiyya to later scholars from the eighteenth-century family of Muḥammad b. ʿAbd al-Wahhāb and how these came to form a kind of exegetical canon, both in essential terms (that is, what exactly should be interpreted) and textually (which sources are 'suitable' to do that with). This hermeneutics also incorporates the problem of translation [*tarjama*] and the limits of interpretation, for example, ideas about which meanings can be explained in Arabic and explicitly transferred to other languages. The chapter also briefly addresses foreign language learning in Saudi Arabia and modern developments in higher education there.

The second chapter, 'The Muslim World League: A Forerunner to International Translational *daʿwa* Networks', outlines the history and impact of one of the earliest Saudi Muslim organisations dedicated to translation, The Muslim World League (MWL), which was established in 1962. It traces the emergence of the idea of 'approved' or 'authorised' Muslim-authored translations of the Qur'an, originally in terms of the adoption and production of pre-existing translations, and later moving on to the commissioning of projects that led to new, bespoke translations. Although the Muslim World League only produced four completely new translations (if one does not count the translations produced as a result of some of its later collaborative projects), its activities represented the first instance of Saudi state intervention in Qur'an translation, motivated by both political and religious factors.

Chapter Three, 'The Hilālī-Khān Translation: The First Interpretation of the Qur'an in a Foreign Language by Saudi Scholars', provides the first comprehensive study of the textual history of this influential Qur'an translation into English— one which was first published in the USA in 1977 and prepared by scholars affiliated with the IUM at the time. The Hilālī-Khān translation provides a good illustrative example of how the original text of Qur'an translations can be subject to significant change in later editions, sometimes to the extent of completely changing the original and introducing new meanings that bear the hallmarks of a Salafi interpretation of the Qur'an. The Hilālī-Khān translation (particularly the later editions published by Darussalam and the KFGQPC) has also paved the way for a growing trend of '*tafsīr*isation' of translation, the idea that the core meanings of the Qur'an will not be understood 'properly' by the reader if it is not supplemented by the 'correct' (in its Salafi or mainstream-Sunni sense) classical interpretation [*tafsīr*]. This approach demonstrates the way that, in general, the Muslim tradition tends to view translation as a kind of commentary, seeing the translator (and also editor and publisher) as interpreters with the religious authority to undertake exegesis.

The fourth chapter, 'The King Fahd Complex Glorious Qur'an Printing Complex: A Turning Point in the History of Qur'an Translations', discusses a unique phenomenon in twentieth-century Muslim intellectual life: the creation of a special institution (in 1984) for the production, revision, and publication of translations. While a significant proportion of the translations published by the KFGQPC are merely revised editions of earlier works, the organisation has also produced more than fifty newly-prepared translations, some of which have become extremely influential in various parts of the Muslim world. Remaining a leading international actor in the field, the KFGQPC has become the gold standard for many Salafi readers of the translations, as well as a broad range of Sunni audiences, with its own set of regulations and requirements for its translations, in terms of both their content and formal features.

Finally, Chapter Five, 'Translation for Everyone: Collaborative Saudi Publishing Projects in Foreign Languages', explores individual and private publishing projects in Saudi Arabia, past and present. These range from standalone, one-off translations such as 'Saheeh International', one of the most widely distributed Qur'an translations in the English-speaking Muslim world; to those produced by commercial publishing projects such as Darussalam, which publishes in a range of languages; to missionary initiatives such as the *Tafsīr al-ᶜushr al-akhīr* project. Additionally, the chapter discusses some examples of how digitisation in the field of Islamic sources is changing the face of translation, rendering the translator less visible and promoting the production of a kind of multi-language translation which aims to provide the same reading and interpretation in every language.

This volume is not an attempt to provide an exhaustive bibliography of all the translations published in Saudi Arabia, nor a comprehensive biographical study of the translators themselves. Instead, it focuses on a select number of case studies with the aim of, for example, identifying any common background among translators and/or editors, their shared exegetical choices, as well as other features that are essentially related to the Salafi hermeneutic trend. A number of excellent studies have already covered the most essential features of Salafi exegetical traditions in modern Qur'an translations.[5] This volume will build on these to show that not every translation that appears from Saudi publishers is positioned as conforming to Salafi reading of the Qur'an; instead, many of them are positioned as mainstream Sunni works (which, in many cases, is fairly accurate). Such variation in interpretation also shows the complexity of what I denote as the 'translation movement'. It is also worth noting that the dynamics of Qur'an translation as a genre and a living field are changing and evolving, with more and more translations published every year. This means that the translation movement may yet experience some intriguing new turns: every translation published quickly passes into history, only to be rewritten with the publication of newer works.

5 See, for example: Johanna Pink, *Muslim Qur'anic Interpretation Today: Media, Genealogies and Interpretive Communities* (Bristol: Equinox, 2019), pp. 49–71, https://doi.org/10.1558/isbn.9781781797051; Massimo Campanini, *The Qur'an: Modern Muslim Interpretations*, trans. by Caroline Higgitt (London and New York: Routledge, 2010), pp. 8–20; Walid A. Saleh, 'Preliminary Remarks on the Historiography of *tafsīr* in Arabic: A History of the Book Approach', *Journal of Qur'anic Studies*, 12 (2010), 6–40, https://doi.org/10.3366/jqs.2010.0103

1. Twentieth-Century Debates on the Translatability of the Qur'an in the Middle East

On even the most cursory comparison of the history of Qur'an translation to that of other sacred books, one particular feature stands out: despite the fact that hundreds, if not thousands, of translations into more than 150 languages have already been printed, many Muslims still maintain that it is impossible to actually translate the Qur'an. Most translations published in the Islamic world begin their introductions by emphasising the notion of Qur'anic inimitability [*iʿjāz al-Qurʾān*], a theological concept used to argue against the validity of any 'translation' as such. This doctrinal stance dates back to the Early Medieval era, when interlinear translations of the Qur'an (at this time, usually treated as 'commentary') into Persian and Turkic languages became established practice, and is held into the present day.

In the context of the Islamic world, it was only relatively recently that a new kind of translation emerged, one that was presented independently from the Arabic original, as a standalone text. Such standalone, or independent, 'Muslim' translations (which usually still described themselves as 'translation(s) of the meanings' of the Qur'an to accord with the idea of Qur'anic *iʿjāz*) did not begin to appear until long after non-Muslims had begun publishing translations of the Qur'an in European languages. These were mainly produced by Western scholars in Islamic Studies or by Christian missionaries who used their translations as tools in their polemical disputes with Muslims. Some non-Arabic-speaking Muslim-majority countries (such as India or Persia), came round to the idea of standalone translations quite quickly, while in

©2024 Mykhaylo Yakubovych, CC BY-ND 4.0 https://doi.org/10.11647/OBP.0381.01

other areas (for example, the late Ottoman Empire and early Republican Turkey and, later, Egypt) this innovation was discussed and debated for much longer periods of time, as it will be shown below. Given the significance of these debates over the legality and legitimacy of Qur'an translation to the Saudi translation movement, this chapter delves into the Middle-Eastern scholarly network of the first half of the twentieth century, examining those who supported or discouraged translations of the Qur'an.

Early Debates on Translatability at al-Azhar University

Who was the first person in the Islamic world to translate the Qur'an? There are a number of topics that have been discussed by scholars since the ninth century that can help us to understand the difficulty involved in arriving at a definitive answer to this question. On the one hand, there is a well-established tradition of interlinear translations/interpretations into Persian and other 'Muslim' languages, which was developed mainly in the context of Sunni-Hanafi scholarship. On the other hand, treating translation as a text that is produced and read mostly independently from the original Arabic scripture is a phenomenon of modern book culture. It is no easy task to reconstruct the history of Qur'an translation into world languages, especially in terms of translations produced by Muslims; in general, however, it can be divided into two periods: before and after the turn of the twentieth century.

As mentioned above, debates over the translatability of the Qur'an emerged first in the Indian subcontinent, Egypt, and the late Ottoman Empire/Republic of Turkey. In the geographical area covered by present-day India, Pakistan, and Iran, the tradition of interlinear translations reached its peak in the eighteenth century with the publication by the reformist Indian scholar Shāh Walī Allāh Dihlawī (1703–1762) of his *Fatḥ al-Raḥmān bi-tarjamat al-Qurʾān* [Inspiration from the Merciful in the translation of the Qur'an] (1738). Both this and its Persian translation were the inspiration for further likeminded endeavours in the field. The bilingual edition of Dihlawī's work, which appeared in 1743, played a particularly significant role in shaping future translations of the Qur'an and was especially influential among mainstream Sunnis.[1] Over a century later, it would also be an important work for the Ahmadi school, who printed their edition of Muhammad Ali's translation of the Qur'an into English in India in 1917.

What was the situation at that time in the Arabic-speaking parts of the Muslim world, where obviously there was no need for Qur'an translations? It would be unreasonable to expect the eighteenth-century Wahhabi movement to have taken a position on the issue of translation, given that its influence was then limited to the Arabian Peninsula. Yet, the legacy of Shāh Walī Allāh Dihlawī (who translated the Qur'an into Persian) is often compared to that of Muḥammad b. ᶜAbd al-Wahhāb (1703–1791), the eponym of the Salafi/Wahabbi school, since they

> shouldered the same mission, namely, to purify Islam and realise its basic teachings as they understood them. Yet, the different backgrounds and social settings that they experienced, as well as the dissimilar challenges that they faced, triggered different visions, approaches, and responses.[2]

Although some attempts have been made to find a connection between Dihlawī and Muḥammad b. ᶜAbd al-Wahhāb (mostly via their common teacher, Muḥammad Ḥayyāt al-Sindī), there is no evidence that they knew each other or that either had any influence on the other.[3] It seems that the beginnings of Salafi theology (including perspectives on Qur'anic hermeneutics) were primarily rooted in the domestic context of local scholarly networks, rather than being influenced by external sources.

The situation, however, changed much during the twentieth century and the development of Saudi religious scholarship during this period has been widely connected to other centres of learning, especially Egypt. Recent, in-depth studies on the translation of the Qur'an in Turkey by

---

1 See Muhammad Qasim Zaman, 'Shāh Walī Allāh of Delhi, His Successors, and the Qurʾān', in *Ways of Knowing Muslim Cultures and Societies*, ed. by Bettina Gräf, Birgit Krawietz, and Schirin Amir-Moazami (Leiden: Brill, 2019), pp. 280–97, https://doi.org/10.1163/9789004386891

2 Hassan Ahmed Ibrahim, 'Shaykh Muḥammad ibn ᶜAbd al-Wahhāb and Shāh Walī Allāh: A Preliminary Comparison, Some Aspects of their Lives and Careers', *Asian Journal of Social Science*, 34.1 (2006), 103–19 (p. 117).

3 Basheer M. Nafi, 'A Teacher of Ibn ᶜAbd al-Wahhāb: Muḥammad Ḥayāt al-Sindī and the Revival of *Ashāb al-Hadīth*'s Methodology', *Islamic Law and Society*, 13.2 (2006), 103–18, http://doi.org/10.1163/156851906776917552.

M. Brett Wilson[4] and discussions on the translatability of the Qur'an in Egypt by Travis Zadeh[5] provide an overview of the ongoing debates that ultimately resulted in the appearance of the concept of *tarjamat al-maʿānī,* or 'translation of the meanings'. Supporters of the idea of Qur'an translation, such as the Shaykh [principal scholar] of al-Azhar, Muḥammad b. Muṣṭafā al-Marāghī (1881–1945), contributed to the development of this concept. By summarising their positions, we can identify a few key milestones in the development of Qur'anic translation.

We know that preliminary discussions of the issue of translation had already begun in 1908, as the well-known Egyptian proponent of Islamic reform Rashīd Riḍā (1865–1935) published in his newspaper, *al-Manār*, a fatwa under the title *'Ḥukm tarjamat al-Qurʾān'* ['A statement on the translation of the Qur'an'].[6] An Islamic scholar from Imperial Russia, Aḥsan Shāh Aḥmad, had asked him about some 'Russian Turks' who were challenging the 'prohibition' on Qur'an translation and had started to publish it part by part [*tadrījan*] in the city of Kazan. Riḍā condemned this endeavour,[7] as did many other scholars of his time, from Muṣṭafā Ṣabrī (1869–1954), the last Shaykh al-Islām of the Ottoman Empire, to the influential Azhari scholars Muḥammad Ḥabīb Shākir (1866–1939) and Muḥammad al-Aḥmadī al-Ẓawāhirī (1887–1944).[8] These scholars were critical of any attempts to publish a translation of the Qur'an itself or even a translation of its meanings. Their position was motivated not only by the fight against the modernist movement that was taking place among religious scholars in a quickly changing scholastic environment but also by the association of the Qur'an translation movement with anti-Arab nationalism and secularism (that is, the 'Kemalism' of the Turkish

4 M. Brett Wilson, *Translating the Qur'an in an Age of Nationalism: Print Culture and Modern Islam in Turkey* (Oxford: Oxford University Press, 2014).

5 Travis Zadeh, 'The *Fātiḥa* of Salmān al-Fārisī and the Modern Controversy over Translating the Qurʾān', in *The Meaning of the Word: Lexicology and Qur'anic Exegesis*, ed. by Stephen Burge (Oxford: Institute of Ismaili Studies/Oxford University Press, 2015), pp. 375–420.

6 Rashīd Riḍā, *'Ḥukm tarjamat al-Qurʾān', al-Manār, 4:11 (1908), 269.*

7 Later in the 1930s, Riḍā took more favourable position on the Qur'an translation. See Johanna Pink, 'Riḍā, Rashīd', in *Encyclopaedia of the Qurʾān*, https://referenceworks.brillonline.com/entries/encyclopaedia-of-the-quran/*-EQCOM_050503#d110807225e792

8 Mykhaylo Yakubovych, 'Qur'an Translations into Central Asian Languages: Exegetical Standards and Translation Processes', *Journal of Qur'anic Studies*, 24.1 (2022), 89–115, https://doi.org/10.3366/jqs.2022.0491

Republican leader Mustafa Kemal Pasha) and, especially in the 1920s and 1930s, the rising influence of Ahmadi translations of the Qur'an.[9]

Without going into the details of the debates of the 1920s and 1930s, the general point can be made that the 'pro-translation' camp finally won out. Al-Marāghī's influential position as the shaykh of al-Azhar (he was initially appointed in 1928 but dismissed the following year; he returned to the office in 1936) played a big part in this. Already in an ongoing dispute with one of his biggest opponents, Muḥammad al-Aḥmadī al-Ẓawāhirī (an active critic of the idea of Qur'anic translatability), al-Marāghī recognised the necessity of translating the Qur'an into other languages as early as the 1920s and wrote his first treatise on this issue in 1932 (although it was not published until four years later). This work, entitled *Baḥth fī tarjamat al-Qurʾān al-karīm wa-aḥkāmuhā* [A study of the translation of the Qur'an and its rules], served as a response to the ongoing debate. In it, he concluded that the Qur'an has to be not only interpreted but also translated in a literal fashion [*tarjama ḥarfiyya*] and that, for the vast majority of verses, this would be eminently possible.[10] He argued that translation should be separated from interpretation as much as possible and referred to as *maᶜānī al-Qurʾān* [the meanings of the Qur'an] rather than as the Qur'an itself—a concept which has been consistently reiterated in every Muslim translation of the Qur'an up to the present day.

Al-Marāghī maintained that some verses—those not subject to debate by *tafsīr* scholars—can be translated 'literally', while others require varying degrees of explanation and discussion [*tarjama maᶜnawiyya*]. He thus upheld the concept that Qur'an translations cannot lay claim to Qur'anic *iᶜjāz*, nor replicate its rhetorical features, but took the stance that its meanings must be opened up for all mankind, insisting that 'the Qur'an was not revealed for the Arabs only, but for all the people in the world'.[11] Ultimately, al-Marāghī concluded that, 'there is no other way to convey the Message [...] than using translation'. In addition to addressing the issue of Qur'anic *iᶜjāz* and translation, al-Marāghī also discussed the

---

9 Moch Nur Ichwan, 'Differing Responses to an Ahmadi Translation and Exegesis: The Holy Qurʾân in Egypt and Indonesia', *Archipel*, 62 (2001), 143–61.

10 al-Marāghī, *Baḥth fī tarjamat al-Qurʾān al-karīm wa-aḥkāmuhā* (Cairo: Maṭbaᶜat al-Raghāʾib, 1936), p. 31.

11 Ibid., p. 35.

role of the Arabic language and its 'sanctity' [*qudsiyya*]: taking a kind of Pan-Arabist view, he asked 'How can we make all the nations Arabised [...] if they cannot comprehend the meanings of the Qur'an in their own language[s]?'. It seems that, for al-Marāghī, translating the Qur'an was one of the starting points for Islamic reform, as he believed it would help make both Islamic and Arabic identity 'simultaneously global'.[12] His efforts to promote Qur'an translation appear to have eventually gained institutional support, as a special committee on Qur'an translation was established at al-Azhar in 1936. However, when Muhammad Marmaduke Pickthall (1875–1936), a British convert to Islam and one of the first Muslim European translators of the Qur'an, visited Egypt in 1929 and met with al-Marāghī and other scholars, he was unable to gain their approval for his draft translation. 'The approval or the condemnation of Al-Azhar, or indeed of all the Ulama of Egypt, could not help or injure my translation much [...] Al-Azhar is a great historic institution which one would wish to see reformed and not demolished', writes Pickthall.[13] He goes on to reveal some of the reasons why a particular Egyptian scholar criticised his *The Meaning of the Glorious Qur'an* after it was first published in 1930:

> I have translated Surah XVII, v.29, thus: 'And let not thy hand be chained to thy neck nor open it with a complete opening lest thou sit down rebuked, denuded'. He considers that, by thus translating the Arabic words literally, I have turned a commandment relating to miserliness and generosity into a commandment concerning the position of a man's hands! How should he know that we speak of 'open-handedness' and 'tight-fistedness' in English and that every English reader will understand my literal translation in precisely the same sense in which the Arabic reader understands the Arabic text. The ban is therefore based upon an altogether false assumption.[14]

Perhaps the most significant development of the time was the appearance of the idea of translation as a collective or, rather, institutional act—one overseen and produced by an institution with perceived religious authority, such as al-Azhar. The committee on translation formed by al-Marāghī just after he came to office as Shaykh of al-Azhar for the

12 Ibid.
13 Qtd. in Anne Fremantle, *Loyal Enemy* (London: Hutchinson & Co, 1938), p. 419.
14 Ibid.

second time in 1936 established a list of eleven rules for the translation of the Qur'an, which were published in the official university journal *al-Azhar* (the following year these same 'rules' also appeared in the Egyptian literary journal *al-Risāla*).[15] These rules seem to constitute the first official set of guidelines for translating the Qur'an, still described as 'the explanation of the meanings of the Qur'an into a foreign language'. From this list, it is apparent that the committee proposed to first draft a work in Arabic that explained the meaning of the Qur'an, and then to translate this into various foreign languages (*'tafsīr al-Qurʾān al-karīm* [...] *tamhīdan li-l-tarjamat maᶜānīhī'* [the interpretation/explanation of the Qur'an [...] is the source that leads to the translation of its meanings]). This official recognition of the term 'translation of the meanings' seems to denote some kind of compromise between the two camps, and the rules set out in *al-Azhar* do not relate to exegetical reasoning but, rather, address problems of text representation and accessibility. Some of the rules direct translators to avoid using specialised scientific terms or referring to any 'scientific theories' in their interpretation of the text, in what seems to be a reaction to the growing trend of scientism in the Muslim world. The committee also recommended excluding any reference to the *madhāhib fiqhī* [legal schools] or *madhāhib kalāmī* [theological schools]. Other rules propose the use of only the Ḥafṣ *ᶜan* ᶜAṣim variant of Qur'an reading (that is, translations should make reference to other texts only 'when necessary') as well as the use of the clearest and simplest wording when reproducing the meaning of the verses. The guidelines also advise that all translations should include an introduction that highlighted the main Qur'anic themes, such as 'the call to God, legislation, stories, and polemics'. Last but not least, they advocate the use of a *ḥadīth*-based exegesis, which entails the use of interpretations that are transmitted as approved traditions [*al-maʾthūr*], 'that which is already accepted'.[16] Thus, we see with these rules a kind of universalisation of Qur'anic textuality being brought into play. It seeks, first of all, to situate the scripture in time, specifically through the avoidance of 'modern' readings and, secondly, to transcend the interpretive confines of any specific legal school. This process of

15 'Aḥkām al-tarjama', *Risāla*, 184 (1937), 3–4 (p. 4).

16 See Muhammad al-Zurqānī, *Manāhil al-ᶜirfān fī ᶜulūm al-Qurʾān*, 4 vols (Beirut: Dār al-Kitāb al-ᶜArabī, 1995), ii, p. 171.

universalisation also fits in with the broad concept of Islamic unity, by promoting only 'well-established' meanings that are (presumably) consistent with the idea of a common, but unspecified, Islamic creed: it could be 'pan-Islamic' in some way, or specifically 'Sunni' or 'Shii', for example.

In some ways, al-Azhar's rules also echo the ideas of another scholar from al-Azhar, the main editor of its official press, Muḥammad Farīd Wajdī (1878–1954). A prominent intellectual and polymath who authored books on many subjects, from history to *tafsīr*, he was educated in the French school system in Egypt and so was more or less familiar with ideas in circulation in Western education systems. Siding with al-Marāghī and his supporters, Wajdī published a treatise in 1936 called 'Scientific Proofs on the Permissibility of Translating the Meanings of the Qur'an into Foreign Languages', which was issued as an appendix to *al-Azhar*.[17] For Wajdī, 'the aims of the Qur'an' [*maqāṣid al-Qurʾān*] that should be represented in a translation are: 'the establishment of the authority of reason, the propagation of freedom of thought [*ḥurriyat al-niẓār*], and the destruction of the idol of imitation [*taqlīd*]'. Moreover, his treatise is a plea for 'general equality [*al-musāwā al-ʿāmma*] between all people [... and] the destruction of national and linguistic borders in the service of human unity'.[18] This and other such statements calling for the establishment of a 'state of truth' [*dawlat al-ḥaqq*] and 'permanent progress in knowledge and action' evince a socialist leaning that was quite popular among Egyptian intellectuals of those times.[19] All of these ideas were synthesised in Wajdī's promotion of the ideas of a 'return to the original roots of Islam' and the concept that translation of the Qur'an is the only way to present the true message of Islam to humanity. Wajdī argues that translation undertaken according to the technique proposed by his colleagues at al-Azhar would the most effective way to perform *daʿwa*, that is, missionary activity. Furthermore, when addressing the question of why books on Islam and the Qur'an cannot substitute for translations of the scripture, Wajdī shows quite a strong understanding

17 Muḥammad Farīd Wajdī, *al-Adilla al-ʿilmiyya ʿalā jawāz tarjamat maʿānī al-Qurʾān ilā al-lughāt al-ajnabiyya* (Cairo: Maṭbaʿat al-Maʿāhid al-Dīniyya, 1936).

18 Ibid., p. 3.

19 A good example of such ideas can be found in Mayy Ziyādah, 'al-Musāwwāh' [The Equality], which first appeared in the journal *al-Muqtaṭaf* in 1922. For a modern edition, see Ziyādah, *al-Musāwwāt* (Cairo: Hindāwī, 2013).

of a Western readership as he explains why 'missionary treatises' are insufficient: firstly, Christian readers already have the same level of prejudice against this type of publication as Muslims do against Christian missionary pamphlets; secondly, the use of such treatises means that Christians can accuse Muslims of imitating their own evangelical methods among Islamic peoples; and, thirdly, 'contemporary people cannot be persuaded by things which are no more than a kind of means [...] they want something to come from the primary sources directly'.[20] So, in Wajdī's ideas about Qur'an translation, we can see support for not only the activity of translation itself but also its primary orientation towards *daᶜwa* at a time that coincides with an era of reform within Egypt.

In the light of this, members of the 'modernist' movement who were affiliated with al-Azhar seem to have used the idea of translating the Qur'an as a way to make the University and its scholarly network globally relevant, so that it represented the Islamic tradition in a way that was meaningful to both East and West. Unsurprisingly, the responses and theories developed in Egypt during this time of modernisation strengthened nationalist feelings and the hope for real self-government and independence from foreign rule, especially after 1936 with the signing of the Anglo-Egyptian Treaty.[21]

When did support for the idea of the Qur'an's translatability finally become the predominant opinion in the Middle East? Following the discussions that took place the 1920s and 1930s, Qur'an translations had to be integrated into the traditional learning discourse, specifically into the voluminous books on the *ᶜulūm al-Qurʾān* [the sciences of the Qur'an] which were used as text books in intermediate and higher Islamic education. One of the best-known of these is the *Manāhil al-ᶜirfān fī ᶜulūm al-Qurʾān* [Sources of Knowledge in the Qur'anic Sciences], first published in 1943. Written by Muḥammad al-Zurqānī, a graduate of al-Azhar, several years earlier, this four-volume book is one of the most important twentieth-century contributions to the field of Qur'anic translation studies. Reprinted dozens of times since its first edition, *Manāhil al-ᶜirfān* remains an influential work and is especially

20 Wajdī, *al-Adilla al-ᶜilmiyya*, p. 7.
21 See Anthony Eden and Moustapha el-Nahas, 'Anglo-Egyptian Treaty of Alliance, 1936', *Current History*, 22.128 (1952), 231–39.

interesting for our purposes because its second volume contains a fairly long chapter entitled '*Fī tarjamat al-Qurʾān wa-ḥukmihā tafṣīlan*' [On the translation of the Qur'an and details of the rules for this].[22] There, the author summarises earlier debates on the subject but also proposes his own strategic vision for Qur'anic translation, which includes many innovative points.

Al-Zurqānī demonstrates a vast knowledge as he discusses the various languages into which the Qur'an has already been translated, both European and Asian. Seeming to take a personal interest in the topic, he mentions thirty-five translations that he considers to have been produced by 'the enemies of Islam' or 'false friends'.[23] He also reveals that the basis of the historical data about the first Latin translations and some missionary works were manuscript copies of the lectures of Viscount Philippe de Tarrazi (1865–1956), a polymath and philanthropist, founder of the National Library of Lebanon, and founding member of the Arab Academy of Damascus.[24] This reference shows Al-Zurqānī's acquaintance with Christian scholarship in Arabic, but he was also influenced by the writings and thought of Abū ʿAbd Allāh al-Zanjānī (1892–1941), a jurist, exegete, and prolific Iranian writer.[25] In 1935, al-Zanjānī had published a short work in Arabic called *Tārīkh al-Qurʾān* [The History of the Qur'an], which closed with a discussion of existing translations of the Qur'an into European languages. Although he did not directly address the question of the permissibility of translating the Holy Book of Islam, he did describe the first Latin translation of the Qur'an and its various editions, as well as the contributions made to the study of the Qur'an by European Orientalists such as the German scholar Theodor Nöldeke (al-Zanjānī actually used the term *afranj* to describe Nöldeke, which literally means 'Frenchmen', but it seems he used this term to refer to all 'Westerners').[26] Notably, al-Zanjānī was himself Shii, but he travelled widely throughout the Sunni world and

22 al-Zurqānī, *Manāhil al-ʿirfān*, ii, pp. 88–135.
23 Ibid., ii, pp. 92–95.
24 Ibid., ii, p. 89. For more on Tarrazi, see 'Viscount Philippe de Tarrazi', http://dbpedia.org:8891/page/Philippe_de_Tarrazi
25 See Seyyed Jaʿfar Sajjadi, 'Abū ʿAbd Allāh al-Zanjānī', trans. by Nacim Pak, in *Encyclopaedia Islamica*, ed. by Farhad Daftary and Wilferd Madelung, https://dx.doi.org/10.1163/1875-9831_isla_COM_0034
26 Abū ʿAbd Allāh al-Zanjānī, *Tārīkh al-Qurʾān* (Cairo: Lajnat al-Taʾlīf wa-l-Tarjama wa-l-Nashr, 1935), pp. 70–72.

lectured at al-Azhar in the mid-1930s, and it is fair to say that his thought provided a new paradigm of Islamic unity and revival. *Tārīkh al-Qurʾān,* which enjoyed wide circulation among both Sunni and Shii scholars, described the legacy of Qur'an in a historical, rather than a theological, way for the first time. It is possible that al-Zanjānī's innovative approach was inspired by Nöldeke's *Geschichte des Qorâns* [History of the Qur'an], which was first published in 1860.[27]

Starting his own discussion on the permissibility of the translation of the Qur'an with a long quote from al-Zanjānī on Latin Qur'an translations, al-Zurqānī argues that the time has come to respond to all the doubts and misconceptions that surround the issue of translation. He seems to have perceived the need for further clarity and ruling [*ḥukm*] on this well-known problem. For, after examining the meaning of the word *tarjama* [translation], he divides translation into two kinds: 'literal' and 'explanatory' [*ḥarfiyya wa-māʿnawiyya*]. Al-Zurqānī defines the first as the kind of interpretation where the word order is observed and the words in the new, target language are selected because they are synonyms for those in the original, source language; he defines the second as the expression of the 'aims' of a text on the level of 'the beauty of its imagination' [*ḥusn al-taṣwīr*].[28] To illustrate his latter point, he takes the example of Q. 17:29, exactly the same verse that was previously employed against Muhammad Marmaduke Pickthall: 'And let not thy hand be chained to thy neck'. Al-Zurqānī explains that a 'literal' translation would not convey the correct image and meaning to the reader, whereas an 'explanatory' interpretation—one that clarified that this Arabic expression refers to avarice—would work better.[29] With this, he corroborated the view of Azhari scholars who had already identified this verse as an example that perfectly illustrated the impossibility of translating the Qur'an literally.

Al-Zurqānī then sets out the pros and cons of translating the Qur'an and draws up his own list of four rules for interpreting the Qur'an in

---

27 Al-Zurqānī used a later edition: Theodor Nöldeke, *Geschichte des Qorāns* (Leipzig: Dieterich, 1909).

28 al-Zurqānī, *Manāhil al-ʿirfān*, ii, p. 99.

29 The meaning of the verse relies on the idea that the hands of ungenerous people, because they are not extended to others, seem to be 'chained' to their neck.

other languages. Translations 'literal or explanatory', he states, should be based on:

1. Translators' knowledge of the lexicography of both the source and target languages;
2. Translators' familiarity with the stylistic and other features of both languages;
3. Aims to achieve full correspondence between the meanings of the source text and the translation; and
4. Aims to produce a target text that is 'independent' from the original, so a reader is able to read and understand the translation as a text in its own right.

The last rule is the most innovative: it proposes, for the first time, that a translation of the Qur'an should be able to be read as a standalone and self-sufficient text rather than as accompaniment comparable to *tafsīr* sources. This provides clear evidence of an established concept of treating translations as independent works, as opposed to interlinear explanations or some other kind of auxiliary text. Al-Zurqānī insists that 'independent form' [*istiqlāliyya*] is one of the main differences between a translation [*tarjama*] and an interpretation [*tafsīr*], and he makes the point that translation 'generally conveys basic meanings fully as well as their aims' while interpretation can work only as more or less profound 'clarification' [*iḍāḥ*] of parts of the source text, depending on the aims and skill of the interpreter.

In this context, al-Zurqānī builds a kind of hermeneutical theory that distinguishes between two kinds of meanings in the Qur'an: 'primary' meanings do not vary from one language to another, but 'secondary' ones do.[30] He clarifies this distinction with examples taken from *Sūrat al-Fātiḥa*, the first part of the Qur'an. Al-Zurqānī suggests that the original text's statements about the oneness of God [*tawḥīd*] and about God's promise of mercy to believers and disgrace to unbelievers can be effectively conveyed through either translation or *tafsīr* [*interpretation*]. These, therefore, are 'primary meanings' engendered by the 'aims' of the Qur'an. Likening this type to the skyline or horizon to emphasise

30 al-Zurqānī, *Manāhil al-ʿirfān*, ii, pp. 110–12.

their constancy, he describes 'secondary meanings' as 'deep sea covered by waves, within which knowledge of God and the greatness of His divinity manifests itself'.[31]

Al-Zurqānī's *Manāhil al-ʿirfān* develops the opinions of Azhari scholars in a new way. It proposes that the Qur'an could be translated, that its content could be accessed in another language, and that this interpretation is understood to take the form of a self-sufficient text. Perhaps most importantly, al-Zurqānī's work paved the way for translation to become a powerful tool for *daʿwa* [missionary activity], as we shall soon see. His writings represent the peak of the translation movement in Egypt of the late 1930s and early 1940s, and *Manāhil al-ʿirfān* influenced nearly all subsequent work on Qur'anic translation.[32] These discussions on Qur'anic translatability made their way from Egypt to Saudi Arabia during the same period and began to bear fruit in the following decades. However, despite theoretical innovations in the field, Egypt's al-Azhar focused in the early 1960s not on the translation of the Qur'an itself but, rather, that of *tafsīr* [accompanying interpretation]. This project was later realised in *al-Muntakhab fi tafsīr al-Qurʾān al-karīm* [Selected Commentaries on the Noble Qur'an] (1961) and its subsequent translations into English, German, Indonesian, Spanish, and Russian.[33]

The Domestic Salafi Context: Wahhabi Hermeneutical Theory and Translation Activities Prior to the Age of Modernisation

The reference materials used in debates surrounding the translatability of the Qur'an in the Egyptian context were primarily Hanafi legal sources, although some other texts were brought in later. For example, al-Zurqānī also quoted writers in the Shafii and Maliki traditions (respectively, al-Ghazālī and al-Shāṭibī). These scholars were not generally opposed

31 al-Zurqānī, *Manāhil al-ʿirfān*, ii, p. 97.

32 Demonstrating its ongoing influence, al-Zurqānī's book was published in a second edition by Dār Iḥyāʾ al-Kutub al-ʿArabiyya in 1952, and numerous copies were reprinted in 1953, 1954, and later years.

33 See 'Mashrūʿ tarjamat al-Qurʾān', *al-Hilāl* (1960), pp. 12–13. The *tafsīr* itself was first published by al-Azhar in 1381/1961. On its later translation, see *al-Muntakhab fī tafsīr al-Qurʾān al-karīm* (Cairo: al-Majlis al-Aʿlā li-l-Shuʾūn al-Islāmiyya, 1381/1961).

to the reproduction of Qur'anic meanings in other languages, but they did establish some limits, such as the impermissibility of interpreting the divine names. Further development of the translation movement, especially in Saudi Arabia, however, was shaped by the Hanbali school.

Historically, the Hanbali school has predominated in Arabic-speaking areas of the Muslim world and, as such, was largely unconcerned with discussions on the translation or explanation of the Qur'an in other languages. One of its thirteenth-century proponents, Ibn Qudāma, exemplifies this thinking. In *Kitāb al-Mughnī* (c. 1223), he prohibits recitation of the Qur'an in languages other than Arabic and urges people to learn Arabic if they are unable to read it, stating that, otherwise, 'prayer is not valid'.[34] Hanbalite teachings became implicated in the translation movement in the nineteenth century, however, because they constituted the primary legal foundation of the modern Salafi tradition, which emerged at that time. The first scholar to address the issue of the translation of the Qur'an was an authority working within the older Salafi tradition, Ibn Taymiyya (1263–1328). Recent researchers understand his theoretical views on language to describe a 'radical hermeneutics' and a kind of 'linguistic philosophy'.[35] Seeking to determine the origin of meaning, Ibn Taymiyya presented 'a fairly well developed defence of the thesis that the meaning of words arose out of their use and that the veridical/metaphorical dichotomy was fundamentally flawed'.[36] This and several other of his ideas merit attention here because they influenced the later development of the translation movement in Salafi scholarship.

In *al-Radd ᶜalā-l-manṭiqiyyin* [Refutation of the Logicians] (1263), Ibn Taymiyya critiques Aristotelian formal logic and, in doing so, offers insightful commentary on the translation of meaning. He delves into the question of how an imaginative concept [*taṣawwūr*] originates from the basic utterance of a word [*lafẓ*] 'if uttered in another

34 Ibn Qudāma, *Kitāb al-Mughnī*, 15 vols (Riyadh: Dār ᶜAlām al-Kutub, 1997), i, p. 526. Despite taking this stance, Ibn Qudāma was not against the use of non-Arabic *tafsīrs* to explain the Qur'an's meaning.

35 Walid Saleh, 'Ibn Taymiyya and the Rise of Radical Hermeneutics: An Analysis of an Introduction to the Foundations of Qur'anic Exegesis', in *Ibn Taymiyya and His Times*, ed. by S. Ahmed and Y. Rapoport (Oxford: Oxford University Press, 2010), 123–62; Abdul Rahman Mustafa, 'Ibn Taymiyya & Wittgenstein on Language', *The Muslim World*, 108.3 (2018), 465–91, https://doi.org/10.1111/muwo.12251

36 Rahman Mustafa, p. 488.

language'.[37] Comprehending the process of translation [*tarjama*] as a transfer of meanings between two languages, Ibn Taymiyya suggests that the translator [*mutarjim*] should know both languages well. Like al-Zurqānī', he distinguishes between two levels of meaning that require different methods of transference. Ibn Taymiyya identifies some 'basic concepts'—such as 'bread', 'water', 'meals', 'drinks', 'heaven', 'earth', 'night', 'day', 'sun', 'moon', etc.—that have conceptual consonancy in different languages. Many other words, however, 'can be translated only according to their approximate meaning'.[38]

Ibn Taymiyya turns to religious vocabulary to demonstrate his theory. Some basic religious concepts, he argues, can be adequately explained through others. He offers as example the phrase *al-ṣirāṭ al-mustaqīm* ['the right way'] (Q. 1:6), advising that this can be interpreted as 'Islam', 'adherence to the Qur'an', 'obedience to Allah and His messenger', and 'useful knowledge and good actions'. Ibn Taymiyya also advances the idea that all terms used 'in the Qur'an and Sunna' can be divided into three categories: (1) words such as 'sun' and 'moon' that can be known easily; (2) legal terms such as *ṣalāt* and *ḥajj*; and (3) words such as 'marriage' [*nikāḥ*], 'bargain' [*biʾya*], and 'debt' [*qabḍ*], which fall into the category of social practice or 'tradition' [*ʿurf*].[39] When explaining those concepts in another language, the meaning of the original can be conveyed through the use of 'particularisation' or 'description' [*waṣf*], in other words, by the use of equivalent examples or synonyms. Ibn Taymiyya, then, generally believed that translation is plausible, that terms in different languages are able to convey the same meaning. Even as *al-Radd ʿalā-l-manṭiqiyyīn* lays out this hermeneutical theory, it remains silent as to whether Ibn Taymiyya himself believed in its applicability to the Qur'an. Did he understand the scripture as a text like any other that, according to his views, can be translated?

For insight into this question, we must look to another of Ibn Taymiyya's works, a treatise named *Naqḍ al-manṭiq* [A Criticism of Logic], which was not published until 1951.[40] The subject of Qur'an

37 Ibn Taymiyya, *al-Radd ʿalā-l-manṭiqiyyīn* (Beirut: al-Rayān, 2005), p. 90.
38 Ibid., p. 95.
39 Ibid., p. 94.
40 Those who brought *Naqḍ al-manṭiq* to light were the Egyptian editor Muḥammad Ḥamīd al-Fiqī and two Saudi scholars, Muḥammad b. ʿAbd al-Razzāq Hamza and Sulaymān b. ʿAbd al-Raḥmān. Al-Fiqī was an active proponent of the Salafi

translation is mentioned in its introduction, and one of its chapters is entitled '*Jawāz tarjamat al-Qurʾān ilā ghayr al-lugha al-ʿarabiyya wa-kāyfiyyat dhālika*' [The permissibility of translating the Qur'an into non-Arabic language, and how to do it].[41] However, both of these parts were penned not by Ibn Taymiyya but by the book's editors, who openly position themselves as supporters of 'the Salafi creed' and want to claim that Ibn Taymiyya had nothing against the translation of the Qur'an. They explain that the publication is based on a manuscript copy of the text dating from 1783 and preserved in the Maḥmūdiyya Library in Medina. A more recent editor has suggested that this copy was at the disposal of earlier scholars.[42] The manuscript also contains references to other copies, which may mean that it was, at some time, viewed as an integral part of a collection of legal treatises. Thus, we can assume that Ibn Taymiyya's text was known to many Salafi-Wahhabi scholars prior to 1951; its appearance in print only made his ideas more accessible. The publication of *Naqḍ al-manṭiq* reflects the growing interest in Ibn Taymiyya and his legacy in the mid-twentieth century.

But, what exactly does this text say about the issue of Qur'an translation? After comparing the rationalism of philosophers to the truth of the Qur'an, Ibn Taymiyya says that the permissibility of translation depends on translators' knowledge of the holy text, 'its meanings, explanation, and translation'. For him, both explanation [*tafsīr*] and translation [*tarjama*] can be of three kinds:

1. 'Translation of the word alone, such as the rendition of one word [in the target language] by [using] a synonym';
2. 'Translation and clarification [*bayān*] of the meaning, in order for the listener to imagine the meaning'; and
3. 'Clarification of the trustworthy meanings and verification of them'.[43]

---

movement in Egypt; he led the Salafi-inspired group Jamāʿat Anṣār al-Sunna al-Muḥammadiyya [Society of the Followers of Muhammad's Sunna] and published many works by Ibn Taymiyya. On this society, see Aḥmad Ṭāhir, *Jamāʿat anṣār al-sunna al-Muḥammadiyya: nashātuhā, ahdāfuhā, minhajuhā wa-juhūduhā* (Algiers: Dār al-Faḍīla, 2004).

41 Ibn Taymiyya, *Naqḍ al-manṭiq*, ed. by Muḥammad Ḥamīd al-Fiqī (Cairo: Dār al-Maʿrifa, 1951), pp. 11, 214.

42 Ibn Taymiyya, *Naqḍ al-manṭiq*, ed. by ʿAbd al-Raḥmān Qāʿīd (Riyadh: Dār ʿAlām al-Fawāʾid, 2013), p. 12.

43 Ibn Taymiyya, *Naqḍ*, ed. by al-Fiqī, p. 96.

The three techniques he outlines here are comparable to the distinctions he makes in *al-Radd ᶜalā al-manṭiqiyyin* between 'grammatical/literal', 'rhetorical/metaphorical', and, finally, 'explanatory' translation. Fully aware of the complexity of translation, then, Ibn Taymiyya at last addresses the question of Qur'anic translation directly:

> It is well-known, that the *umma* [community] is obliged to convey the Qur'an, its word and its meaning, just as the Messenger was obliged to do so, and conveyance of the Message from God cannot be done without such translation. So, if [this] conveyance to foreigners requires translation, it should be translated for them as well as possible.[44]

He seems to understand translation as a necessary process to allow the community to fulfil its obligation to convey the message of the Qur'an widely.

Ibn Taymiyya's views on the subject quickly caught the attention of Salafi scholars after the publication of *Naqḍ al-manṭiq*. For instance, Muḥammad Bahja al-Bayṭār, an eminent Salafi scholar from Syria, published a review of *Naqḍ al-manṭiq* in the influential *Mujammaᶜ al-ᶜilmī al-ᶜarabī* [Journal of the Arabic Academy of Sciences] in 1952.[45] The Academy had been founded in 1918, and its board comprised not only local scholars, but also European Orientalists, and it served as a bridge connecting Islamic religious networks with modern Western approaches to Oriental Studies.[46] Al-Bayṭār represents his institution's expansive view; his review contained not only a general description but also his opinions on its treatment of 'the Qur'an translation issue'.[47] He brings Ibn Taymiyya's theory to bear on contemporary debates over the 'literal' [*ḥarfiyya*] and 'explanatory' [*tafsīriyya*] translation of the Qur'an, comparing it favourably to a popular opinon of the time that some Arabic words cannot be rendered into other languages at all.

44 Ibid., p. 98.

45 Al-Bayṭār had studied under the famous exegete Jamāl al-Dīn al-Qāsimī and later became a lecturer at a number of Saudi mosques and schools. He was also the first director of the Saudi Teaching Insitute (Maᶜhad al-ᶜIlmī al-Saᶜūdī), established in Mecca in 1926. See William Ochsenwald, 'The Transformation of Education in the Hijaz, 1925–1945', *Arabian Humanities Journal*, 12 (2019), 1–25, https://doi.org/10.4000/cy.4917

46 Agatangel Kryms'kyi and Ol. Bogolybskyi, *Do istorii wyschoi osvity u arabiv* (Kyiv: Vseukrainska Akademiya Nauk, 1928), p. 23.

47 Muḥammad Bahja al-Bayṭār, 'Naqḍ al-manṭiq', *Majallat mujammaᶜ al-ᶜilmī al-ᶜArabī*, 27 (1952), 300–02.

Al-Bayṭār concludes his review with the assessment that 'if the heads of other nations do hear the call to Islam [...] this will urge them to learn Arabic for their worship'.[48] With this, he echoes the sentiments of the pro-modernist scholars of al-Azhar but also demonstrates a general unwillingness to challenge the pre-eminence of Arabic as the language of the Qur'an. However, al-Bayṭār does support the use of translation for *daᶜwa* [missionary] purposes. His review is significant because it is one of the first examples in mid-twentieth-century Salafi literature of a scholar taking a global perspective on the role of translation.

Ibn Taymiyya's writings were not universally understood to support the idea of Qur'anic translation. Opponents of translation, including the traditional Hanafi scholar and Iraqi activist Kamāl al-Dīn al-Ṭāᶜī, read Ibn Taymiyya's texts differently. Al-Ṭāᶜī positions the early thinker as a Hanbali scholar who prohibited the translation of the Qur'an, based on the following quotation from Ibn Taymiyya's *al-Sabᶜiyya* [Refutation of Ibn Sabᶜīn, written around 1300]:

> It is impossible to find any word [in one language] that explains [or replicates] the meaning [of a given word in another language] in exactly the same way, and this is why religious scholars have said it is not permissible to recite the Qur'an in any language other than Arabic.[49]

These words have been used to support the widely disseminated assumption that scholars are unanimously agreed about the Qur'an's inability to be translated. Yet, another of Ibn Taymiyya's works, his *al-Tisᶜīyniyya* [The Ninety Arguments]), also includes the above quotation, but there it is followed by a significant final codicil. The addition specifies 'however, its translation is allowed in the same way as *tafsīr* is allowed' [*lākin yajūzu tarjamatuhu kamā yajūzu tafsīruhu*].[50] Al-Ṭāᶜī's characterization of Ibn Taymiyya's anti-translation position appears to be based on a misquotation. For, the codicil clearly indicates that Ibn Taymiyya's final position is that translation itself is acceptable, just not for use in recitation.

48 Ibid., p. 302.
49 Kamāl al-Dīn al-Ṭāᶜī, *Muᶜjiz al-bayān fī al-mabāḥith takhtaṣṣu bi-l-Qurʾān* (Baghdad: Maṭbaᶜat al-Tafayyiḍ al-Ahliyya, 1940), pp. 169–70.
50 Ibn Taymiyya, *al-Tisᶜīyniyya* (Riyadh: Maktabat al-Maᶜārif, 1999), p. 819.

Returning to the influence of Ibn Taymiyya on the field of Qur'anic translation, his views on language and its theological dimension in particular were widely accepted by the earliest generations of Wahhabi scholars. They, too, considered translation to be a valid hermeneutical tool to aid understanding at a theoretical level. That at least some eighteenth- and nineteenth-century scholars were interested in deeper investigation of the problem of meaning can be seen in instances of polemical literature that were written by early Wahhabi authorities, which aimed to persuade their opponents of the universality of their understanding of the Qur'anic message of divine oneness [*tawḥīd*].

One such authority was a man called ᶜAbd al-Raḥmān b. Ḥasan Āl al-Shaykh (1779–1869).[51] He received several *ijāza*s [certificates] in various branches of the religious sciences, primarily in grammar, rhetoric, and comprehension, but also in *tafsīr* and became a prominent teacher. ᶜAbd al-Raḥmān b. Ḥasan was one of the first scholars to use the now-common term *al-salafiyyūn* to describe 'those who follow verified traditions' [*al-muḥaqqīqūn al-muttabiᶜūn*], and he was influential in establishing the Wahabbi *tafsīr* canon.[52] Writing that 'the only correct *tafsīr* is that which corresponds to the *tafsīr* of *al-salaf*' [the traditionally approved *tafsīr*], he advises that 'the best commentaries available to people are those by Abū Jaᶜfar Muḥammad b. Jarīr al-Ṭabarī, al-Ḥusayn b. Masᶜūd al-Baghawī, and also al-ᶜImād Ismāᶜīl Ibn Kathīr', following Ibn Taymiyya's footsteps on that issue.[53] This reference is one of the earliest to Ibn Kathīr's *tafsīr* (c. 740), which was almost unknown until it became popular in the late twentieth century.[54]

---

51 He was the nephew of Muḥammad b. ᶜAbd al-Wahhāb who, unusually for a Wahhabi, studied at al-Azhar University after being taken to Egypt as a prisoner of war during the Ottoman/Egyptian-Wahhabi war of 1811–18. See Abd al-Raḥmān b. Ḥasan Āl al-Shaykh, *Mashāhir ᶜulamāᵓ al-Najd* (Riyadh: Dār al-Yamama, 1974), p. 80.

52 ᶜAbd al-Raḥmān b. Ḥasan Āl al-Shaykh, *al-Muḥajja* (Riyadh: Maktabat Dār al-Hidāya, [n. d.]), p. 38.

53 Ibid., p. 42.

54 An Indian scholar, Muḥammad Siddīq Ḥasan Khān, who died in 1890, may have used it as one of the sources for his own *tafsīr*. See Younus Y. Mirza, 'Tafsīr Ibn Kathīr: A Window onto Medieval Islam and a Guide to the Development of Modern Islamic Orthodoxy', in *The Routledge Companion to the Qur'an*, ed. by George Archer, Maria Dakake, and Daniel Madigan (London: Routledge, 2022) pp. 245–52 (p. 248), http://doi.org/10.4324/9781315885360-26

While advocating for the use of a specific set of *tafsīrs*, ᶜAbd al-Raḥmān b. Ḥasan was careful not to speak against others that were popular. Rather, he restrained himself to warning against their overindulgence in theology [*kalām*]. Such '*tafsīrs* are "good" only in those parts where they rely on early traditions', he advised, 'with the most problematic question relating to [their treatment of] the attributes of God and *irjā*ᶜ [postponement of judgment]'.[55] In ᶜAbd al-Raḥmān b. Ḥasan's writing, then, one may see a formalisation of the Salafi *tafsīr* tradition. For, all of the exegetical works he explicitly approves, particularly Ibn Kathīr's commentary, went on to constitute the core of the Salafi tradition. He also delineates the problems that would require further explanation and investigation by future scholars. His approach did much to shape the Salafi discourse on Qur'an interpretation in foreign languages over the next century.

One of ᶜAbd al-Raḥmān b. Ḥasan's most important works is his *al-Radd ᶜalā-l-Kashmīrī* [Response to al-Kashmīrī] (1926).[56] This book is important in the current context because it contains a discussion of hermeneutical theory and the question of whether language is given by God directly or established by divine inspiration. ᶜAbd al-Raḥmān b. Ḥasan wonders if some fixed meanings are identical in different languages and, in answer, confirms that 'all languages were inspired by God, and after they were first established no changes took place [...] the name of every thing is set'.[57] Later, while talking about the notion of divine oneness, and using this pretext to prove the Qur'an's universal accessibility, ᶜAbd al-Raḥmān b. Ḥasan follows Ibn Taymiyya in understanding certain Qur'anic meanings as intelligible in all languages. This raises a broader question: if some meanings are universal, can they be 'safely' translated from one language to another without any distortion at all? This query would not be answered until much later, during the 1940s.

55 Āl al-Shaykh, *al-Muḥajja*, p. 42.

56 This book is a criticism levelled at someone called ᶜAbd al-Maḥmūd al-Kashmīrī, whose identity remains unknown (he may have been a member of a Sufi brotherhood or some other Sunni anti-Wahhabi circle). See ᶜAbd al-Raḥmān b. Ḥasan Āl al-Shaykh, *Bayān kalimat al-tawḥīd wa-l-radd ᶜalā al-Kashmīrī ᶜAbd al-Maḥmūd*, in *Majmūᶜ al-rasāᵓil wa-l-masāᵓil al-Najdiyya*, 4 vols (Cairo: al-Manār, 1926), iv, pp. 325–26.

57 Ibid., p. 327.

One reason for growing interest in Qur'an translatability in Saudi Arabia was the introduction of the printing press. With it came discussions about the accessibility of the Qur'an and the wider religious tradition accelerated. The first printing house to be established in the Middle East was established by the Ottomans in Mecca in 1882.[58] This was followed by the establishment of the first 'official' Saudi publishing press in 1926, again in the holy city. These institutions, at least during the last years of the Ottoman Empire and the Kingdom of Hijaz [a region in the western part of the Arabian peninsula] (1916–25), printed literature that mostly conformed to the mainstream Sunni tradition, including books by Abū Ḥāmid al-Ghazālī, Jalāl al-Dīn al-Suyūṭī, and other scholars.[59] The establishment of a printing industry (which, though quickly accepted by the public, was not entirely above suspicion) prompted initiatives to print and distribute the Qur'an. There is, however, no indication of any interest in publishing Qur'an translations during this initial period.

The first printed edition of the (Arabic) Qur'an to be published in Saudi Arabia was produced in 1949 by a private institution known as the Sharikat Muṣḥaf al-Makka al-Mukarrama [The Holy City of Mecca Qur'an Company]. The project began as a commercial initiative to distribute copies of the Qur'an among the pilgrims who came to Saudi Arabia to perform Hajj and Umrah.[60] Later, it was supported by the founder of the Saudi Kingdom, ᶜAbd al-ᶜAzīz al-Saᶜūd (who reigned from 1932–53). This Qur'an, known as *Muṣḥaf al-Makka al-mukarrama* remained in print until 1979. According to an anecdote from a calligrapher who worked on the project, Muḥammad b. Ṭāhir al-Kurdī al-Makkī, he personally copied the text from the Cairo edition then sent it to relevant authorities in Saudi Arabia for approval, while also requesting approval from al-Azhar in Egypt. He relates his memories in a book entitled *Tārīkh al-Qurʾān wa-gharāʾib rasmihi wa-ḥukmuhu* [The

---

58 Ibrāhīm al-ᶜUtaybī, 'Bidāyat tārīkh al-maṭābiᶜ wa-l-nashr fī al-mamlaka', *Majallat al-fayṣal*, 247 (1997), 60–64 (p. 63).

59 Aḥmad al-Ḍubayb, *Bawākīr al-ṭibāᶜa wa-l-maṭbūᶜāt fī bilād al-ḥaramayn al-sharīfayn* (Riyadh: KFNL, 1408/1987), p. 9.

60 One of the co-founders of this press was a well-known Saudi writer Muḥammad Sarūr al-Ṣabān (1898–1972). He supported Abdullah Yusuf Ali's English Qur'an translation, which was reprinted in Mecca in 1965 (and will be discussed in Chapter Two). For more on al-Ṣabān, see Saudi Archive [in Arabic], https://www.darah.org.sa/index.php/media-library/st-and-rep/dignitaries/155-2019-01-30-09-57-47

History of the Qur'an, the Wonders of its Orthography and Opinions on it] (1946) that was first published in Jeddah, and then, a few years later, in Cairo. Al-Kurdī's work offers great insight into the prevailing views of printing and translation at that time.[61] The author, who was born in Mecca in 1900, studied at al-Azhar in Egypt then returned to his homeland where he worked as one of the foremost calligraphers in the holy city. Some of his works, such as *Tabarruk al-saḥāba* [Seeking Blessing through the Prophet's Companions] (1987), reveal that he was not a Salafi.[62] Indeed, some of the *fiqh* [Islamic law] books he published were mainly devoted to the teachings of the Shafii legal school.[63]

In al-Kurdī's 'History', which gives a general overview of the history of the Qur'an in print, he mentions that the first versions appeared in Europe and the Ottoman Empire, and then, later, Egypt.[64] While Al-Kurdī acknowledges 'the absence of permission to recite the Qur'an in a non-Arabic language', he insists that this prohibition does not extend to Qur'anic commentary:

> When it comes to explanatory translation [*al-tarjama al-tafsīriyya*], there are no problems with it, since it clarifies [the Qur'an's] meanings and reveals their depth; since there are many books on that topic, it is enough here to just say that.[65]

Al-Kurdī further explains his position with the claim that any 'literal' translation of the Qur'an is simply an impossible undertaking, and any 'explanatory' translation is not the Qur'an itself. His casual references to the issue of Qur'an translation suggest that debate on the subject

61 Muḥammad b. Ṭāhir al-Kurdī al-Makkī, *Tārīkh al-Qurʾān wa-garāʾib rasmihi wa-ḥukmihi* (Jeddah: al-Fatḥ, 1946), p. 5. Since the book appeared two years before his edition of the Qur'an went into print, the author speaks of his copying out the muṣḥaf in terms of a completed project awaiting release. In the second edition (Cairo: Maṭbaᶜat Muṣṭafā al-Bābī al-Ḥalabī, 1953), he was described on the cover as *'kātib muṣḥaf al-Makka al-mukarrama'* ('a Qur'an copyist from the Holy City of Mecca').

62 Muḥammad b. Ṭāhir al-Kurdī al-Makkī, *Tabarruk al-saḥāba* (Cairo: Maktabat al-Qāhira, 1987).

63 For example, Muḥammad b. Ṭāhir al-Kurdī al-Makkī, *Irshād al-zumra li-manāsik al-ḥajj wa-l-ᶜumra ᶜalā madhhab al-Imām al-Shāfiᶜī* (Cairo: Maṭbaᶜat Muṣṭafā al-Bābī al-Ḥalabī, 1955).

64 al-Kurdī, *Tārīkh al-Qurʾān*, p. 163. Al-Kurdī omits from his history the Qur'ans printed in Kazan and Crimea in the nineteenth and early twentieth century, but this is excusable as these editions were largely unknown in the Arab World.

65 Ibid., p. 166.

was a well-accepted phenomena in the Muslim world by the mid-twentieth century, and he makes clear on which side his opinions fall: al-Kurdī's promotion of explanatory translations situates him firmly in the modernist camp alongside Azhari scholars such as al-Wajdī and al-Marāghī, whose views were discussed earlier in this chapter. As if to underscore his 'progressive' position, al-Kurdī also references a book called *The Messenger: The Life of Mohammad*, written by R. V. C. Bodley and first published in both English and Arabic translation in 1946.[66] The mention is significant as Bodley, a British-American Orientalist, describes the untranslatability of the stylistic beauty of the Qur'an. Thus, al-Kurdī not only takes a typical Azhari position on the question of Qur'an translation but also demonstrates some level of interest in Western Orientalist approaches. Having said that, al-Kurdī's main interest was in the Arabic Qur'an, and he only mentions the issue of translation in passing. Al-Kurdī's *Tārikh al-Qurʾān* [History of the Qur'an] is relatively well known in the Muslim world; it has been republished recently by the Saudi publishing house Dār Aḍwāʾ al-Salaf li-l-Nashr wa-l-Tawzīᶜ [Salafī House for Publishing and Dissemination].[67] In some ways, this relatively humble scribe was one of the many points of connection between al-Azhar, Western Orientalism, and the growing Salafi tradition in Saudi Arabia. He was not, of course, unique in this. During the 1920s and 1930s, most religious teaching activities in the Hijaz were carried out by scholars from Egypt and Syria, and many graduates from the area went on to undertake further studies at al-Azhar.[68] This exchange helped to develop Salafi networks in the Middle East, but it also opened the door to the theological discussions and trends happening outside the Salafi community, including debate over the translatability of the Qur'an.

Another reason for the upsurge in interest in Qur'an translation in Saudi Arabia in the early twentieth century is the increasing level of engagement with foreign languages throughout the Middle East at this time. English-language courses began being taught in schools in

66 R. V. C. Bodley, *The Messenger: The Life of Mohammad* (New York: Doubleday & Company, Inc. 1966).

67 The recent Saudi edition is Muḥammad b. Ṭāhir al-Kurdī al-Makkī, *Tārīkh al-Qurʾān wa-garāʾīb rasmihi wa-ḥukmihi* (Riyadh: Dār Aḍwāʾ al-Salaf li-l-Nashr wa-l-Tawzīᶜ, 2008).

68 See Ochsenwald, 'The Transformation'.

the urban areas of the Hijaz in 1926. A decade later, specialised English courses aimed at adults began to appear; these were mostly attended by members of the local merchant elite and the upper classes. Exemplifying that interest in language-learning extended beyond English, a 1936 issue of the newspaper *Ṣawt al-Ḥijāz* [The voice of the Hijaz] promotes courses in English, Persian, and Urdu.[69] The local Wahhabi clergy generally tolerated this development, especially in the case of courses aimed at mature students. Some, including Taqī al-Dīn al-Hilālī, actively encouraged Muslims to study foreign languages, even while warning them against reliance upon translations of religious texts that may 'distort' the true divine message and lead to 'the deception of the Ummah'.[70] Such a caution is standard; it does not indicate that al-Dīn took any kind of serious anti-translation stance. Generally speaking, in the late 1940s, there was no strong Salafi opposition to translation. In fact, there is a notable contrast between the enthusiasm for Qur'an translation in Saudi Arabia and the anti-translation discourse that dominated in other Arab countries at the same time.

The absence of any sustained opposition to translation in Saudi Arabia effectively facilitated the rise of the translation movement over the following decades. This open attitude was not only the result of the influential discussions that disseminated outwards from al-Azhar, but also of their application in the Salafi theological context, which promoted the universal self-evidence of basic Qur'anic values such as *tawḥīd* [divine oneness]. The concept of 'translation of meanings' imported from Egypt seemed to reinforce the pre-existing discourses of Qur'anic hermeneutics—ones based largely on the modern reception of Ibn Taymiyya's approach to issues of textuality.

The Salafi movement, in calling for a return to the textual sources (such as the Qur'an and Sunna) and stressing the irrelevance of the *madhhabī* ['confessional' tradition], promoted the belief that the basics of Islam should be available without the need for any further intercessions or intermediaries. Such direct access was the promise of Qur'an translations, especially those made in accordance with Salafi

---

69 'al-Madrasa al-layliyya li-taᶜlīm al-luga al-Injliziyya al-Fārisiyya wa-l-Urdiyya', *Ṣawt al-Ḥijāz*, 28 April 1936, p. 4.

70 Taqī al-Dīn al-Hilālī, 'Taᶜlīm al-lugāt: ḥukmuhu wa-fīᶜīdatahu', *Lisān al-Dīn*, 3.10 (1949), p. 10.

hermeneutical theory. This raises the question of who, ultimately, could authorise translations and would define the interpretive boundaries? In general, the Saudi clergy can be divided into establishment and non-establishment ulema [teachers with specialist knowledge]. The first type hold official positions in religious institutions, while the second preach independently or are affiliated with educational structures inside the country.[71] During the 1950s and, especially, the 1960s, the non-establishment ulema were gradually incorporated into a semi-official network by the Ministry of Islamic Affairs, and their rejection or acceptance of specific religious approaches and issues came to play an important role in the religious life of the country. Their views on the concept of Qur'an translation would also influence the Saudi state's approach to the issue, as will be discussed in the following chapters. Originating beyond the borders of the Kingdom of Saudi Arabia; in Turkey, Egypt, Syria, and India; the concept of Qur'an translation was firmly embraced by ulema working in official circles. Influential political institutions such as the Ministry of Islamic Affairs (later the Muslim World League) were guided by the Saudi royal family to understand translation as a tool through which the state could gain influence abroad. Support for the speedy instrumentalisation of translations to accelerate global Islamic missionary activism met with no strong opposition inside religious circles, even among non-establishment groups.

71 See Raihan Ismail, *Saudi Clerics and Shia Islam* (Oxford: Oxford University Press, 2019), pp. 18–21, https://doi.org/10.1093/acprof:oso/9780190233310.001.0001

2. The Muslim World League: A Forerunner to International Translational *daᶜwa Networks*

The MWL: An Innovative Step in the International Promotion of Islam

The Muslim World League (MWL, known in Arabic as Rābiṭat al-ᶜĀlam al-Islāmī) officially came into being on 15 December 1962. This global Muslim organisation, with headquarters in Mecca, remains one of the most influential transnational Islamic institutions. It has realised many different goals, from the cultural and religious to the political, and now maintains offices in more than a hundred countries, including many Western states. As an organisation formed from the policies and ideology of Saudi Arabia's then crown prince who would become king Fayṣal b. ᶜAbd al-ᶜAzīz Āl Saᶜūd (1906–1975), it has been described as an attempt to 'impose respective moral and the political authority on the entire Muslim world'.[1] During its sixty-year history, the MWL has had a significant impact on the global level, playing a role, for example, in the Saudi response to the threat posed by Nasser's pan-Arab radical regime in Egypt and, more recently, in the 'globalisation' of Saudi Salafism as the 'most correct' version of Islam. It has shaped many of the discourses surrounding the modernisation of Islam and is involved in even secular developments within the Kingdom (for example, progress in

1 Samir Amghar, 'The Muslim World League in Europe: An Islamic Organization to Serve the Saudi Strategic Interests?', *Journal of Muslim in Europe* 1.2 (2012), 127–41 (p. 129), https://doi.org/10.1163/22117954-12341234

©2024 Mykhaylo Yakubovych, CC BY-ND 4.0
https://doi.org/10.11647/OBP.0381.02

modernising education) that are considered to be implicated in Islamic revival: as Abul Hasan Ali Nadwi from MWL noticed in late 1970s, 'The future of Islam depends on Saudi Arabia [...]. The circumstances are also conductive to the promotion of Islamic ideals.'[2]

Since its inception, the MWL has been actively engaged with current political trends in the Islamic world. For example, during the 1960s and 1970s, a time when Saudi Arabia supported the Muslim Brotherhood and was also active in the mobilisation of Muslims against the 1979 Soviet invasion of Afghanistan, the MWL contributed significantly to these initiatives.[3] Reinhard Schulze's comprehensive study of the organisation's early years shows that it not only built on previous Muslim activist achievements but also introduced new structural forms of international influence.[4] Nowadays, the MWL is registered as an NGO in Saudi Arabia and is headed by a Supreme Council made up of sixty members from all over the world.[5] Publishing has always been one of the MWL's priorities. Its Department of Press and Publication was established in the organisation's first year. This chapter asks how this office of the MWL has contributed to the Qur'an translation industry and which of its works have had the most crucial impact.

As mentioned in Chapter One, translation of the Qur'an was not considered problematic in the Saudi context in the 1950s and 1960s. The first plans to produce translations were announced in this era of modernisation, soon after the establishment of the MWL. During its first two years of operation, 1962 and 1963, in fact, the Department of Press and Publication released details of at least five projects to produce Qur'an translations in English, French, Japanese, Chinese, and Yoruba.[6] A few articles on the rationale for and the methodology of Qur'an

2 Abul Hasan Ali Nadwi, 'Education and Society in Saudi Arabia', in *Education and Society in the Muslim World*, ed. by M. W. Khan (Jeddah: King Abdulaziz University, 1981), 89-99 (p. 98).

3 Muhammad Haniff Hassan, 'Mobilization of Muslims for Jihad: Insights from the Past and their Relevance Today', *Counter Terrorist Trends and Analyses*, 5.8 (2013), 10–15.

4 Reinhard Schulze, *Islamischer Internationalismus im 20. Jahrhundert: Untersuchungen zur Geschichte der Islamischen Weltliga* (Leiden: Brill, 1990). This study remains the most profound investigation on the establishment and early activities of the MWL.

5 'Affiliated Councils and Organizations', *The Muslim World League*, https://themwl.org/en/Bodies

6 Schulze, pp. 333–34.

translation appeared in the MWL journal at the time. One editorial piece, entitled 'Lights on the translation of the Noble Qur'an', insisted on the 'permissibility' of translating the holy book by emphasising the importance of translating its 'meanings' for *daᶜwa* [missionary] purposes.[7] The following issue of the same journal included a ten-page article by Muhammad Asad, the translator working on the English-language edition, with the title 'Introduction to the Translation of the Meanings of the Qur'an'.[8] From these preliminary publications, it is clear that, even in its early years, the MWL considered translations of the Qur'an to be part of the institution's long-term strategy for the global promotion of Islam.

The First Translations

The MWL focused first on publishing a French translation of the Qur'an, perhaps because it was the simplest project. An edition, translated by Muhammad Hamidullah, had been already published in 1959 by Le Club français du livre, and it was decided to reprint this existing French translation without mentioning that Saudis had not been involved in its production.[9] The MWL's approach to the English-language edition, however, was very different. The production of this version was the first Saudi-sponsored Qur'an-translation project, and it has an interesting, if rather controversial, history.

The translator on the English project was Muhammad Asad (1909–1992), a convert to Islam who worked as a journalist, traveller, writer, and diplomat.[10] Widely travelled in both the East and West, Asad had many connections all over the Middle East, particularly in Saudi Arabia. He had stayed at the court of the first ruler of the modern Saudi State, King ᶜAbd al-ᶜAzīz between 1927 and 1932. From that point onwards, even after years of living and working in Pakistan and finally moving back to the West in 1959, Asad enjoyed a level of support from the

7 'al-Ḍawʾ ᶜalā tarjmāt al-Qurʾān', *The Muslim World League Journal*, 10 (1964), 42–44.
8 Muḥammad Asad, 'al-Muqaddima fī tarjmat al-Qurʾān', *The Muslim World League Journal*, 11 (1964), 42–54.
9 Muhammad Hamidullah, *Le Saint Coran* (Paris: Club Francais du Livre, 1959).
10 His real name was Leopold Weiss. He was born in the Austro-Hungarian city of Lemberg, now Lviv in Ukraine.

royal family and other Saudi authorities.[11] He developed an interest in translating the Qur'an around 1960 and began his first draft just before the establishment of the MWL. Asad describes his motivation to undertake the project in his introduction to the first edition of his English translation:

> Familiarity with the bedouin speech of Central and Eastern Arabia—in addition, of course, to academic knowledge of classical Arabic—is the only way for a non-Arab of our time to achieve an intimate understanding of the diction of the Qur'an. And because none of the scholars who have previously translated the Qur'an into European languages has ever fulfilled this prerequisite, their translations have remained but distant, and faulty, echoes of its meaning and spirit.[12]

Seeking to use his knowledge of Arabic-language variants to reproduce the true meaning of the Qur'an in English, then, Asad embarked on his translation with approval from King Fayṣal, the successor of ᶜAbd al-ᶜAzīz. Fayṣal continued Asad's Saudi patronage and, in 1963, directed the MWL in Mecca to subscribe in advance to Asad's forthcoming translation.[13] During his first three years of work, Asad completed nine suras [chapters], which he published under the title *The Message of the Qur'ān* in 1964.[14] Its copyright page lists both Geneva and Mecca as its places of publication, acknowledging that the translation was authorised by Asad's local Swiss Islamic centre and also by the MWL. *The Message* was initially distributed in Switzerland and beyond, with some copies sent to Saudi Arabia as well. Although published under a dual Swiss-Saudi banner, it was printed in the Netherlands by Mouton and Co, the Hague, a publisher that was later incorporated into De Gruyter, the well-known German academic press. The book's cover includes the price of the volume in three currencies—details which gives some indication of the intended areas of distribution: Saudi Arabia (16 riyals), Austria

11 Elma Ruth Harder, 'Muhammad Asad and the Road to Mecca: Text of Muhammad Asad's Interview with Karl Günter Simon', *Islamic Studies*, 37.4 (1998), 533–44.

12 Muhammad Asad, *The Message of the Qur'ān, Translated and Explained by Muhammad Asad* (Gibraltar: Dar al-Andalus, 1980), p. 5.

13 See Martin Kramer, 'The Road from Mecca: Muhammad Asad (born Leopold Weiss)', in *The Jewish Discovery of Islam: Studies in Honor of Bernard Lewis*, ed. by Martin Kramer (Tel Aviv: The Moshe Dayan Center for Middle Eastern and African Studies, 1999), pp. 225–47.

14 Muhammad Asad, *The Message of the Qur'ān (Suras 1–9)* (Mecca: MWL, 1964).

(25 shillings) and Switzerland (15.50 Swiss Francs). The copyright is cited as belonging to Pola Hamida Asad, Muhammad Asad's second wife, his first reader, and sometimes even the editor of his books. She is also mentioned in the acknowledgements, as is the Secretary General of the MWL, Muḥammad Sarūr al-Ṣabbān (1898–1972), a prominent Saudi writer and intellectual who secured MWL funds for Asad.15

The MWL leaders seem to have trusted Asad completely, as he was allowed to produce his translation without any directives or supervision. After publication, however, the members of the publishing board examined the translation and found it rather challenging. Raising serious objections to some of Asad's interpretations, they took the decision to destroy virtually the entire print run of *The Message's* first edition and never to print another. Among the points that most troubled the MWL, Abdul Majid Khan explains, were

> [Asad's understanding of] Isra᾿ and Miᶜraj not as physical occurrences but as purely spiritual [...]; the view that the jinn in some cases should be understood as 'elemental forces of nature'[; and ...] his interpretation of 24:31 and 33:59 as to whether women had to wear the hijab.[16]

The MWL representatives disagreed with Asad's 'rejection' of (or, more precisely, his attempt to rationalise) wonders and miracles described in the Qur'an. Asad's response, included in the complete edition finally published in 1980, was the following:

> But even such extraordinary, 'miraculous' messages cannot be regarded as 'supernatural': for the so-called 'laws of nature' are only a perceptible manifestation of 'God's way' (sunnat Allah) in respect of His creation—and, consequently, everything that exists and happens, or could conceivably exist or happen, is 'natural' in the innermost sense of this word, irrespective of whether it conforms to the ordinary course of events or goes beyond it.[17]

This position on miracles was one Asad shared with Egyptian commentators, including Muḥammad al-Marāghī (see Chapter One)

15 Ibid., p. 4.
16 Abdul Majid Khan, 'A Critical Study of Muhammad Asad's *The Message of the Qur'an* (1980)' (unpublished doctoral thesis, Aligarh Muslim University, 2005), p. 120.
17 Muhammad Asad, *The Message of the Qur'an* (Gibraltar: Dar al-Andalus, 1980), p. 427, fn. 71.

and the earlier Grand Mufti, Muḥammad ᶜAbduh.[18] Saudi scholars of the time, however, especially those in academic religious circles who were becoming more familiar with the English language, considered such readings to be completely irreconcilable with their Sunni-Salafi beliefs.[19] Although there was no specific campaign to discourage or discredit Asad's translation, some fatwas [legal opinions] issued in the 1970s (and, especially, after the publication of the entire, finished work) were extremely critical.

An illuminating example is the 1992 ruling by the Permanent Committee for Scholarly Research and Ifta (PCSRI [Lajnat al-Dāʾima li-l-Buḥūth al-ᶜIlmiyya wa-l-Iftā']) that advises against a plan to republish *The Message of the Qur'an* in Dublin, Ireland.[20] Although a first printing of Asad's complete translation had been produced in the city in 1980, officials were aware that this reissue of *The Message* had a good chance of reaching a wide range of readers and libraries via one of the biggest networks of academic publishers. The key objection raised with the committee about Asad's translation in this case centred on his claim that the prophet Isa [Jesus] has already died and will never return as Muslims falsely believe. Historically, the Islamic exegetical tradition had not been concerned with the issue of how to understand Jesus's disappearance from the material world, but this changed in the twentieth century due to the Ahmadi movement's specific stance on the issue. For Ahmadi Muslims, Jesus's death, as reported in Q. 3:55, is a pure historical fact. Many Sunni Muslims, however, believe that Jesus was taken to Heaven while alive; they interpret the relevant Qur'anic verb, *mutawaffika*, to mean 'taking away' as opposed to 'causing to die' in any real, physical sense. The issue at hand in Dublin was that Asad's translation of the relevant phrase as 'Verily, I shall cause thee to die' was similar to that used by the Ahmadi translator Muhammad Ali in his 1917 translation ('I will cause you to die') and unlike that of, for example, Abdullah

18 See Muhammad al-Marāghī, *Tafsīr al-Marāghī*, 30 vols (Cairo: Sharikat al-Ḥalabbī, 1946), xxx, pp. 241–44. I am grateful to Johanna Pink for this reference.

19 An example is the translation committee that worked with Muḥammad Taqī al-Dīn al-Hilālī and Muḥammad Muḥsin Khān in the late 1960s. On this, see Chapter Four.

20 See *Fatāwā al-lajna al-dāʾima li-l-buḥūth al-ᶜilmiyya wa-l-iftāʾ*, 4 vols (Riyadh: Maktabat al-ᶜUbaykān / Riʾāsat Idārat al-Buḥūth al-ᶜIlmiyya wa-l-Iftāʾ, 1412/1992), esp. iv, p. 213.

Yusuf Ali's post-1938 translation ('God said: 'O Jesus! I will take thee'). Asad was never entirely clear on the rationale for his rendition of this phrase, but his approach generally fits with his stated effort to show that the Qur'anic text accords with the natural world order. Opinion among the PCSRI was that the translator had not been concerned enough with the implications of Ahmadi-Sunni theological conflicts. Thus, after a long apologetic statement on the single issue of whether or not Jesus was taken to heaven alive, the committee issued a decisive statement on Asad's entire work:

> In his translation, there are brutal mistakes and disgusting disbeliefs, and this is why the Consulting Board of the Muslim World League in the Holy City of Mecca has prohibited its printing and distribution.[21]

The mentioned prohibition by the MWL may relate to the organisation's decision to destroy its copies of *The Message*, as discussed above.

That one of the authors of the PCSRI fatwa was the religious authority Ibn Bāz is surprising as he was well known for championing the translation of the Qur'an.[22] His involvement in the ruling suggests that other motivations were at work in the committee's disavowal of Asad's work. The translator had fallen out of favour with the Saudi authorities after his main patron, King Fayṣal, was killed in 1975. Asad was unable to maintain his ties with the Saudi religious elite while living in the West, and he was supplanted by other translators working locally. His background—as a practising Jew who converted to Islam or, at a broader level, as an educated Westerner who embraced an 'Eastern' identity and was engaged in the struggle for the global Muslim Ummah—may have allowed him and his translation of the Qur'an to rise above the controversies surrounding it; however, the fact remains that Asad's translation has never been printed in Saudi Arabia. Today, it is one of the most influential Qur'an translations worldwide. Not only

---

21 Ibid., p. 215.

22 According to Ahmad Totonji (Aḥmad Tūtūnjī), one of the founding members of the International Insitutte of Islamic Thought, who had forged close ties with Saudi establishment ulema while in Saudi Arabia during the 1980s and 1990s, Ibn Bāz frequently secured funds for his numerous assistants from various parts of the Muslim world to go on *daʿwa* missionary trips. Such activities could be hardly imagined without a favourable approach to the translation of various Muslim texts. See Aḥmad Tūtūnjī, *Sittūn ʿāmman bayna al-sharq wa-l-gharb: al-takhṭīṭ wa-l-muthābara wa-l-tanfīdh* (Amman: Dār Fan, 2022), p. 287.

has Asad's edition itself been translated into many languages (including German, Spanish, Bosnian, Turkish, and Swedish), it is now viewed by many as a kind of *tafsīr*. Nevertheless, it has never been considered part of the Salafi religious domain. The Saudi press, even now, prefers to gloss over the controversy generated by Asad's translation, mentioning simply that the MWL 'had some concerns about this work and thus prevented its distribution'.23 And criticism continues to be levelled at *The Message of Qur'an*. For example, M. I. R. Elnemr recently wrote that

> the translator [Asad] ignores the occasion of revelation so he misrepresents the meaning of some verses; moreover, he has a confusion because of unawareness the principles of Tafsir and Hadith that lead him to stick to the ideology of rational school.[24]

Such views are representative of Salafi and mainstream Sunni objections towards this work. Other translations, including those fully endorsed by the MWL, however, have also met with similar critique.

(Dis)Approved for Publication: The First MWL Translation of the Qur'an into English

Following the controversy over Asad's work, the MWL decided to publish an English translation that was already widely accepted rather than one which had yet to be reviewed and revised. The Department of Press and Publication accordingly published a limited print run of Abdullah Yusuf Ali's 1917 translation in Mecca in 1965.[25] To this researcher's knowledge, this was the first-ever complete English translation of the Qur'an to be printed in Saudi Arabia. It came out just one year after the controversial publication of Asad's *The Message*, and the speed at which it was produced reflected the simplicity of the production process: the two-volume edition comprised no more than a reprint of an edition Yusuf Ali first published in New York in 1946, with

23 ʿAbd al-Raḥman al-Shibaylī, 'Risālat al-Qurʾān: tarjamat Muḥammad Asad li-l-muṣḥaf al-sharīf', *al-Sharq al-Awsaṭ*, 15 June 2017, 7.

24 M. I. R. Elnemr, 'The Ideological Impact on the English Translations of the Qur'an: A Case Study of Muhammad Asad's Translation', *International Journal of Linguistics, Literature, and Translation*, 3.7 (2020), 30–41 (p. 39).

25 Abdullah Yusuf Ali, *The Holy Qur'an: Text, Translation and Commentary by A. Y. Ali* (Mecca: Muslim World League, 1965).

no revisions, additions, or any other kind of corrections.26 The decision suggests that the MWL was deeply concerned about the controversy over Asad's translation and sought to hastily replace it with something already widely known and popular in the Muslim world.

A similar publishing project came to fruition a few years later. In 1977, the MWL published Muhammad Marmaduke Pickthall's English translation of the Qur'an to distribute gratis via its office at the United Nations in New York.[27] Like the hasty Ali reprint, this bilingual edition was an 'as-is' reproduction of a work— one originally published in India in 1938.[28] Although Pickthall's work has never since been republished by the Saudi government, some pro-Salafi commentators remain positive towards this translation and its translator into the twenty-first century. '[T]he appeal of his Quran translation and his other remarkable writings on Islam', one recently observed, 'rank as a native English speaker Muslim's valuable gift which has superbly served the cause of Islam for almost a century'.[29] This praise suggests why Pickthall's translation might have been selected by the MWL as a good alternative to Asad's: although both authors are Westerners who had converted to Islam, Pickthall was a native speaker of English. His translation found a readership in both the Muslim world and the West.

These two translations, by Yusuf Ali and Pickthall, were the only complete Qur'an translations into English to be published by the MWL. After the establishment of the KFGQPC in 1984 (see Chapter Four), all translation publishing projects were carried out by the new organisation. The MWL may never have succeeded in developing and producing its own translation of the Qur'an into English (or French, as the announced translation by Muhammad Hamidullah was never published), but it was able to produce translations in other languages. These editions merit

26 Abdullah Yusuf Ali, *The Holy Quran: Text, Translation and Commentary by A. Y. Ali* (New York: Hafner Publishing Company, 1946).

27 Muhammad Marmaduke Pickthall, *The Meaning of the Glorious Qur'an: Text and Explanatory Translation by Muhammad Marmaduke Pickthall* (Mecca: Muslim World League, 1977).

28 Muhammad Marmaduke Pickthall, *The Meaning of the Glorious Quran* (Hyderabad–Deccan: Government Central Press, 1938).

29 Abdul Raheem Kidwai, 'Muhammad Marmaduke Pickthall's English Translation of the Quran (1930): An Assessment', in *Marmaduke Pickthall: Islam and the Modern World*, ed. by Geoffrey P. Nash (Leiden: Brill, 2017), pp. 230–47 (p. 247), https://doi.org/10.1163/9789004327597_013

attention because they exemplify how the organisation increasingly sought to use translation of the Qur'an for missionary purposes.

The MWL's Japanese Translation

The MWL's Japanese edition was produced with the help of a domestic reviser named ᶜAbd Allāh ᶜAbbās al-Nadwī (1925–2006). He was an Islamic scholar of Indian origin who played quite an important role in the development of Qur'anic Studies in Saudi Arabia. Al-Nadwī moved to Saudi Arabia in 1950 and joined the MWL from its very beginnings in 1962. After completing his doctoral studies in Linguistics in the UK and a *daᶜwa* mission to South Korea, the Philippines, and Singapore on behalf of the MWL, he was appointed as the head of the Translation and Muslim Minority Affairs unit, a position he held from 1971 to 1976. Al-Nadwī published many books, including a bilingual (Arabic-English) dictionary entitled *Vocabulary of the Holy Qur'an* (1983), on which project Ibn Bāz, the head of the PCSRI, acted as editor.30 In this work, al-Nadwī cites at least nine different Qur'an translations, showing himself to be well-acquainted with the issues and problems inherent in translating the holy book. In another, *Tarjamāt maᶜānī al-Qurʾān al-karīm wa-taṭwīr fahmuhu ᶜinda-l-gharb* (1996) [Translation of the Meanings of the Qur'an and Development of Its Understanding in the West], he discusses the many theoretical implications of the great demand for translations of the Qur'an throughout the Muslim world. Thus, al-Nadwī was not only one of the MWL's top-ranking experts on foreign languages but also someone with very high-level connections in the Saudi religious hierarchy.

In the aforementioned *Tarjamāt maᶜānī al-Qurʾān al-karīm wa-taṭwīr fahmuhu ᶜinda-l-gharb*, al-Nadwī shares his experience of working on the MWL's Japanese Qur'an translation project, which began in 1963.[31] The translator, Umar Mita (Ryoichi Mita, 1892–1983), was a Japanese Muslim convert and one of the founders of the Association of Japanese Muslims. He lived in Saudi Arabia for three years, between 1962 and 1965, during

30 ᶜAbd Allāh ᶜAbbās al-Nadwī, *Vocabulary of the Holy Qur'an* (Jeddah: Dār al-Shurūq, 1983).

31 ᶜAbd Allāh ᶜAbbās al-Nadwī, *Tarjamāt maᶜānī al-Qurʾān al-karīm wa-taṭwīr fahmihi ᶜinda-l-gharb* (Mecca: Muslim World League, 1996), p. 7.

which time he improved his Arabic language skills, explored the idea of translating the Qur'an into Japanese, and completed his first draft.[32] Al-Nadwī' revised this draft, despite having no knowledge of Japanese, and his discussion of the process is fascinating: Mita would translate his 'understandings of the verse' into English from Japanese orally, while al-Nadwī would listen carefully and compare his colleague's rendition with existing English translations and the Arabic text.[33] The pair spent two years and eight months working in this way, painstakingly going through the entire translation. In 1972, the final product was printed in Hiroshima, Japan under the label of the Association of Japanese Muslims and the MWL.

The Mita-al-Nadwī collaboration was the first Muslim-authored translation of the Qur'an in that language. Reprinted several times, this version remains one of the most popular in Japan, especially among local Muslims, and it has been praised for its language choices: Hans Martin Krämer, in his recent study of the reception of Qur'an translations in Japan, points out that this edition makes good use of specific linguistic phenomena. As example, he notes how Mita's translation of Q. 4:

> [...] shows how language choices for Allah are different from language choice for husband against their wives and for wives themselves. Language choice is apparent in the use of nouns referring to Allah [...] and verbs addressing Allah's act as shown with respectful sentences [...] These differences in language choice aim at educating humans not to be arrogant and to be humble since only Allah is the most high.[34]

Krämer also suggests that Mita makes a conscious cultural choice to use more Christian than Buddhist Japanese vocabulary in his translation.[35]

Saudi sponsorship of Mita's Japanese translation took place against a wider political background, particularly the Saudi establishment's

---

32 Hans Martin Krämer, 'Pan-Asianism's Religious Undercurrents: The Reception of Islam and Translation of the Qurʾān in Twentieth-Century Japan', *The Journal of Asian Studies*, 73.3 (2014), 632–35, http: doi.org//10.1017/S0021911814000989

33 During this process, he came to the conclusion that Pickthall's translation was much more accurate than Yusuf Ali's, and it is safe to assume that it was al-Nadwī's idea that the MWL publish Pickthall's work in 1977.

34 Ely Triasih Rahayul and Ahmad Fauzan, 'The Language Choice as a Reflection of Islamic Communication in the Quran-Japanese Translation', *Madania*, 24.1 (2020), 73–82 (p. 82), http://dx.doi.org/10.29300/madania.v24i1.3073

35 Krämer, p. 635.

activities in the East. In 1971, King Fayṣal made an official visit to Tokyo.[36] The publication of the MWL's Japanese translation, when viewed in this context, appears to be part of a cultural diplomatic strategy, an attempt to strengthen cultural ties between the two countries. The Mita-al-Nadwī edition is also notable because it constituted the first successfully published translation of the Qur'an into a foreign language to be produced at the behest of the MWL. It was not the last translation into Japanese to be printed by a Saudi institution, however. In 2018, a new translation by Saeed Sato was published by the KFGQPC.

The MWL's Turkish Translation

Translating the Qur'an into 'non-Muslim' languages proved to be problematic due to a lack of available scholars with the appropriate combination of skills in linguistics and Qur'anic/Islamic studies. This led the MWL to embark on projects to translate the Qur'an into 'Muslim' languages, such as Turkish. Interest in religion grew in Turkey during the 1960s and 1970s as the Demokrat Parti, which had come to power in 1950, implemented policies that increased religious liberty.[37] There was a strong demand for a new translation of the Qur'an to replace Muhammed Hamdi Efendi Elmalılı's 1935 *Hak Dini Kur'an Dili* [God Religion Quran's language] because it contained a large amount of Arabic and Persian words that were difficult for many readers to understand. Several new translations appeared as a result. Perhaps the most comprehensive of these was *Kur'an-ı Kerim Meali* [The Meanings of the Noble Qur'an] by Süleyman Ateş, which was published in two volumes in, respectively, 1974 and 1977.[38] With the increase in religious freedom, more and more Turkish people began traveling to Saudi Arabia's holy cities to perform the Hajj, and the Muslim World League did not have an approved translation to distribute to these pilgrims.

36 J. A. Allan and Kaoru Sugihara, *Japan and the Contemporary Middle East* (London: Taylor and Francis, 2005), p. 148.

37 Muhammet Abay, 'Türkçedeki Kur'an Meâllerinin Tarihi ve Kronolojik Bibliyografyası', *Türkiye Araştırmaları Literatür Dergisi*, 10.19–20 (2012), 232–303 (pp. 252–54).

38 Süleyman Ateş, *Kur'an-ı Kerim Meali* (Istanbul: Yüksel Matbaası, 1974); Süleyman Ateş, *Kur'an-ı Kerim ve Yüce Meali* (Ankara: Kılıç Kitabevi, 1977).

The MWL responded by publishing *Kur'an-ı Kerim ve Açıklamalı Meali* in 1982.[39]

This latter translation was prepared by a team of Turkish scholars in cooperation with the MWL. It is unusual in being a collectively authored work; the majority of modern Turkish interpretations until that point had been produced by an individual translator. The six members of the original translation team were, at the time, affiliated with the theological department at Marmara University in Istanbul. Their introduction to the translation states that the project was initiated by the MWL but does not give any further information about the organisation's involvement in the production. It does not say, for example, whether the MWL maintained any degree of oversight. It does, however, describe the working process of the translation team: each member was allocated approximately one-sixth of the Qur'anic text to translate individually, then all worked together in a later stage to ensure the entire translation was stylistically cohesive.

The *Kur'an-ı Kerim ve Açıklamalı Meali* contains some innovative features. Like almost all Turkish Qur'an translations, it prefaces each sura [chapter] with a short introduction. However, it also appends comments to the main text; these offer some clarification but do not refer to exegetical or other sources. The volumes also include an unusually detailed thematic index, beginning with the topic of *ahlak* [ethics] and finishing with *muhtelif mevzular* [varieties]. Within the text itself, some interpolations set in brackets offer further auxiliary information, such as explanations of pronouns or interpretations of some key concepts. The style of the translation seems to be rather late Ottoman/Early Modern Turkish and resembles that of Elmalılı's 1935 work. The very beginning of the chapter *Sūrat al-Baqara* uses Qur'anic vocabulary in almost every verse: 'müttakîler' (for *muttaqīn*) in verse 2; 'gayb' (for *al-ghayb*) and 'rızıktan infak' (for *mimmā razaqnāhum yunfiqūna*) in verse 3; 'azap' (for *ʿadhāb*) in verse 7, etc. Another good example of this reliance on Arabic as well as Arabic loan words can be seen in Q. 2:218, where almost all of the key concepts in the translation are expressed in language based on Arabic words:

39 Ali Özek, Hayrettin Karaman, Ali Turgut, Mustafa Çağrıcı, İbrahim Kafi Dönmez, and Sadrettin Gümüş, *Kur'an-ı Kerim ve Açıklamalı Meali* (Istanbul: Ayyıldız Matbaası, 1982).

> İman edenler (*alladhīna amanū*) ve hicret edip (*hājarū*) Allah yolunda cihad edenler (*jāhadū*) var ya, işte bunlar, Allah'ın rahmetini (*raḥmat Allāh*) umabilirler. Allah, gafur (*ghafūr*) ve rahîmdi (*raḥīm*)
>
> [Indeed, those who have believed and those who have emigrated and fought in the cause of Allah—those expect the mercy of Allah. And Allah is Forgiving and Merciful].

Generally, the translators of MWL's Turkish edition follow the 'literal' trend found in twentieth-century Saudi exegesis related to theological issues. However, some noteworthy exceptions exist, and one example is the phrase *yawma yukshafu ᶜan sāqin* in Q. 68:42. It is translated literally as '*O gün incikler açılır*' [the Day the shin will be uncovered], but a comment explains that 'this may refer to hardships, or [the Day] when all truths are revealed clearly' [*işlerin güçleşmesi veya bütün hakikatlerin apaçık ortaya çıkması kasdedilir*]. This comment offers two competing interpretations: one, the more widespread, is that this expression refers to some kind of 'horrifying things' [*shiddat al-amr*] that will happen during the Day of Resurrection; the second (about 'revealed truths' [*ḥaqāʾīq al-umūr*]) is found in a number of late Ottoman *tafsīr* works, such as those by Abū Suᶜūd, Ismāᶜīl Ḥaqqī, and a recent edition of Shihāb al-Dīn al-Alūsī's called *Rūḥ al-maᶜānī*.[40] A third interpretation of this verse, one quite popular in Salafi circles that understands the phrase to refer literally to 'Allah's shin', is not mentioned here at all.

The influence of the modern Turkish exegetical tradition can also be seen in the commentary provided on Q. 3:7, which states that God has sent down the Book, in which are verses that are *muḥkamāt* [of clear meaning] and also verses that are *mutashābihāt* [ambiguous]. The *Kur'an-ı Kerim* translators render the phrase '*wa-mā yaᶜlamu taʾwīlahu illā-llāhu wa-l-rāsikhūna fī-l-ᶜilmi yaqūlūna* [...]' in this verse in the most widely accepted way, as '*Halbuki Onun tevilini ancak Allah bilir. İlimde yüksek pâyeye erişenler ise* [...]' [No one knows its interpretation except Allah. And those who are firmly grounded in knowledge say [...]], that is, they include a full stop after 'Allah'. Yet, they also mention an alternative reading—one that carries on to suggest it is not only God who knows the true meaning of the Qur'an's verses but also 'those grounded

40 See Shihāb al-Dīn al-Alūsī, *Rūḥ al-maᶜānī fī tafsīr al-Qurʾān al-ᶜaẓīm wa-l-sabᶜa al-mathānī*, 11 vols (Beirut: Dār al-Kutub al-ᶜIlmiyya, 2014), x, p. 39.

in knowledge' [*al-rasikhūna fī-l-ʿilmi*]. In accordance with this alternative interpretation, the Turkish translation comments that '*müteşâbih âyetlerin manaları, zaman içinde ilmin gelişmesi ile çözülecektir*' [the meanings of the *mutashābih* verses in the Qur'an will become clear with the development of science over time]. Also, the index to the translation includes a list of so-called '*kevni/kozmolojik*' [cosmological] verses, a popular trend in the 1960s and 1970s. Such scientifically inflected exegesis was later criticised in some Salafi circles as being 'pseudo-rationalism'.

The *Kur'an-I Kerim ve Türkçe Açıklamalı Meali*, therefore, blends two exegetical styles. It is a conservative Sunni rendition of the Qur'an insofar as it follows contemporary Saudi-Salafi discourse by relying on literal/grammatical translations and many 'Arabicised' wordings. Further editions of this translation were published within only a few years by both the KFGQPC, in 1987, and the state-supported Turkish Religious Foundation (TDV), in 1993. These editions preserve much of the original 1982 work, introducing only very minor changes. This translation remains popular in Turkey, being distributed under the name *Türkiye Diyanet Vakfı Meali* [The Turkish Religious Foundation Translation], but has also become an important source for Qur'an translations into other languages.[41] Published in both Saudi Arabia and Turkey by state-supported organisations, it is one of the most successful projects of the MWL and of the KFGQPC, which later adopted it and still publishes the translation as its only Turkish edition.

MWL Translations into African Languages

Another of the MWL's successful translation projects, realised between 1962 and 1973, was a translation into the Yoruba language, which is mainly spoken in Nigeria and has more than fifty-million speakers.[42] The translation was initiated by the Nigerian political leader Ahmadu Ibrahim Bello in reaction to early missionary translations and as part of a pro-Islamic agenda led by local elites. Bello was a Nigerian statesman

41 For example, it is the basis of the Russian translation by Fazıl Karaoğlu (1994) and the Crimean Tatar translation by Riza Fazıl (1998).

42 Abdul Kabir Hussain Solihu, 'The Earliest Yoruba Translation of the Qur'an: Missionary Engagement with Islam in Yorubaland', *Journal of Qur'anic Studies*, 17.3 (2015), 10–37.

who was heavily involved in the independence of Northern Nigeria (an autonomous division within the country), and served as its first and only premier from 1954 until 1966.[43] He had close ties with the MWL, serving as a member of al-Majlis al-Tāʾsīsī, its Constituent Council, and established links between this organisation and the local scholars who carried out the translation. The work itself was another collaborative effort: the Muslim Council of Nigeria, specifically its Lagos branch, commissioned a committee to undertake the actual translation.[44] Their text was revised by a further board of scholars from Lagos, handed over to the MWL for approval in 1972, and finally published in 1973 (together with the Arabic source text) by the Lebanese company Dār al-ᶜArabiyya. After publication, it was distributed by The Light of Islam publisher in Maiduguri, Nigeria.[45] The translation used Roman script and soon gained popularity. According to one study, 25,000 copies were distributed in the first two years.[46] The initial print run was followed by two more, one in 1977 and the other in 1983. This translation, with some revisions, was republished by the KFGQPC in 1997.

In 1979, the MWL also published a translation in Hausa, which currently has some fifty-million speakers, again through the publisher Dār al-ᶜArabiyya.[47] This edition was later revised by the KFGQPC and republished by them in 1991. Its translator was Shaykh Abu Bakr Mahmud Gumi (1924–1992), who was also a member of the Constituent Council of the MWL and its representative in Lagos. He is considered to be 'the first Nigerian ever to write a complete translation of the Qur'an into Hausa'.[48] A close friend of Ahmadu Bello, he was an active protagonist of the Salafi movement in West Africa, criticising local Sufi orders for their 'misinterpretations' and promoting the idea of Islamic

43 Hassan Ma'ayergi, 'Translations of the Meanings of the Holy Qur'an into Minority Languages: The Case of Africa', *Institute of Muslim Minority Affairs Journal*, 14.1–2 (1993), 156–80 (p. 172).

44 The committee included Muhammadul-Awwal Augusto, Tijani A. Akanni, Hasani Yusau Dindey, and some other scholars.

45 *Al-Kurani ti a tumo si ede Yoruba* (Beirut: Dār al-ᶜArabiyya, 1973).

46 Mofakhkhar Hussain Khan, 'Translation of the Holy Qurʾān in the African Languages', *The Muslim World*, 77.3–4 (1987), 250–58 (p. 255).

47 *Al-Kur'ani mai girma. Da Kuma Tarjaman Maᶜanōninsa Zuwa Ga Harshen Hausa* (Beirut: Dār al-ᶜArabiyya, 1979). A partial translation into Hausa had previously been published in 1975 and distributed in Nigeria (see Khan, p. 255).

48 Andrea Brigaglia, 'Two Published Hausa Translations of the Qurʾân and Their Doctrinal Background', *Journal of Religion in Africa*, 35.4 (2005), 424–49 (p. 428).

governance in Nigeria. In some senses, he continues to be a heroic figure for local Muslims.[49]

As some researchers have noted, the Saudi state used the activities of the MWL to help create a network of religious schools and centres in Nigeria during the 1970s.[50] It is no coincidence that both of the MWL's successful publishing projects in African languages also emerged from this context: the Kingdom of Saudi Arabia deliberately established ties within Nigerian Muslim political circles. Both the Yoruba and Hausa translations were part of a soft-power strategy to spread the Salafi-Wahhabi view of Islam, especially in the case of Gumi's translation. In contrast to the Japanese and Turkish translations produced by the MWL, a 'Salafi hermeneutics' was broadly applied to both the African-language interpretations.

The MWL's Bulgarian Translation

Perhaps the last MWL project to be more or less successful in terms of the eventual production of a published text was the Bulgarian translation that appeared in 1993, *Sveschen Koran. Prevod Nedim Gendzhyjev.*[51] Published by the Saudi-run King Fahd bin ᶜAbd al-ᶜAzīz Foundation with support from the MWL representative in Vienna and the Eastern European Muslim Council (EEMC) based in Vienna, this work sought to fill the gaps in Islamic learning that emerged in Eastern Europe during the years of communist rule. The introduction to *Sveschen Koran* was written by one of EEMC's directors, al-Fātiḥ ᶜAlī al-Ḥasanayn. A scholar from Sudan who later obtained a degree from the University of Belgrade (in Yugoslavian times), al-Ḥasanayn played an active role in the Islamic revival in the Balkan states. He developed close ties with local politicians through membership of various Middle-Eastern relief organisations, including becoming an advisor to Alija Izetbegović (1925–2003), the first president of the newly independent Republic of Bosnia and Herzegovina. Al-Ḥasanayn's introduction to the Bulgarian

49 See Usman Faruk, *The Life and Times of Sheikh Abubakar Mahmud Gumi: Lessons for the Muslim Ummah* (Zaria: Ahmadu Bello University Press Limited, 2013).

50 See Sahabi Maidamma Jabo and Umar Ubandawaki, 'Nigeria-Saudi Arabia: Socio-Cultural and Educational Relations', *RIMA International Journal of Historical Studies* (*RIJHIS*), 4.1 (2019), 29–37, http://dx.doi.org/10.36108/IJSI/2202.11.0140

51 *Sveschen Koran. Prevod Nedim Gendzhyjev* (Sofia: Kral Fahd bin Abdul Aliz, 1993).

translation states that 'almost all translations and interpretations of the Qur'an in Eastern Europe were written by Christian priests or Jews, not counting those from Bosnia and Herzegovina'.[52] This claim is somewhat confusing since, while translations by Christian missionaries certainly existed prior to the Soviet era (including in Bulgaria)[53], none are known to have been produced by Jewish translators; perhaps al-Ḥasanayn was referring to conspiracy narratives that could be found in many Muslim apologetic texts of the time as a result of the Palestinian-Israeli conflict. His introduction continues, then, to explain that a few leading Muslim institutions (the MWL, the KFGQPC, and the World Assembly of Muslim Youth, known as WAMY) came together to undertake 'this Bulgarian translation as the first in the region'.[54] The translator, Nedim Gendzev, who was Mufti of Bulgaria at the time, went further, asserting that his was 'the only correct translation of the Qur'an'.[55] *Sveschen Koran* was published together with the Arabic text (based on the KFGQPC *muṣḥaf* [recitation]) and can, at least, be called the first Muslim translation of the Qur'an in Bulgarian, if one does not count an earlier Ahmadi Qur'an translation made from previous English translations.[56] It was edited by a professor of Turkic Studies, Ivan Dobrev, and a few local Muslim scholars who were editorial board members.[57] A browse of this Bulgarian translation suggests that the text was based on Ali Özek's translation into Turkish, as it provides almost identical introductions to the suras.

In 1997, another translation of the Qur'an into Bulgarian appeared. Tsvetan Teofanov worked from an Arabic source text to create this edition, which was published by a locally operating Saudi foundation that goes by the name Taybah Foundation.[58] This work hints that Saudi influence in the country was not limited to the MWL's translation

52 *Sveschen Koran*, p. 3.
53 See, on this translation, Natanail Nazifoff, 'The Bulgarian Koran', *The Muslim World*, 23.2 (1933), 187–90.
54 *Sveschen Koran*, p. 3.
55 Ibid., p. 5.
56 *The Qur'an in Bulgarian* (Tilford: IIPH, 1989).
57 Ivan Dobrev later published his own translation into Bulgarian—one based largely on Russian and Turkish sources. See Ivan Dobrev, *Svescheniyat Koran, prevod od Ivan Dobrev* (Sofia: BMK, 2008).
58 Tsvetan Teofanov, *Prevod na Sveschenija Koran. Prevede Tsvetan Teofanov* (Sofia: Tayba, 1997).

activities. Bulgaria's relatively liberal laws on religion allowed many Saudi-sponsored Islamic NGOs to be established there in the 1990s.[59]

The Bulgarian translation project was the only one planned by the MWL for the whole of Eastern Europe. Other translations of the Qur'an into the languages of neighbouring countries (Macedonian, Hungarian, Russian, and Ukrainian) were only produced years later—by the KFGQPC.

Concluding Remarks

After the establishment of the KFGQPC in 1984, all of the MWL's projects (as well as its human resources, experts, and contacts in the area of translation) were moved to this new institution. The MWL did have initial discussions with the Complex about producing Qur'an translations in other languages, such as Italian, but all of these were eventually published solely by KFGQPC or as collaborations between the two organisations.[60] Despite bringing to fruition only a modest number of translations, the MWL clearly promoted the idea of Qur'an translation in its modern sense (as 'translation of the meanings'), firmly establishing this notion within scholarly networks of Salafi scholarship across the world. It can thus be said that, by the 1960s, the issue of the translation of the Qur'an had already become a part of both Salafi doctrine and, especially, Salafi missionary endeavours. The most important contribution the MWL made to the Saudi translation movement was to build local and international networks of translators and revisers but also of publishing and distribution companies. Its policy of approving some translations and rejecting others also established the idea of institutional translation—that state or inter-state bodies were authorised to confirm the 'correctness' of a given translation. Due in no small part to the MWL's adoption of this approach, almost all of the translations it published remain in use today.

To summarise the situation as it stood in 1984 when the KFGQPC was established, the MWL had overseen the successful completion of

59 See Ismail Telci and Aydzhan Peneva, 'Turkey and Saudi Arabia as Theo-Political Actors in the Balkans', *Insight Turkey*, 21.2 (2019), 249–52.

60 'Tarjamat maᶜānī al-Qurᵓān al-karīm ilā al-Iṭāliyya', *Alfaisal Magazine*, 128 (1987), 113–14 (p. 114).

translation projects into Japanese (1972), Yoruba (1973), Hausa (1979), and, finally, Turkish (1982), to which we can add one more cooperative project in Bulgarian (1993). There is also some reference to the MWL in an Albanian translation published in 1988, but it looks as if the organisation simply provided logistical and/or financial support rather than being involved in any revision process.[61] The Eastern European market that appeared in the late 1980s and early 1990s with the collapse of communism helped to establish the KFGQPC, as it was given full authority and responsibility for the promotion of Qur'an translations in the region. Given the Complex's dominant position, the MWL has taken almost no further steps towards publishing translations of the Qur'an into any other world languages (the only exception to this is a Portuguese edition but, as this was later republished by the KFGQPC, it will be discussed in Chapter Four); their activities have been constrained to proposing some revisions of Yusuf Ali's English interpretation. The establishment of the KFGQPC marks the start of a new and much more productive phase of the Saudi Qur'an-translation industry. Before discussing this organisation, however, we turn in the next chapter to consider one of the most globally influential translations to come from Saudi Arabia. Widely known as the 'Hilālī-Khān', after the names of its translators, it was the first English translation to be produced in the scholarly environment of the Islamic University of Madinah in the late 1960s and early 1970s. The history of the work illustrates well how the translation movement developed in the Saudi Kingdom at the very same time that the idea of 'authorised' institutional translations of the Qur'an was crystallising.

61 Same is true for the Taiwan edition of earlier translation into Chinese by Wang Jingzhai. See: https://www.taiwan-panorama.com/en/Articles/Details?Guid=03d4d3fb-c186-4856-bce1-d58f62c7a0f4&langId=3&CatId=11&postname=Sacred%20Task—Shen%20Hsia-huai%27s%20New%20Translation%20of%20the%20Qur%27an.

3. The Hilālī-Khān Translation: The First Interpretation of the Qur'an in a Foreign Language by Saudi Scholars

It may be hard to believe, given the state involvement in the Qur'an-translation industry over several decades outlined in the previous chapter, but there exists only one Saudi-produced English translation of the Qur'an that can be considered entirely state-supported. The Hilālī-Khān translation, developed in the late 1960s and early 1970s, has a complex history. Initially neglected in the first few decades after its publication, it was subsequently published on a massive scale and presented as an exemplar for other translations.[1] The work, known as 'Hilālī-Khān' because it was authored by Muḥammad Taqī al-Dīn al-Hilālī and Muḥammad Muḥsin Khān, two scholars working at the Islamic University of Madinah, is one of the most important sources to be addressed in this study. This translation has survived multiple revisions and editions and been subject to widespread and intensive critique, especially in recent times. For some readers it represents the most accurate interpretation of the text and holds a status similar to that of the King James Bible in many Protestant communities, while for others it exemplifies a conservative and fundamentalist 'Wahhabi' interpretation of the Qur'an that distorts God's word. Consequently, even after the introduction of many other translations to the market,

1 As of 2023, seventeen editions of the Hilālī-Khān translation are listed in WorldCat (the global catalogue of library holdings). The number rises to somewhere between twenty and thirty if we add reprints that are not given a unique ISBN.

©2024 Mykhaylo Yakubovych, CC BY-ND 4.0 https://doi.org/10.11647/OBP.0381.03

the Hilālī-Khān translation can be found in almost any Sunni mosque or Islamic centre in the West, including those that are not specifically Salafi-leaning. Moreover, the translation and *tafsīr* provided in 'Hilālī-Khān' has come to be a standard reference text for other translations of the Qur'an into a variety of languages. Beyond its lasting global impact, the 'Hilālī-Khān' merits special attention here because the history of this work and its textual development illuminates the evolution of views on Qur'an translation in Saudi Arabia. The original text has undergone three extensive revisions in Saudi hands, and the story of this translation answers how and why the state came to use Qur'an translation as a tool for global Salafi missionary activity. This chapter examines the target text but also the almost legendary personae of the translators who were behind it.

Al-Hilālī and His Legacy

Muḥammad Taqī al-Dīn al-Hilālī (1893–1987) was a Muslim activist, translator, scholar, and prolific writer. His background and context have been the subject of recent interest for English-language scholars: Umar Ryad has discussed al-Hilālī's experiences working for the Arabic-language section of Radio Berlin in Nazi Germany,[2] while another profound study, by Henri Lauzière, meanwhile, considers al-Hilālī's Islamic missionary vision and offers a valuable perspective on Muslim scholars' encounter with modern technologies in the mid-twentieth century.[3] Lauzière has also authored what is probably the only comprehensive biography of al-Hilālī, which discusses his contribution to the development of Salafi missionary activities.[4] The Hilālī-Khān translation itself has also received much attention, attracting reviews

2 Umar Riyad, 'A Salafi Student, Orientalist Scholarship, and Radio Berlin in Nazi Germany: Taqi al-Din al-Hilali and His Experiences in the West', in *Transnational Islam in Interwar Europe*, ed. by G. Nordbruch and U. Ryad (New York: Palgrave Macmillan, 2014), pp. 107–55. https://doi.org/10.1057/9781137387042_6.

3 Henri Lauzière, 'Islamic Nationalism through the Airwaves: Taqī al-Dīn al-Hilālī's Encounter with Shortwave Radio 1937–39', *Die Welt des Islams*, 56.1 (2016), 6–33, https://doi.org/10.1163/15700607-00561p03.

4 Henri Lauzière, 'The Evolution of the Salafiyya in the Twentieth Century Through the Life and Thought of Taqi al-Din al-Hilali' (PhD dissertation, Georgetown University, 2008).

that range from the laudatory[5] to the critical[6] but also some neutral ones.[7] This is unsurprising because, as Stefan Wild rightly suggests, 'the Hilālī-Khān translation is the most widely disseminated Qur'an in Islamic bookstores and Sunni mosques throughout the English-speaking world'.[8] What remains almost completely unexplored, however, is the textual history of this translation and al-Hilālī's role in it. This is somewhat surprising because, as this study will show, the differences in the many versions produced since 1977 are appreciable.

Al-Hilālī authored a number of books in *tafsīr* studies, including the voluminous exegesis *Sabīl al-rashād fī hudā khayr al-ᶜabbād* [The Correct Path, Leading to the Happiness of the Servants [of God]] and a few commentaries on single suras.[9] From these, it is possible to glean his approach to the translation of the Qur'an into English in terms of his personal hermeneutical experience and methodology. One example is his monograph on modern Arabic linguistics called *Taqwīm al-lisānayn* [Correcting the Two Tongues] (1978).[10] In it, al-Hilālī challenges the application of Western semantics to Arabic as a sign of colonialism, utilising examples from George Sale's 1734 English translation of the Qur'an to demonstrate the loss of meaning that can occur in translation.[11] He had been interested in the representation of Islam in foreign languages since 1949, when he published an article 'Taᶜlīm al-lughāt' [The Study of Languages].[12] Although 'translating the Qur'an was, by all means,

5 For example, Abdul Raheem Kidwai, 'Review on Hilali's and Khan's *Noble Quran*', *Muslim World Book Review*, 15.3 (1995), 3–5.

6 For example, Zaidan Ali Jassem, '*The Noble Quran*: A Critical Evaluation of Al-Hilali and Khan's Translation', *International Journal of English and Education*, 3.2 (2014), 237–73.

7 For example, Mohammad Hawamdeh and Kais Kadhim, 'Parenthetical Cohesive Explicitness: A Linguistic Approach for a Modified Translation of the Quranic Text', *International Journal of Applied Linguistics & English Literature*, 4.5 (2015), 161–69, http://dx.doi.org/10.7575/aiac.ijalel.v.4n.5p.161

8 Stephan Wild, 'Muslim Translators and Translations of the Qur'an into English', *Journal of Qur'anic Studies*, 17.3 (2015), 158–82 (p. 173), https://doi.org/10.3366/jqs.2015.0215

9 Taqī al-Dīn al-Hilālī, *Sabīl al-rashād fī hudā khayr al-ᶜabbād*, 4 vols (Amman: al-Dār al-Athriyya, 2006).

10 By this expression, he meant both oral and written tongue [*al-lisān wa-l-qalām*].

11 Taqī al-Dīn al-Hilālī, *Taqwīm al-lisānayn* (Cairo: Maktabat al-Maᶜārif, 1978), p. 13.

12 Taqī al-Dīn al-Hilālī, '*Taᶜlīm al-lugāt: ḥukmuhu wa-fīᶜīdatahu*', *Lisān al-dīn*, 3.10 (1949), 7–10 (p. 8).

a religiously risky venture' at the start of the 1970s[13], it was one that al-Hilālī had been contemplating for some time. It also fit well into the emerging translation movement in Saudi Arabia, which, as was shown in Chapter Two, had much in common with discussions that had been taking place on the issue of Qur'anic translatability in Egypt and Turkey. Where this 'venture' differed was in its orientation toward missionary activity and the promotion of 'true Islamic doctrine' [*al-ᶜaqīda al-ṣaḥīḥa*] in its Salafi understanding.

Many unanswered questions remain about what led al-Hilālī to the idea of translating the Qur'an and about the relevance of the Saudi milieu of the late 1960s and early 1970s on the realisation of this project. The translation was first printed in 1977 by a publisher based in the USA, and it was not reprinted in the Kingdom of Saudi Arabia until the middle of the 1980s. Why was its promotion there delayed? The answer is complicated, but some clarity can be found in the story behind the first edition of the Hilālī-Khān and the individuals responsible (that is, not only its original translators but also those who revised and published the text). Key among these is its co-translator, Muḥammad Muḥsin Khān (1927–2021). Though often overshadowed in comparison to al-Hilālī, Khān took primary responsibility for all revisions, and even copyrights, after al-Hilālī's death in 1987. He was also very much involved in the edition published by the KFGQPC in 1997—one which led to a vast increase in the translation's popularity. The story behind the subsequent editions, how the translation was changed each time, is also an important one, given the status of the Hilālī-Khān as an exemplar for other translators of the Qur'an from both Salafi and non-Salafi backgrounds. When viewed from a broader perspective, these revisions reflect the dynamics of a specifically Saudi approach to missionary activity: intellectual, political, and especially religious trends can be seen at work in the text. The Saudi trajectory marks the emergence of a new type of hermeneutics in modern Qur'an translations.

The Background to the First Edition

In contrast to English-language sources, quite a lot of biographical material on Muḥammad Taqī al-Dīn al-Hilālī is available in

13 Lauzière, 'The Evolution of the Salafiyya', p. 357.

contemporary Arabic and Muslim sources[14]. Al-Hilālī himself published an autobiography, *al-Da^c^wa ilā Allāh fī aqṭār mukhtalifa* [The Call to God in Various Regions], in 1971. This memoir recounts his various travels, with the last chapters covering the late 1960s, when the influential Saudi authority and later Mufti of the Kingdom ^c^Abd al-^c^Azīz b. Bāz invited him to teach at the Islamic University of Madinah (IUM) in 1968.15 It was here that al-Hilālī met Khān and undertook the work of translating the Qur'an into English.

Born in 1893 in Sijilmasa in Morocco, al-Hilālī later moved first to Algeria to pursue his studies, and then to Egypt. Influenced by such notable Muslim thinkers as Rashīd Riḍā (1865–1935) and Ḥasan al-Bannā (1906–1949), al-Hilālī was an active member of the anti-colonial movement. He escaped a death sentence in French Morocco by fleeing to India, where he learned English. Establishing strong ties with Middle Eastern scholarly networks and Arab political elites (above all, the royal family of Āl Sa^c^ūd), al-Hilālī later used his ties with European Muslim leaders like Shākib Arslān to enrol at the University of Bonn (in 1936), where he obtained a doctorate in 1941 with a thesis on a section of al-Bīrūnī's 'India' on mineralogy.[16] His time in Germany and service as a translator for the Nazi-run Radio Berlin is well researched,[17] and his attitude towards the Nazi 'liberation' of the Muslim people colonised by British and French imperial powers seems to have aligned with the 'Pan-Islamist' thinking of the time. In his memoir at least, al-Hilālī disassociated himself from the Nazis when, in a meeting with the British Ambassador in Spain, he identified himself as merely a 'fighter against British colonialism' and no more.[18]

In 1959, al-Hilālī left a teaching position at the University of Baghdad to take up a similar role in his homeland. During his time at the Muhammad V University in Rabat, he became one of the most active proponents of Salafism in Morocco, providing religious instruction and

14 See www.alhilali.net/ for an informative website (in Arabic) dedicated to al-Hilālī.

15 Taqī al-Dīn al-Hilālī, *al-Da^c^wa ilā Allāh fī aqṭār mukhtalifa* (al-Shārqa: Maktabat al-Ṣaḥāba, 2003), p. 214.

16 Taki Ed Din Al Hilali, *Die Einleitung zu al-Bīrūnīs Steinbuch. Mit Erläuterungen übersetzt.* Dissertation unter Aufsicht von Richard Hartmann und Hans Heinrich Schaeder. Mit einer Widmung an Herbert W. Duda (Leipzig: Harrassowitz, 1941).

17 See, for example, David Motadel, *Islam and Nazi Germany's War* (Cambridge—London: The Belknap Press of Harvard University Press, 2014), pp. 94–95.

18 al-Hilālī, *al-Da^c^wa ilā Allāh*, pp. 101–02

giving sermons in a number of mosques.[19] In the mid-1960s, however, he experienced quite a lot of opposition to his teachings from local scholarly circles in the cities of Fez and Meknes. Al-Hilālī's somewhat radical response was to accuse his opponents of 'being polytheists' for simply preventing him from teaching a classical Wahhābī source, *Kitāb al-Tawḥīd* [The Book of Oneness].[20] Perhaps because of this conflict, he seized the opportunity to work in Saudi Arabia when it was offered by Ibn Bāz (then vice-rector, and later rector of IUM) in 1968. Unfortunately, al-Hilālī's autobiography does not tell us anything significant about his time in Saudi Arabia, despite the fact that he lived there until he retired and returned to Morocco in 1974, at the age of eighty-one. We do know that he undertook teaching duties for the Department of the Mission and Basics of Religion [Kulliyat al-Daᶜwa wa-Uṣūl al-Dīn] and was also an active author. For example, al-Hilālī frequently published articles on various issues in the IUM journal *Majallat al-jāmiᶜa al-Islāmiyya*. The very first of these, which he wrote in 1968, was entitled 'al-Taqaddum wa-l-rajᶜiyya' [Progress and Backwardness].21 In it, he discussed his negative perception of the West and its values, coming to the conclusion that nations do not 'progress' in a linear fashion and that the 'hegemony of the West' is not eternal. Al-Hilālī also praised Saudi Arabia for its social justice, security, and other advantages. Interestingly, he cites Nazi Germany as a second example of a secure country while pointing out that, in contrast to Hitler's regime, the state politics of the Saudi Kingdom are not derived from secular institutions but from its Qur'anic schools [*madrasas*].[22]

The first systematic moves to provide educational opportunities in the West to Saudi students had begun in the 1950s.[23] Nevertheless, the number of students travelling to Europe and America remained quite low until the end of the 1960s, especially those in conservative Islamic circles. Al-Hilālī's academic and religious experience of the West, therefore, was fairly unique. To the religious establishment in

19 Ibid., p. 205.
20 Ibid.
21 Taqī al-Dīn al-Hilālī, 'al-Taqaddum wa-l-rajaʾiyya', *Majallat al-jāmiᶜa al-Islāmiyya* 1.2 (1389/1969), (pp. 18–22).
22 Ibid., pp. 19–20.
23 In the US context, for example, the 'Saudi Arabian Cultural Mission to the US' was established in 1951. See 'SACM History', http://www.sacm.org/about/history

the context of the Islamic educational systems in Saudi Arabia, which were changing and adapting to modern times, he represented an opportunity: here was a scholar with experience of life in both the East and the West who would attest the validity of the Salafi interpretation of Islam. Al-Hilālī embraced the term, using it from at least the mid-1950s to describe himself and his fellow believers in various parts of the world. For example, in the first two editions of his Qur'an translation, he identifies himself with the phrase 'as for his belief, he is a Salafi'.[24] Al-Hilālī's persona as a 'Western-educated Salafi' was quite unusual for the time, and thus he was warmly welcomed in conservative Saudi circles whose members, like the aforementioned Shaykh Ibn Bāz, dreamed of a global call to Islam.

While al-Hilālī is nowadays well known in both the East and the West as a twentieth-century hero of the Salafi mission, his co-author, Muḥammad Muḥsin Khān (1927–2021), remains quite an enigmatic figure. No systematic biography of Khān has yet been written, but the popular Saudi publisher Darussalam has compiled a few details about his life.[25] This brief sketch informs readers that Khān was born into a family of Afghani refugees in the city of Qasur (now in Pakistan). After graduating from the University of Punjab (Lahore), and later the University of Wales in the UK, he moved to Saudi Arabia where he was employed as a respiratory specialist. He worked for the Ministry of Health and a couple of hospitals before moving to the IUM to be the head of the local medical clinic there in the early 1960s.

Khān's experience with translation began while he was at the IUM. In an interview with the university's journal in 1971,[26] he explained that he began translating the *Ṣaḥīḥ al-Bukhārī* in 1956 after having a dream in which he saw the Prophet. This vision was interpreted by Ibn Bāz, the rector of IUM, as signifying that the work would 'provide a benefit' to Islam.27 Khān's aim in translating the *Saḥīḥ*, he said, was

24 Taqī al-Dīn al-Hilālī and Muḥammad Muḥsin Khān, *Explanatory English Translation of the Holy Qur'an, by Taqī al-Dīn al-Hilālī, Muḥammad Muḥsin Khān* (Chicago: Kazi Publications, 1977), p. 7,

25 Dar-us-Salam Publications, 'Muhammad Muhsin Khan', https://dar-us-salam.com/authors/muhsin-khan.htm

26 'Liqāʾ ṣuḥufī maʿa al-duktūr', *Majallat al-jāmiʿa al-Islāmiyya*, 12 (1971), 4–6.

27 'Dr. Muhammad Muhsin Khan Passes Away', *Muslim Mirror*, https://muslimmirror.com/eng/dr-muhammad-muhsin-khan-passes-away/

to fulfil this prediction and make the Sunna [Islamic traditions and practices] accessible for all English speakers, '[so that] no one on the Day of Resurrection could say that message of the Prophet has not been delivered'. It was not until 1971, some twelve years later, that he was able to present his finished work to the General Secretary of the MWL, a number of scholars who were highly proficient in English, and his friend al-Hilālī. Khān's translation of *Ṣaḥīḥ al-Bukhārī* was printed in Pakistan later that year, with the support of Muhammad Yusuf Sethi, the owner of Sethi Straw Board Mills Ltd (a paper mill based in the city of Ghakkar Mandi in Pakistan). The copyright belonged to the publisher, who covered all the expenses of printing.[28]

It seems odd that Khān makes no reference to his joint Qur'an translation project with al-Hilālī in a 1971 interview. As the preface to the first edition is dated 3 May 1972, the project must have been in progress at the time. Perhaps the initiative was deliberately kept under wraps until its completion and publication in 1977. Alternatively, Khān's role in this project may have been fairly minor; however, this is unlikely as al-Hilālī had no previous experience in translation and would have needed assistance. One way of identifying each scholar's contribution could be to determine which Qur'an translation(s) Khān used in his translation of *Ṣaḥīḥ al-Bukhārī* (if any), as this contains many quotations from the Qur'an, and to compare this with the first edition of Hilālī-Khān.

One place to look for similarity is in the introduction to Khān's *Ṣaḥīḥ* translation, which contains a particularly high number of Qur'anic citations. For example, the first verse cited is Q. 29:65, which Khān translated as follows: 'And when they embark on the ships they invoke Allah, making their faith pure for him only but when He brings them safe to land, behold, they give a share of their worships to others'. In the first edition of Hilālī-Khān this verse is rendered nearly identically—the only difference is the use of 'safely' instead of 'safe'. The same, low level

28 al-Bukhārī, *al-Jāmi*ᶜ *al-ṣaḥīḥ*, trans. by Muhammad Muhsin Khan (Ghakkhar: Sethi Straw Board Mills Ltd, 1971). In the interview, Khān mentions that the (then forthcoming) translation would consist of ten volumes, but it was finally published in nine.

of variation is seen in the next citation, Q. 11:15–16. Khān's *Ṣaḥīḥ Bukhārī* reads

> Whoever desires the life of the world and its glitter, to them We shall pay (the wages of) their deeds therein and they will have no diminution therein. They are those for whom there is nothing I in the Hereafter but Fire; vain are the deeds they did therein, and of no effect is that which they used to do.[29]

In the 1977 edition of the Qur'an translation, the addition 'in full' has been inserted after 'We shall pay', thereby interpreting the Arabic *nuwaffī ilayhim* more precisely.

All other verses cited by Khān in his translation of *Ṣaḥīḥ al-Bukhārī* mostly correspond with those found in the first version of the Hilālī-Khān translation. The minor nature of the changes to both English and Arabic wording suggests that the former translation served as a kind of draft text that was corrected in the latter translation. Thus, it appears that Khān may well have already been working on his own translation of the Qur'an in the 1960s and already had some kind of draft at this point. If so, he may initiated the project, with the trained exegete al-Hilālī coming in as co-author to make corrections only after 1968, when the latter began working in Medina. This idea finds support in the words of Shaykh Yāsir Qāḍī, who wrote in the obituary for his teacher and, later, close friend Khān:

> Sh. Ibn Bāz assigned him Dr. Taqī al-Dīn al-Hilālī [...] Although Dr. Hilālī was more fluent in French and German than English, he knew enough English to help Dr. Muḥsin, and together they embarked on the translation of the Quran, after which Dr. Muḥsin continued onwards to translate the *Ṣaḥīḥ* on his own.[30]

From these indications, we can surmise that the primarily author of not only the first edition but also the more recent revised editions published since 1994 was Muḥammad Muḥsin Khān, with Taqī al-Dīn al-Hilālī playing only a secondary role.

29 This translation seems to have been influenced by Abdullah Yusuf Ali's translation of the Qur'an. The latter's popular edition of 1946, at least, renders these verses as follows: 'Those who desire the life of the present and its glitter,—to them We shall pay (the price of) their deeds therein,—without diminution'.

30 'Dr. Muhammad Muhsin Khan Passes Away'.

The First Edition

The very first edition of the Hilālī-Khān translation appeared in 1977 and was published far from Saudi Arabia, by a publisher and distributor of Islamic texts called Kazi Publications based in Chicago. The company, established in 1972[31] by the Pakistani immigrant Liaquat Ali, is the oldest Islamic publisher in North America.[32] By the end of the 1970s, Kazi Publications was already selling books that had been published in US and elsewhere, and it seems that the owner's Pakistani connections played a decisive role in the publication of the Hilālī-Khān translation. The text's first page says that the translation was produced courtesy of Sethi Straw Board Mills Company from Ghakkhar Mandi in Pakistan, the same company that financed the publication of Khān's translation of *Ṣaḥīḥ al-Bukhārī*. Using funds from Pakistan to publish the translation and distributing it through a Pakistani publisher in the US helped to establish the work with a global audience. It is worth noting, however, that this edition bears no official stamp of approval from any state or international institutions, including Saudi authorities. Their attention, in the year that the Hilālī-Khān translation first appeared, was focused on the MWL's reprinting of Muhammad Marmaduke Pickthall's 1833 translation into English, *The Glorious Qur'an*.[33] This edition, which was published for gratis distribution by the United Nations office of the Muslim World League in New York, constitutes the first official Saudi effort to promote the translation of the Qur'an in the West. Important in relation to their subsequent efforts, this publication did not involve any exegetical intervention, as the text faithfully reproduces the first edition of Pickthall's translation—one based on an Ottoman lithography.

Turning back to the first edition of the Hilālī-Khān translation, its arrival on the scene, bearing the long title *Explanatory English Translation of the Meanings of the Holy Qur'an: A Summarised Version of Ibn Kathir,*

---

31 Mohamed Nimer, *The North American Muslim Resource Guide: Muslim Community Life* (London—New York: Taylor & Francis Ltd, 2002), p. 110.

32 David Lepeska, 'Islamic Publishing House Flourishes in US', *The National News*, https://www.thenationalnews.com/world/the-americas/islamic-publishing-house-flourishes-in-us-1.436788

33 Muhammad M. Pickthall, *The Meaning of the Glorious Qur'an. Text and Explanatory Translation by Muhammad Marmaduke Pickthall* (Mecca: Muslim World League, 1977).

Supplemented by At-Tabari with Comments from Ṣaḥīḥ al-Bukhārī (with the Arabic text), does not seem to have made any immediate impact, and it did not gain a large readership. The edition soon became a bibliographical rarity as the number of copies printed and sold was extremely limited. According to the WorldCat database, the original Hilālī-Khān translation is available in only a few libraries nowadays; and the first review of it was not written until the 1990s (by which time, thoroughly revised versions were being published by popular global publishing companies). In this instantiation, the translation in no way competed with influential Muslim interpretations of the Qur'an, such a those by Abdullah Yusuf Ali or Muhammad Marmaduke Pickthall.

Despite the initially tepid reception of the Hilālī-Khān translation, a second edition appeared the following year (1978), produced by another publisher and in a very different geographical context. This version was published by Hılâl Yayınları, which is located in Ankara, in Turkey. It is not immediately apparent why a Turkish publisher would opt to publish this translation, given that Turkey is not a logical market for an English Qur'an translation, or who its intended target audience was. Hılâl Yayınları ('Crescent Publications') was established in 1956 by Salih Özcan (1929–2015), a well-known Turkish religious and political leader, and a student of the famous theologian Badiuzzaman Said Nursi (1877–1960). Originally from the southern Turkish city of Akçakale (in Şanlıurfa province), Salih Özcan embarked on a political career, promoting Pan-Islamism in Turkey and beyond. He was involved in politics at a national level, and was an active supporter of Adnan Menderes, the Turkish prime minister between 1950 and 1960, and one of founders of the Democratic Party (DP). In the aftermath of the 1960 military coup and the subsequent execution of the prime minister, Salih Özcan had to leave the country for a few years until the political situation calmed down: he was able to return to Turkey in 1965, where he again became politically active.[34] During his extensive travels throughout the Arab world, he is reported to have met with Muhammad Hamidullah in Beirut, as well as to have had strong ties with well-known figures from the Muslim world such as Abul A'la Maududi and Muhammad Iqbal. He was the editor of two Turkish journals, *İslam Mecmuası* (1956–65) and

34 His biography is yet to be written, but for a brief outline, see Salih Özcan https://rinap.uskudar.edu.tr/uploads/site/6/content/files/salih-ozcan.pdf.

Hilal (*1958–93*), both of which were deeply concerned with the issue of Islamic unity and were heavily critical of communism, materialism, and other 'anti-Islamic' ideologies. Notably, *İslam Mecmuası* also included 'Kur'an tercümeleri' ('Qur'an translations') within its publishing remit. The editorial committee listed in the first issue of *İslam Mecmuası* includes the names of such eminent personalities as Edige Mustafa Kirimal and Muhammad Hamidullah.[35] The first, a scholar of Polish Tatar origin born in Crimea, was the nephew of Jakub Szynkiewicz (1884–1966), the former mufti of Lithuania and translator of the Qur'an into Polish and English.[36] Muhammad Hamidullah (1908–2002), a renowned Indian-Muslim scholar of the twentieth century, is known for his translation of the Qur'an into French (already mentioned in the previous chapter), which Salih Özcan published through Hilâl Yayınları in 1973.[37] Later on, a number of European Muslims were added to *İslam Mecmuası*'s editorial committee, all of whom had a similar background in Qur'anic studies. For example, Hulusi Achmed Schmiede (1935–2010) was a German convert to Islam and the editor of a popular Qur'an translation into German (by Max Henning) that was later published by the Turkish-Islamic Union for Religious Affairs in Germany (DITIB).[38]

Salih Özcan was also active internationally during the 1960s: he is reported to have been a founding member of the MWL, serving as a representative of Turkey, and acted as an agent and intermediary between Turkish and Saudi Arabian business circles.[39] Later, in 1984, Özcan became a shareholder in the Faisal Finance group, which is owned by Saudi businessmen, including members of the royal family.[40]

35 *İslam Dergisi*, 1 (1956), 1.

36 A Polish translation of selected verses was published in Sarajevo in 1935, while the English text was published later on, in the 1950s (again as a partial translation). See Mykhaylo Yakubovych, 'Nieznane tłumaczenie Koranu', *Przegląd Tatarski*, 1 (2023), 23–25.

37 Hamidullah, Muhammad, *Le Coran: Texte original en arabe et traduction française par M. Hamidullah* (Ankara: Hilal Yayinlari; Beyrouth: Salih Ozcan, 1973).

38 For one of the first editions published by the DITIB (Türkisch-Islamische Union der Anstalt für Religion e.V), see Max Henning, *Der Gnadenreiche Koran* (Ankara: DITIB, 1991).

39 Behlul Ozkan, 'Cold War Era Relations Between West Germany and Turkish Political Islam', in *Islam, Populism and Regime Change in Turkey: Making and Re-making the AKP*, ed. by M. Hakan Yavuz and Ahmet Erdi Öztürk (London—New York: Routledge, 2020), pp. 31–54.

40 *The Edinburgh Companion to Shariᶜah Governance in Islamic Finance*, ed. by Syed Nazim Ali, Wijdan Tariq, and Bahnaz Al Quradaghi (Edinburgh: Edinburgh

He had a longstanding concern with the fate of Muslims living under communist rule, and one of his closest friends and supporters was a Turkish industrialist and businessman called Sabri Ülker (1920–2012), whose family escaped from Soviet Crimea in 1929.[41] And, in addition to all this, Özcan continued to propagate the legacy of his teacher, Said Nursi, through association with the Hizmet Vakfı religious foundation (established in 1973 in Istanbul).

The question remains, his personal interest in the propagation of Islam and the promotion of Islamic unity in different languages aside, why did Özcan become interested in the Hilāli-Khān translation specifically? The answer becomes clearer when one considers Özcan's connections with Saudi religious circles. Although it appears that neither al-Hilālī nor Khān was personally associated with either of Özcan's journals, two of al-Hilālī's articles dated to 1972[42] and 1977[43]—a period coinciding with the peak of al-Hilālī's popularity as a global Islamic scholar—appeared in translation in other Turkish periodicals.

Özcan's Hilâl Yayınları edition bears two titles: in English, it was called *Explanatory Translation of the Meaning of the Holy Qur'an in English* and, in Arabic, *Tarjamat maᶜānī al-Qurᵓān al-karīm li-Ibn Kathīr* [sic]. The work was published as a single volume in 1978, with a print run of 10,000 copies. The confusing Arabic title (literally, 'Translation of the Meaning of the Glorious Qur'an by Ibn Kathīr') is probably based on the English subtitle ('A Summarised Version by Ibn Kathīr, Supplemented *by* al-Tabri [sic], with Comments from Sahih-al-Bukhari'). This edition includes the Arabic text of the Qur'an on one page, and the English text on the facing page. Özcan chose to include an Arabic text that follows the standard Ḥafṣ reading—one popular among followers of Said Nursi, who is said to be the first Islamic scholar to explore this 'wonder' of the

University Press, 2020), p. 333.

41 'Asım ve Sabri Ülker kardeşlerin 43 yıllık ortaklığını, yönetimdeki uyuşmazlık bitiriyor', http://sabriulkerinhayathikayesi.com/hikaye/asim-ve-sabri-ulker-kardeslerin-43-yillik-ortakligini-yonetimdeki-uyusmazlik-bitiriyor

42 On 'Christian missionary' and Orientalists' activities, see Muhammed Takıyüddin el-Hilâlî, 'Misyoner ve Müsteşriklerin İslam Düşmanlığı', *İslamᶜın İlk Emri Oku*, 10.120 (1972), 16; part two is published in *İslamᶜın İlk Emri Oku*, 11.12 (1972), 12.

43 The article was published in the official TDRA periodical and discusses Christian beliefs. See Muhammed Takıyüddin el-Hilâlî, 'Hz. İsaᶜnın İnsan Olduğuna ve İlahlıkla İlgisinin Bulunmadığına Dair İncilᶜden Kesin Deliller', *Diyanet İlmi Dergi Yazı*, 16.2 (1977), 101–16.

Qur'anic text.[44] The Ḥafṣ edition has been distributed under copyright by Hizmet Vakfı in Turkey and beyond since 1974, and the company is still actively printing Said Nursi's books and translations in a number of languages. From a contemporary perspective, Özcan's choice of texts is somewhat paradoxical: he pairs a specifically Salafi translation alongside the Arabic text used by Said Nursi's school, which follows the Sunni-Hanafi tradition. However, at the time it was printed, at the end of the 1970s, Islamic missionary activity was not yet so affected by intra-Islamic divisions as it is today.

The Turkish edition acknowledges the involvement of Sethi Straw Board Mills Ltd. and, for the first time, the IUM. It includes a letter, signed by the university's General Secretary, ᶜUmar Muḥammad Fulāta, that confirms the affiliation of both translators with the university. Moreover, it asserts that al-Hilālī and Khān are known for their 'correct religious doctrine' and that their work is 'much needed for the Muslim world'. However, it essentially says nothing about the text of the translation itself. Thus, the question of whether this or that translation is 'good enough' remains completely unanswered. This reflects a continuing trend in the introductions of Qur'an translations published by the KFGQPC and other Saudi institutions, according to which there is never any attempt to establish the merits of a given translation, it is simply described as a 'sincere effort for the sake of Allah' to convey the true meanings of the Qur'an, or rather, of course, 'the interpretation of the meanings'. The letter included in the Turkish edition of the Hilālī-Khān translation is dated to 10/4/1398 AH, which corresponds to 19 March 1978; given that the translation was published in May 1978, according to its copyright page, it looks as if the letter was prepared specifically for this print run. Its introduction, which was written by a group of Muslims scholars from Saudi Arabia's IUM (F. ᶜAbd al-Raḥīm, M. Amīn al-Maṣrī, and Muḥī ad-Dīn al-ᶜAẓmī, the latter two of whom are graduates from UK universities), notes the limits inherent to any translation while making quite an interesting observation about the target text:

> Again, if the book is reprehended for not being written in a high and advanced style of English, as it occurs, in modern contemporary English

44 See, for example, their illustrated booklet: Bedîüzzaman Said Nursî, *Tevafukat i-Kuraniye Dair*, https://hizmetvakfi.org/ekitap/TEVAFUK-kitapcigi.pdf

> Literature, there, it is only from its advantages. The reader's intention is to enjoy himself by understanding the meaning of the Book, and not to enjoy himself through an English style.[45]

It also includes some words in praise of al-Hilālī, telling readers that 'he qualified for his Doctorate in Germany, which is renowned for its being strict in everything [...] as for the Belief, he is a Salafi (traditional follower of the way of the Prophet)'.

The introduction generally discusses the approach taken in the translation: here we have Muslims scholars with Western academic accreditation, which likely indicates a hope that the translation will be accepted by Western readers, while, because they are also Muslims, the doctrinal aspect of the work prevails over its literary value. Of the three authors of the IUM introduction (who presumably were among the first readers of the translation), one, F. ᶜAbd al-Raḥīm, went on to be one of the most active figures in the field, later becoming the head of the KFGQPC's translation unit. The others were active in religious education. Muḥammad Amīn al-Maṣrī (1914–1977), who had already passed away before the second edition of the translation appeared in print, was a Syrian scholar who graduated first from al-Azhar, and later from Cambridge (he defended a PhD on the Sunna corpus in 1959), and who moved to Saudi Arabia in the 1960s, where he remained until his death.[46] Al-Maṣrī was a student of Ḥasan al-Bannā, the founder of the Muslim Brotherhood, and a proponent of Islamic revivalist ideas who insisted on the necessity of lessons on *jihād* in Muslim educational programs. He published a few books, including a *tafsīr* on selected suras.[47] The third co-author, Muḥyī al-Dīn al-ᶜAẓmī, was originally from Egypt and joined the IUM after attaining degrees in English from Aberdeen University in the UK and the American University in Cairo. Although his biography is elusive, he was active in translation and editing until the mid-1990s.[48]

---

45 al-Hilālī and Khān *Explanatory English Translation* (1978), p. iii.

46 Muḥammad Ḥāmid al-Nāṣir, *Ulamāʾ al-Shām fī qarn al-ᶜashrīn* (Kuwait: Dār al-Maᶜālī, [n. d.]), p. 193.

47 Muḥammad Amīn al-Miṣrī, *Min hudā Sūrat al-Anfāl* (Kuwait: Dār al-Arqam, [n. d.]).

48 *Pillars of Islam: Shahadah & Salah* (Riyadh: Darussalam, 1995).

The Turkish edition of the text, like the first Kazi edition and the KFGQPC edition mentioned above, also contained prefatory matter, presumably composed by al-Hilālī, that emphasised the preeminent status of the Arabic language in Islam. Its discussion of the translatorial approach taken generally focuses on four main topics: the 'attributes of Allah' (Q. 20:5 is specifically mentioned in this context), 'correction of serious mistakes which the previous translators have committed', the use of two *tafsīrs*, those of al-Ṭabarī and Ibn Kathīr, and, finally, the use of 'modern' (as opposed to 'archaic') English. This seems to be the first Muslim translation into English that deliberately sets out to use modern language rather than using an archaic style that was mostly inspired by the King James Bible translation, with its use of 'thou', 'hath', etc.

All four topics were quite innovative for the time: the prioritising of doctrinal topics, the polemical dialogue with other translations, the use of modern style, and the active commitment to Ibn Kathīr's commentary, an emerging exegetical trend in late twentieth-century Muslim hermeneutics. Finally, al-Hilālī mentions in his introduction an anti-Soviet Uzbek fighter he met years ago in Afghanistan. This man used only Arabic, on the basis that it was the language of the Qur'an, and prohibited his family members from talking in Russian, designating it 'the language of the enemy'. Al-Hilālī seems to have borrowed this quotation from the autobiographical book *al-Daᶜwa ilā Allāh.*[49] The anecdote reads like a pious disclaimer that urges Muslims to pursue the study of Arabic as the language of Qur'an, and it reiterates the truism that no translation can substitute for the original text. What is particularly interesting is the article on the rules of *jihād* which is included as an appendix (in both Arabic and English), published under the name 'The Call to Jihad (Fighting for Allah's Cause) in the Holy Qur'an'.[50] This appears to be drawn from a book by ᶜAbd Allāh b. Muḥammad b. Ḥāmid, and constitutes the text of a lecture delivered in the headquarters of the MWL on 5 June 1971, and subsequently published as a small booklet.[51] The author, ᶜAbd Allāh b. Muḥammad b. Ḥāmid, was a well-known Saudi scholar who once served as imam of the Great Mosque of Mecca. A Saudi scholar from the older generations,

49 al-Hilālī, *al-Daᶜwa*, p. 190.

50 al-Hilālī and Khān, *Explanatory English Translation* (1978), pp. 607–32.

51 ᶜAbd Allāh b. Muḥammad Ibn Ḥāmid, *al-Jihād fī al-Qurʾān wa-l-Sunna* (Qasim-Burayda: Dār al-Bukhārī, [n. d.]).

ᶜAbd Allāh b. Muḥammad b. Ḥāmid generally does not go into any political discussions in his treatise on *jihād*, instead addressing the idea as a prerequisite of Muslim revivalism (that is, talking about 'enemies of Islam' but not specifying who they are in any detail). This fits in with the general atmosphere of the Muslim world in the 1970s, as it experienced the rise of various Islamic movements and the growth of ideology that opposed leftist thought such as Soviet-inspired socialism. The mention of 'foreign oppressors' in the introduction, along with the inclusion of a treatise on *jihād* contextualises this Qur'an translation as one intended to promote Islamism: later, in the 1980s, during the Soviet invasion of Afghanistan, these references come across as describing current events in the Cold War era.

The third and last imprint of this edition appeared a few years later, in 1985, this time sponsored by al-Hilālī and Khān's great friend, the late Shaykh Ibn Bāz, who held the position of Director General (al-Rāᶜīs al-ᶜĀmm) of the Boards of Academic Studies, Fatwa, Islamic Call, and Guidance (Idārāt al-Buḥūth al-ᶜIlmiyya wa-l-Iftāʾ wa-Daᶜwa wa-l-Irshād) at the time. In a letter included at the beginning of the edition, dated to 21 Dhū-l-Qaᶜda 1404/18 August 1984), Ibn Bāz confirmed that this translation of the Qur'an, and also some books on Sunna, by both scholars are 'correct' [*tarjamatan saḥīḥatan*] and thus cannot be denied distribution inside the KSA.[52] This edition was published by the Saudi Office of the Director General, and the man holding its most senior position, Maktab al-Raʾīs al-ᶜĀmm, is credited as publisher. The initial print run was limited. This was the first and last appearance of the Hilālī-Khān translation in its original, unedited form in Saudi Arabia. Nevertheless, Ibn Bāz's offical seal of approval set in motion its long journey from this first Saudi edition to the later, much revised, editions produced by Darussalam and the KFGQPC.

The Second, Revised Edition(s): from Darussalam to the KFGQPC

In 1994, Darussalam Publishing House in Riyadh published its first edition of the Hilāli-Khān translation. Darussalam had been set up in 1986 and quickly established a good international distribution network,

52 al-Hilālī and Khān, *Explanatory English Translation* (1985).

from the UAE to South Africa. The owner, Abdul Malik Mujāhid, was interested in promoting translations of Islamic literature to meet the growing market for *daʿwa* books, which had been fuelled in no small part by the generous investments in this field by many state and private institutions within the Kingdom. At the very end of the 1970s, the Saudis had become involved in the anti-Soviet campaign in Afghanistan, while during the 1980s the longstanding campaign to promote the Saudi perspective on Islam and the Islamic creed had already reached the peak of its development.[53] The KFGQPC was already a pioneer in the field of Qur'an printing (as will be discussed in the next chapter), and their activities effectively provided official sanction for other publishers to do so as well. The flourishing of Qur'an printers, coupled with the growing demand for English Qur'an translations, inspired Darussalam to prepare its own edition of Hilālī-Khān.

Darussalam published a new edition in 1994. It was notable for the inclusion of a new introduction by Muḥammad Muḥsin Khān (al-Hilālī had passed away seven years earlier) in which he refers to new corrections made to the text and commentary and prohibits the publishing of 'all previous editions'. Nothing more specific is said on the nature of the revisions that had been implemented in this version. However, the second version of the edition (published in 1996) is more informative: first, readers are told that the Arabic text used for the bilingual edition is taken from *Muṣḥaf al-Madīna al-nabawiyya* (the KFGQPC 1985 edition of the Arabic Qur'an) and that some corrections have been made to improve the English. Perhaps the most obvious change is the inclusion of a third column of text alongside the Arabic text and English translation, which provides a transcription of the Qur'anic verses into romanised Arabic. With this new edition, it seems that Darussalam was trying to promote the whole work as a practically oriented and comprehensive text that could be used by non-Arabic-speaking Muslims living in the West and beyond.

The preface, by the General Manager of Darussalam, ʿAbd al-Malik Mujāhid, identifies the revision committee as consisting of two people: Dr Abdul Ahad from Aligarh Islamic University in India, and one

53 Mohd Faizal Musa, 'The Riyal and Ringgit of Petro-Islam: Investing Salafism in Education', in *Islam in Southeast Asia: Negotiating Modernity*, ed. by Norshahril Saat (Singapore: ISEAS Publishing, 2018), pp. 63–88.

Mohammad Monavar. There are also some new appendices—a glossary of Qur'anic terms, for example. It appears that most of the revisions were undertaken by Khān himself as the only copyright owner of the text. A later version of this edition, printed in 1997, includes a few more names in the acknowledgments, but the role of these individuals in the editing process is not entirely clear; it may be that they undertook final proofreading, for example.[54]

Although the introductions to both the 1994 and 1996 versions of this second edition (each of which has been republished more than ten times) are silent on the specific corrections implemented, it is clear from even a cursory look at the text that quite extensive changes were made. First of all, the English translations of 1977 and 1978 are almost completely free from the inclusion of Arabic glosses, that is, hardly any transliterated Arabic words are inserted in brackets in the text. Consider, for example, Q. 2:43. In the 1977/1978 edition, this verse reads as follows:

> And offer the prayer perfectly and give the obligatory charity (Zakat) and submit yourselves with obedience to Allah (with Muhammad a.s.) as the Muslims have done (i.e., embrace Islam, worshipping none but Allah alone and doing good with the only intention of seeking Allah's Pleasure).

Yet, in the 1996 Darussalam edition, we have the following amended translation instead:

> And perform Aṣ-Ṣalāt (Iqāmat-aṣ-Ṣalāt), and give Zakāt, and bow down (or submit yourselves with obedience to Allāh) along with Ar-Rākiᶜūn.

Later editions make the text more complicated. They not only use Arabic words to retranslate (or reinterpret) the basic Qur'anic vocabulary, but they also add explanations in brackets, thereby erasing the line between translation and commentary. To give another example, both the 1977 and 1978 versions of the first edition translate Q. 24:36 as follows:

> In houses which Allah has ordered to be raised, to be cleaned, and to be honoured, in them His Name is glorified in the mornings and in the evenings.

54 Taqī al-Dīn al-Hilālī and Muḥammad Muḥsin Khān, *The Noble Qur'an, tr. by Taqī al-Dīn al-Hilālī and Muḥammad Muḥsin Khān* (Riyadh: Darussalam, 1997), p. 7.

Darussalam's second edition from 1994 again introduces many changes to the target text:

> In houses (mosques) which Allâh has ordered to be raised (to be cleaned, and to be honoured), in them His Name is remembered [i.e., Adhan, Iqamah, Salât (prayers), invocations, recitation of the Qurᶜân etc.]. Therein glorify Him (Allah) in the mornings and in the afternoons or the evenings.

Here we see the insertion of comments explaining that the verse refers to only Islamic religious practices, while this is not so apparent in the earlier edition (for example, 'houses' is used for the original Arabic *buyūt* without adding that, in the context, this word actually refers to mosques).

The first edition also contains traces of scientific exegesis of the Qur'an, which was quite a popular trend in the Muslim world during the 1970s. One instance is its rendition of Q. 41:9. The first edition provides 'Do you verily disbelieve in Him Who created the earth in two Days (Periods)?', translating the Arabic word *yawmayn* literally as 'two days' but adding the gloss 'Periods'. Darussalam's second edition removes the word 'Periods', thus reducing the meaning of the verse to a literal one. This choice reflects a particular ideological stance, as modern Salafi hermeneutics considers any interpretation of the Qur'an in the light of contemporary science to be objectionable pseudo-rationalism.

Such ideological differences are even more visible in the respective translations of the word *al-burūj* from the phrase *wa-l-samāʾi dhāti-l-burūj* in Q. 85:1. Both versions of the first edition render this 'By the heaven holding the Zodiacal Signs of the Stars', while the later Darussalam edition simply provides 'By the heaven holding the big stars'. The reading of *al-burūj* as *al-nujūm al-ᶜaẓẓām* ('the big stars') can be traced back to Ibn Kathīr, but it seems that his opinion was not taken into account in the first edition but became influential in the second. From this we can see that the Darussalam editors intervened and proposed a 'more orthodox' (at least in terms of Salafi hermeneutics) reading of the text.

Probably the most illustrative case is that of Q. 1:7, *ṣirāṭa-lladhīna anᶜamta ᶜalayhim ghayri-l-maghḍūbi ᶜalayhim wa-lā al-ḍāllīn* ['the Path of those You have blessed, those who earned Your Anger, and not those who went astray'], specifically in terms of who is meant by 'those who earned Your Anger' (*maghḍūbi ᶜalayhim*) and 'those who went astray' (*ḍallīn*). In many classical *tafsīrs*, from al-Ṭabarī to al-Jalālayn, it is common to interpret this as referring to Jews and Christians based on information given in *ḥadīths* and, in the 1977/1978 translations, the groups mentioned are glossed accordingly:

> [...] not (the way) of those who earn Your anger (such as, Jews) not those who go astray (such as the Christians).

However, in both the Darussalam 1994 and 1996 editions, the translation has changed:

> The way of those on whom You have bestowed Your Grace, not (the way) of those who earned Your Anger, not of those who went astray.

The initial interpretation of the verse, which includes mention of Jews and Christians reappears in both a later Darussalam edition of 1997 and the first KFGQPC edition published in 1997. However, later editions (2013, 2019, and onwards), revert back and render this verse in a more neutral way, amending the translation to:

> [...] not (the way) of those who earned Your Anger (i.e., those who knew the Truth, but did not follow it) nor of those who went astray (i.e., those who did not follow the Truth out of ignorance and error).

Thus, we see some quite interesting dynamics at work in the translation of this verse: 'Jews and Christians' are mentioned in the first edition of 1977 and 1978, and then erased in 1994 and 1996, only to appear once more in 1997 and, finally, disappear again in the newest editions published since 2013. The reason behind these shifts can be attributed to the fact that Darussalam was selling its translations in the West and considered this interpretation a bit controversial, while the KFGQPC came to this perspective only a few years ago.

Stylistic Changes

In general, Darussalam's editorial changes rendered the translation more 'explanatory', especially in the core text and the selections from *tafsīr* added in the footnotes. A very good illustration can be seen if one compares changes in the translation of Q. 5:5. Both the 1977 and 1978 versions of the first edition translate this verse as follows:

> This day are made lawful to you (all) good things. The food (slaughtered cattle, eatable animals etc.) of the people of the Scripture (Jews and Christians) is lawful to you and yours is lawful to them. (Lawful to you in marriage) are chaste women from the believers and chaste women from those who were given the Scripture before your time when you have given their due dowers (Mahr), desiring chastity (i.e., taking them in legal wedlock) not committing illegal sexual intercourse, nor taking them as girl-friends. And who-so-ever rejects Faith, then fruitless is his work; and in the Hereafter he will be among the losers.

In contrast, the second, 1994, edition reads it in a completely different way. The Darussalam editors specify what the 'good things' mentioned in the verse actually are and what 'faith' really is, interpreting the last term according to a standard Salafi exegetical perspective:

> Made lawful to you this day are At-Tayyibât [all kinds of Halâl (lawful) foods, which Allâh has made lawful (meat of slaughtered eatable animals, milk products, fats, vegetables and fruits)]. The food (slaughtered cattle, eatable animals) of the people of the Scripture (Jews and Christians) is lawful to you and yours is lawful to them. (Lawful to you in marriage) are chaste women from the believers and chaste women from those who were given the Scripture (Jews and Christians) before your time when you have given their due Mahr (bridal-money given by the husband to his wife at the time of marriage), desiring chastity (i.e., taking them in legal wedlock) not committing illegal sexual intercourse, nor taking them as girl-friends. And whosoever disbelieves in Faith [i.e., in the Oneness of Allâh and in all the other Articles of Faith i.e., His (Allâh's) Angels, His Holy Books, His Messengers, the Day of Resurrection and Al-Qadar (Divine Preordainments)], then fruitless is his work; and in the Hereafter he will be among the losers.

It is not surprising that major theological issues were treated in different ways. For Q. 20:5 in the 1977/1978 edition presents the reader with the following wording:

> The Beneficent (Allah) arose over the (mighty) Throne.

The 1994 edition, meanwhile, provides:

> The Most Gracious (Allâh) rose over (Istawâ) the (Mighty) Throne (in a manner that suits His Majesty).

Darussalam also erased any kind of Christian vocabulary that had been used the previous editions. For instance, for Q. 2:138, the 1997/1998 edition gives:

> (Our Religion is) the Baptism of Allah and Who can baptise better than Allah? And we are His worshippers.

While, in the 1994 edition, this has been replaced with:

> [Our Ṣibghah (religion) is] the Ṣibghah (Religion) of Allāh (Islām) and which Ṣibghah (religion) can be better than Allāh's? And we are His worshippers. [*Tafsīr Ibn Kathīr*].

This case illustrates how deep the changes are. The Darussalam editors did not consider usage of the word 'Baptism', referring to the Christian practice, to be appropriate in association with the word *ṣibgha*, especially as it is interpreted here. *Ṣibgha* was earlier translated, literally, as 'hue', 'colour'; however, in this version, it is glossed to suggest that 'religion' is its real meaning. So, once again, Ibn Kathīr's interpretation is asserted here over the literal meaning of the verse.

The Third Edition: The KFGQPC Edition

A third edition of the Hilālī-Khān translation was published by KFGQPC in 1997 under the title *The Noble Qur'an: Translation of the Meanings and Commentary.*[55] Why did the KFGQPC wait so long to publish their version of the Hilālī-Khān translation, some twenty years after it was first printed, given that it was the first complete Salafi/Saudi-authored English translation of the Qur'an? As discussed in Chapter Two, in the early 1960s, the newly established Saudi-based MWL had been interested in supporting Muhammad Asad's translation, although they later completely disavowed his work after the first nine suras were published in 1964 in Geneva. And, as it will be shown in the next chapter, Chapter Four, in the years between 1985 and 1997, the KFGQPC also prepared at least two editions of the popular Abdullah Yusuf Ali translation, each time making some minor and major revisions. Thus, Saudi-based religious publishers were clearly interested in producing English Qur'an

55 Taqī al-Dīn al-Hilālī and Muḥammad Muḥsin Khān, *The Noble Qur'an: Translation of the Meanings and Commentary* (Medina: KFGQPC, 1997).

translations. There are two possible answers to the question of why it took so long for a Saudi-backed edition of the Hilālī-Khān translation to be produced: first of all, the work was likely neglected in Saudi Arabia because the KFGQPC, which was only founded in 1984, was trying to establish itself. It made more sense for them to republish a translation that was already well known and which would thus be more likely to find a wider readership. The second possibility is that the Saudis regarded the existing Hilālī-Khān translation as simply not 'good' enough to promote at a global level. A comparison of the earlier and later editions (that is, the 1994 Darussalam edition and the 1997 KFGQPC edition) reveals quite a significant number of differences. The KFGQPC amended both the text and commentary to a conspicuous extent.

The first KFGQPC edition of 1997 follows the typical pattern of other imprints, with the English text located in verse-by-verse format facing the Arabic original. An introduction to the volume says that the translation has been revised by a committee comprised of four scholars: Fazal Elahi Zahir, Amin al-Din Abu Bakr, Wajīh ^{c}Abd al-Raḥmān, and V. ^{c}Abd al-Raḥīm. The last of these figures was known in local circles in Medina as Abu-l-Tarjamāt ['the father of translations'] and has been the head of the Translation Center at the KFGQPC since 1994. He seems to have undertaken much of the work on this translation, including its strategic planning. The other named members of the committee were, respectively, a Pakistani religious scholar who is a graduate of Imam Muhammad Ibn Saud Islamic University, a Nigerian *da^{c}wa* activist and imam,[56] and a professor of linguistics at King Abdulaziz University (later dean of the Faculty of Arts at the Imam Muhammad bin Saud University, who was also a producer and interpreter for the BBC Arabic Service).[57] Thus, we can see that three of the four scholars comprising the team were affiliated with Saudi academic circles, with quite a wide background of international research experience.

Overall, this edition does not differ much from Darussalam's 1996 edition: one can find only few minor changes (for example, the phrase

56 For more on Amin al-Din Abu Bakr, see A. I. Lawal, 'Sheikh Aminuddeen Abubakar: A Scholar per excellent', *The Pen*, 2.8 (1987), 7.

57 'Dr Wajih Abderrahman, Major Linguistics Scholar Passes Away', *Muslim World Journal*, https://www.muslimworldjournal.com/dr-wajih-abderrahman-major-linguistics-scholar-passes-away/

'Glory is to You' is changed to 'Glory be to you' in Q. 2:32). Other changes include moving some of the explanations included by Darussalam as commentary into the core text of the translation: for instance, for Q. 2:275 the Darussalam edition has: 'Those who eat Riba will not stand [...]', while the KFGQPC adds in an explanatory gloss: 'Those who eat Riba (usury) will not stand [...]'. Dots, commas, and hyphens were added or removed, and some small changes were made to the division of sentences. As all subsequent copies and editions include a similarly minor level of minor amendment, it seems that the Darussalam edition and the first KFGQPC edition of 1997 mark the peak of the textual development of this translation.

What is noteworthy about this edition is how additional materials were used to make this translation something a bit more than simply an interpretation. In the case of the first edition of 1977, the only actual addition to the translation itself was the inclusion of Ibn Ḥāmid's letter on *jihād* in the Qur'an; in comparison, the Darussalam editions included appendices with much more additional material. As well as a glossary and list of prostration places in the Qur'an, the 1997 edition includes the same treatise on 'The Call to Jihād', a comparison of Jesus and Muhammad in the Bible and the Qur'an (written by al-Hilālī himself), and a chapter explaining God's reasons for sending prophets and messengers to humanity, along with a fairly standard Salafi outline of the concepts of *tawḥīd* ('monotheism'), *shahāda* ('confession of faith'), *shirk* ('polytheism'), and *nifāq* ('hypocrisy'). KFGQPC edition replicates all of this, with the exclusion of the text on *jihād*, but some of the later American editions (including Darussalam's 2003 version) omit almost all of these complementary texts. In some ways, this reflects recent developments in the Salafi tradition: whereas, in the late 1970s and 1980s, the idea of military *jihād* may not have been perceived in the West as completely unacceptable (due primarily to support for anti-Soviet Islamic movements), in the 1990s and, especially, the first decade of this century, much has changed. It is thus no coincidence that al-Hilālī mentions the anti-Soviet Uzbek in his original introduction, nor that this reference has been removed in more recent editions. The exclusion of the supplementary material from the later editions reflects the fact that the translation has been undergoing a process of de-politicisation, lest it be too controversial for the post-9/11 world.

Warmly accepted by many readers and critically evaluated by others, the Hilālī-Khān translation eventually played quite an important role in the rise of Salafi exegetics among a non-Arab readership, and even more so in promoting the extensive use of traditional *tafsīr* in translation. The first edition of 1977/1978 was eventually republished at least twice: once in Pakistan in 1989–92 (by the Lahore branch of Kazi Publications, in nine volumes) and once in India (Delhi: Maktaba Dar-Ul-Qur'an, 1993). The second and third editions have only ever been published in Saudi Arabia by Darussalam and the KFGQPC, with the exception of one, now rare version published in Istanbul. Printed by the Hilal publishing house, the text is almost completely taken from the 1994 Darussalam edition, while the publisher claims to be the successor of the now inactive older Hilal Yayınları publishing house that published the 1978 version of the first edition.[58] Thus, the textual history of the translation can be generally summarised as follows:

First edition
Chicago, 1977
Ankara, 1978
Lahore, 1989–1992
New Delhi, 1993

Second edition
Riyadh, since 1994
Istanbul, 2018

Third edition
Medina, since 1997

Currently, the only two editions being printed are those published by Darussalam and the KFGQPC (which distributes it gratis). However, dozens of translations based on these two later imprints can be found on almost all global Islamic websites, such as Quran.com and QuranEnc.

58 Taqī al-Dīn al-Hilālī and Muḥammad Muḥsin Khān, *Interpretation of The Meaning of The Noble Quran* (Istanbul: Hilal Yayınları, 2018). Interestingly, the cover also contains the text of the permission from Muḥammad Muḥsin Khān to publish this text. Since the text is very similar to the Darussalam 1994 edition (with only a few differences), it is not clear who actually edited it. It may have been Muḥammad Muḥsin Khān himself, as in case of the Darussalam edition (for which he confirmed the changes), or someone working on behalf of the Turkish publisher using the previous revisions as a basis for his or her own.

Many of the problems inherent to the Hilālī-Khān translation, such as obvious internal inconsistences in the use of language, have not been completely resolved in the latest editions, as most of the editorial changes implemented were concerned with doctrinal aspects and Islamic legal meanings (which is why the second and third editions are full of Arabisms, in contrast to the first). The later editions also depend less on Abdullah Yusuf Ali's translation than the first edition, which includes many unacknowledged borrowings.[59] Compare, for example, the translation of Q. 2:232–233 provided in Yusuf Ali's translation (first edition, 1934) and in the Hilālī-Khān 1977–1978 edition:

Abdullah Yusuf Ali (1934)[60]

232. When ye divorce women and they fulfil the term of their (`Iddat) do not prevent them from marrying their (former) husbands if they mutually agree on equitable terms. This instruction is for all amongst you who believe in God and the Last Day. That is (the course making for) most virtue and purity amongst you and God knows and ye know not. 233. The mothers shall give suck to their offspring for two whole years if the father desires to complete the term. But he shall bear the cost of their food and clothing on equitable terms. No soul shall have a burden laid on it greater than it can bear. No mother shall be treated unfairly on account of her child nor father on account of his child. An heir shall be chargeable in the same way if they both decide on weaning by mutual consent and after due consultation there is no blame on them. If ye decide on a foster-mother for your offspring there is no blame on you provided ye pay (the mother) what ye offered on equitable terms. But fear God and know that God sees well what ye do.

Hilālī-Khān (1977/1978)

232. And when you have divorced women and they have fulfilled the term of their prescribed period, do not prevent them from marrying their (former) husbands, if they mutually agree on reasonable basis. This (instruction) is an admonition for him among you who believes in Allah and the Last Day. That is more virtuous and purer for you. Allah knows and you know not. 233. The mother shall give suck to their offspring for the two whole years (that is) for those parents who desire to complete the term of sucking, but the father of the child shall bear the cost of the

59 Jassem, 'The Noble Quran', p. 268.

60 Taken from the original first edition: A. Yusuf Ali, *The Holy Qur'an. An Interpretation in English, with the Original Arabic Text in Parallel Columns, a Running Rhythmic Commentary in English, and Full Explanatory Notes, by Allamah Abdullah Yusuf ʿAli* (Lahore: Shaikh Muhammad Ashraf, 1934).

> mother's food and clothing on reasonable basis. No soul shall have a burden laid on it greater than it can bear. No mother shall be treated unfairly on account of her child, nor father on account of his child. And on the father's heir is incumbent the like of that (which was the incumbent on the father). If they both decide on weaning, by mutual consent, and after due consultation there is no blame on them. And if you decide on a foster-mother for your offspring, there is no blame on you, provided you pay (the mother) what you agreed (to give her) on reasonable basis. And fear Allah and known that Allah is All-Seer of what you do.

Comparison between the treatment of this passage in the 1977/1978 edition of Hilālī-Khān and the later 1996 and 1997 edition reveals a few changes (indicated below in italics) that make the text less dependent on Yusuf Ali's translation:

> 232. And when you have divorced women and they have fulfilled the term of their prescribed period, do not prevent them from marrying their (former) husbands, if they mutually agree on reasonable basis. This (instruction) is an admonition for him among you who believes in Allâh and the Last Day. That is more virtuous and purer for you. Allâh knows and you know not. 233. The mothers shall give suck to their children for two whole years, (that is) for those (parents) who desire to complete the term of suckling, but the father of the child shall bear the cost of the mother's food and clothing on a reasonable basis. No *person* shall have a burden laid on him greater than he can bear. No mother shall be treated unfairly on account of her child, nor father on account of his child. And on the (father's) heir is incumbent the like of that (which was incumbent on the father). If they both decide on weaning, by mutual consent, and after due consultation, there is no sin on them. And if you decide on a *foster suckling-mother for your children, there is no sin* on you, provided you pay (the mother) what you agreed (to give her) on reasonable basis. And fear Allâh and know that Allâh is All-Seer of what you do.

Although at least half of the passage completely coincides in terms of both grammar and vocabulary, the later edition of Hilālī-Khān explains a key term in a different way, changing 'foster-mother' to 'foster suckling-mother'.

Another good example can be seen in Q. 100:1–7. The comparison looks like this:

> **Abdullah Yusuf Ali (1934)**
>
> 1. By the (Steeds) That run, with panting (breath), 2. And strike sparks of fire, 3. And push home the charge In the morning, 4. And raise

the dust In clouds the while, 5. And penetrate forthwith Into the midst (of the foe) En masse;— 6. Truly Man is, To his Lord, Ungrateful; 7. And to that (fact) He bears witness (By his deeds).

Hilālī-Khān (1977/1978)
1. By the (steeds) that run, with panting (breath), 2 Striking sparks of fire (by their hooves). 3 And scouring to the raid at dawn. 4. And raise the dust in clouds the while. 5. And penetrating forthwith as one into the midst (of the foe). 6. Verily, man is ungrateful to his Lord. 7. And to that he bears witness (by his deeds).

Hilālī-Khān (1996/1997)
1. By the (steeds) that run, with panting. 2 Striking sparks of fire (by their hooves). 3 And scouring to the raid at dawn. 4. And raise the dust in clouds the while. 5. And penetrating forthwith as one into the midst (of the foe). 6. Verily, man (*disbeliever*) is ungrateful to his Lord. 7. And to that he bears witness (by his deeds).

As we can see, the verses are almost identical, the only differences being that the latest editions omit '(breath)' and add an explanatory insertion that the man who is ungrateful to his Lord is a 'disbeliever'. The Hilālī-Khān translation was at least partially influenced by Yusuf Ali's interpretation, insofar as some parts of the verses are replicated almost word for word. However, a more thorough comparison suggests that al-Hilālī and Khān were doing their best to introduce a new literary style to the translation, one that was far removed from the old-fashioned English used in previous translations. We can clearly see this at work in the translators' respective renditions of Q. 2:252:

Yusuf Ali (1934)
These are the Signs of God; We rehearse them to thee in truth: verily Thou art one of the apostles.

Yusuf Ali (1989 revision)
These are the Signs of Allah, we rehearse them To thee in truth: verily Thou art one of the Messengers.

Hilālī-Khān (1977/1978)
These are the Verses of Allah, We recite unto you (O Muhammad) with truth, and truly you are one of the apostles.

Hilālī-Khān (1996/1997)
These are the Verses of Allah, We recite unto you (O Muhammad) in truth, and surely you are one of the Messengers (of Allah).

It is easy to note a kind of textual development here: on the one hand, the translation from the first edition of Hilālī-Khān sounds much more modern than that of Yusuf Ali; still, it has the adjective 'truly' and uses the rather Biblical term 'apostles' (*rusul*); the later edition of Yusuf Ali changes this to 'Messengers', and the Darussalam revision of Hilālī-Khān replicates this.

The Hilālī-Khān Translation in Contemporary Islamic Discourse

The Hilālī-Khān translation is still used as a main reference by many English-speaking Salafi Muslims (and those in the mainstream Sunni community). Its wide distribution and its extensive use of *tafsīr* sources marked a very important turn in Qur'an translation movements. However, although it has its supporters, many Muslim scholars have spoken out against the translation over the last few decades, and their objections have really challenged the popularity of this work. One of the more critical reviews, by Khaleel Mohammed, suggests that this translation reads 'more like a supremacist Muslim, anti-Semitic, anti-Christian polemic than a rendition of the Islamic scripture',[61] while, in contrast, another suggests that it conveys 'true Islamic teaching'.[62] Due in no small part to such criticism, and the appearance of new translations, the Hilālī-Khān translation is unlikely to retain the predominance it had ten or twenty years ago. Most of the negative reviews it has received seem to be related to the rendition of Q. 1:7, specifically in terms of its mention of Jews and Christians, since, as Stefan Wild notes,[63] this is the only English translation of the Qur'an to promote this reading.

Looking at the recent publishing history of this translation, it seems that Darussalam continues to reprint the 1996 edition and sell it widely (new reprints came at least five time in 2000, 2003, 2007, 2011, and 2017), as do the KFGQPC (with their 2019 edition). The latest version of the KFGQPC edition also contains a new introduction. This document, 'A General Introduction to the Glorious Qur'an', articulates a somewhat

61 Khaleel Mohammed, 'Assessing English Translations of the Qur'an', *Middle East Quarterly*, 12.2 (2005), 58–71.
62 Kidwai, 'Review'.
63 Wild, 'Muslim Translators'.

surprising statement on the so-called 'scientific miracles of the Qur'an', given the contemporary Salafi exegetical stance on this issue:

> Numerous scholars of physics, astronomy, biology, and medicine, etc. are astonished by the information contained in the Glorious Qurʾān relating to scientific facts [...] This led to a number of them embracing Islam, for they realised that what is mentioned in the Glorious Qurʾān is impossible to be the words of a human being.[64]

In line with the usual perspective that 'the translation of the meanings of the Glorious Qurʾān cannot be called the Qurʾān', the introduction asserts that 'it is imperative that the requirements laid down by scholars for explaining the meanings of the Glorious Qurʾān are met in it'. It is clear that the basis for this view on the 'permissibility' of translation is Ibn Taymiyya, since it goes on to refer directly to his *Majmūᶜ al-fatāwa,* after stating that:

> Despite the difficulty of translating the Glorious Qur'an however, scholars have reiterated the necessity of conveying the Glorious Qur'an and its message to all the nations of the world, whatever their languages may be. This cannot be realised except by way of translation.

The introduction then levels some quite harsh criticism against other translations:

> Unfortunately, this is what some Orientalists and some so-called Muslims, who hold wrong beliefs which seek to destroy the values of the great religion of Islam, and to harm its correct beliefs, and its noble sharīʿah laws have done in their translations.[65]

It is hard to come to any conclusion about who exactly the phrase 'so-called Muslims' is aimed at—Ahmadi communities? reformists?—but obviously this declaration is an attempt to contextualise this translation as the 'real Muslim endeavour' intended to replace or correct all possible 'distortions', generally fitting into the monovocal view of Saudi-Salafi hermeneutics of the Qur'an. Many of the problematic issues that were inherited from the very first editions also remain unsolved in

64 Taqī al-Dīn al-Hilālī and Muḥammad Muḥsin Khān, *The Noble Qur'an: Translation of the Meanings and Commentary* (Medina: King Fahd Glorious Qur'an Printing Complex, 2019), pp. 16–18.
65 al-Hilālī and Khān, *The Noble Qur'an* (2019), p. 19.

the new version of the translation. To give one example, sometimes the Qur'anic expression *fī sabīli-llāh* is translated as 'in the Cause of Allah' (as in Q. 2:195, 'And spend in the Cause of Allāh') but at other times as 'in the Way of Allah' (as in Q. 2:218, 'and have striven hard in the Way of Allāh'). This discrepancy indicates that the overall editorial strategy applied to the translation during its revision(s) was concerned with changing readings that did not accord with Salafi theological and other ideas on an ad hoc basis, rather than implementing any kind of systematic revision.

As Henri Lauzière remarks, when evaluating this translation in terms of its 'Wahhabi/Salafi' leanings 'one cannot but conclude that the chief Wahhabi scholars of Saudi Arabia demanded the translation to conform to their own views rather than al-Hilālī's'.[66] Likewise, one should always remember the textual history of this work: its earliest version was much more dependent on al-Hilālī's and, to an even greater extent, Khān's personal exegetical efforts; later institutional editions did their best to revise it into a really 'exemplary' Salafi hermeneutical work. A good example of this process at work can be seen in the treatment of the issue of face-covering for women. Lauzière argues that al-Hilālī personally was not a supporter of the *niqāb* (that is, the practice of covering the face) but that, due to the demands of Wahhabi scholars, the later editions of the translation were amended to advocate the practice.[67] Accordingly, in their respective renditions of Q. 24:31, the 1977/1978 first edition uses the wording: 'and tell the believing women [...] to draw their veils over their necks and bosoms', while all of the Darussalam/KFGQPC editions read as follows: 'tell the believing women [...] to draw their veils all over *juyūbihinna* (i.e., their bodies, faces, necks and bosoms)'. Here, this justification of wearing *niqāb*, a Saudi practice promoted by many Salafi scholars on the global level, is a later insertion made by the publishers.

Can we finally conclude that the Hilālī-Khān is one of the most important contemporary works in English in terms of the representation of the Salafi reading of the Qur'an? Perhaps the answer is both yes and no at the same time. Of course, many of the verses are translated and interpreted in accordance with contemporary Salafi hermeneutics, and the reading is based mostly on the views expressed in Ibn Kathīr's *tafsīr*.

66 Henri Lauzière, 'The Evolution of the Salafiyya', p. 358.
67 Ibid.

On the other hand, many of the verses are rendered in a way that is no different to the predominant Sunni mainstream interpretation. This means that the translation still has a place in the wider, non-Salafi, English-speaking world, even though it has recently been overtaken by newer projects such as the Saheeh International translation, which has been in print since 1997. What also keeps the Hilālī-Khān translation relevant is its wide use of classical Muslim commentaries (including many references to *hadīth*), and it can be justly said that al-Hilālī and Khān were really innovative in this regard. The numerous interpolations that appear in the newer editions, drawn from exegetical traditions, have only strengthened the translation's reputation among many readers as 'promoting the Qur'an as Muslims understand it'.

4. The King Fahd Complex for the Printing of the Qur'an: A Turning Point in the History of Qur'an Translations

King Fahd b. ᶜAbd al-ᶜAzīz (1921–2005) is usually associated with the most conservative period in Saudi Arabian modern history. The crown prince of Saudi Arabia from 1975 to 1982 and its king from 1982 to 2005, Fahd established the basic principles of the late-twentieth-century politics of the country, especially its religious aspects. Three momentous events that took place in 1979—the Islamic revolution in Iran, the siege of Mecca by a radical religious opposition seeking to overthrown the ruling family, and the Soviet invasion of Afghanistan—had already predetermined the attitude of the new Saudi ruler when he came to power. While his predecessor, King Fayṣal, is known for opening the door to the modernisation of the KSA, King Fahd added a strong Islamic component to the foreign policy of the country, and the vigour with which this was pursued can be measured by the fact that it is impossible to count the number of mosques and Islamic centres all around the globe that are named after him. King Fahd supported Islamic activism (from publishing to supporting jihadist fighters in Afghanistan) not only through foreign policy but also through internal policy, by strengthening alliances between the state and local ulema. This alliance was even strong enough to survive his decision to permit foreign troops to be stationed in the region (especially during and after the Gulf War). King Fahd came to power at a time when the Middle East was, in general, moving from a time of Pan-Arabist political sentiment

©2024 Mykhaylo Yakubovych, CC BY-ND 4.0 https://doi.org/10.11647/OBP.0381.04

to a more Pan-Islamistic way of thinking[1] and, during the 1980s, his regime deliberately built on and developed this political trend.[2] It is also worth mentioning that King Fahd played a significant role in shaping educational reform in Saudi Arabia, and according to Abdulmohsen Al Saud, this was one of the main priorities of his rule.[3] At the very beginning of the 1980s, the Saudi Ministry of Education began to devote many more hours of the curriculum to the study of Islamic subjects than had previously been the case.[4] In addition, King Fahd supported many initiatives like the establishment of the National Library in 1990 (nowadays, it is known as the King Fahd Library). Thus, under his leadership, the 1980s and 1990s saw mass religious education in the country rise, and all of these educational efforts were oriented towards promoting the Salafi approach to Sunni Islam. One of the leading components of King Fahd's religious policies was the establishment of the KFGQPC, which remains the world-leading institution for Islamic publishing and, especially, Qur'an translation.

The Emergence of the KFGQPC

Early sources suggest that the KFGQPC was established to address concerns about the printing of the Qur'an in Arabic. For example, in a 2010 issue commemorating twenty-three years of KFGQPC activities, the Saudi newspaper *al-Madīna* told the story of al-Sayyid Ḥabīb b. Maḥmūd Aḥmad (1920–2002), one of the locals responsible for initiating Qur'an printing in the country.[5] The biographical sketch revealed that al-Sayyid Ḥabīb b. Maḥmūd, who claims descent from the family of the Prophet and held a few professional positions in local courts and schools, was

1 Haifaa A. Jawad, 'Pan-Islamism and Pan-Arabism: Solution or Obstacle to Political Reconstruction in the Middle East?', in *The Middle East in the New World Order*, ed. by H. A. Jawad (London: Palgrave Macmillan, 1997), 140–61 (p. 161).
2 Madawi al-Rasheed, 'God, the King and the Nation: Political Rhetoric in Saudi Arabia in the 1990s', *Middle East Journal*, 50.3 (1996), 359–71 (p. 360).
3 Abdulmohsen Al Saud, 'The Development of Saudi Arabia in King Fahd's Era', *Asian Culture and History*, 10.1 (2018), 48–57 (p. 48), http://doi.org.10.5539/ach.v10n1p48
4 Raihan Ismail, *Saudi Clerics and Shia Islam* (Oxford: Oxford University Press, 2019), p. 21, 22.
5 Ṣarḥ ᶜālamī mundhu 23 sana wa-yahdī al-ᶜālam al-muṣḥaf al-sharīf, https://www.al-madina.com/article/25824/صرح-عالمي-منذ-23-سنة-ويهدي-العالم-المصحف-الشريف

particularly interested in the development of print culture in the region. He generously invested in a number of projects, including a rich private library in Medina called Maktabat al-Sayyid Ḥabīb al-ᶜĀmma, which houses a special collection of handwritten and printed Qur'ans and also serves as a museum of Qur'anic print.[6] Sayyid Ahmad was not alone in his enthusiasm for Qur'anic print culture. Nāṣir al-Shaghār (1913–2007), an influential chief from the tribe of al-ᶜUtayb who had close ties with the royal court, was also interested, and it is he who is reported to be the first person to raise with King Fahd the idea of a Qur'an printing complex. According to a popular story, al-Shaghār objected to printing the Qur'an abroad, proposing instead the creation of a facility in the *mahbīṭ al-waḥī* ['place of revelation'], that is, Mecca and Medina.[7] Whether this story is true or not, by the late 1970s, regret was felt over the lack of Qur'an printing facilities in the Kingdom. While Syrian, Lebanese, and Egyptian publishers were successfully filling the market with Cairo editions of the Qur'an, other countries were also active in the Qur'an publishing field. Perhaps the best example is the Libyan World Islamic Call Society's (WICS) 1982 edition of the Qur'an in Arabic according to the *qālūn* reading variant, which is predominantly used in West Africa. This edition of the Qur'an is generally known as *muṣḥaf al-Jamāhīriyya* [The Qur'an of Jamahiriyya], and was used to send a political message to the Muslim world, demonstrating Gaddafi's reverence for Islam: it is reported that the leader himself wrote the last word of the Qur'an, *al-nās* from Q. 114:4, in the handwritten prototype. Meanwhile, there was only one printing press in Saudi Arabia that published the Qur'an, Muṣḥaf al-Makka al-Mukarrama, and this did not have the capacity to meet growing demand, especially as new mosques opened inside the Kingdom and beyond. This is why the first task of the KFGQPC, which was initiated by royal decree in 1982, was to print the Qur'an in Arabic.[8] Other aims mentioned in early sources include translation of the meanings of the Qur'an, the production of audio recordings of the Qur'an and of the Qur'an in translation, the publication of research

6 Aḥmad Ḥabīb, *al-Sayyid Ḥabīb b. Maḥmūd Aḥmad: lamaḥāt min sīra ḥayāt wa-masīra injāz* (Medina: [n. pub.], 1434/2013).

7 *Muṣḥaf al-Madīna al-sharīf wa-iqtirāḥ al-amīr Nāṣir al-Shaghār*, http://www.otaibah.net/m/archive/index.php/t-117246.html

8 'Mujammaᶜ al-Maliki Fahd', *Fayṣal Magazine*, 13 (1990), 51–57.

in Qur'anic Studies, and the collection of manuscripts relating to the biography of the Prophet.[9]

The idea of a printing 'complex' [*mujamma^c*] was realised very quickly, between 1982 and 1984. The main contractor was a company named Saudi Oger Ltd (est. 1978), which was owned by the influential al-Hariri family from Lebanon. Located near the outskirts of Medina on the road to Tabuk, the Complex looks from the outside like a typical industrial facility. At the entrance, which is heavily secured, there is a picturesque square with a mosque for the use of the staff, as well as an administrative building. The main building just behind houses the general printing facility and quality-control line. Using mostly German printing equipment (specifically, the Manroland AG printing press), the KFGQPC has been able to print up to ten million books annually. Every work, after being designed and proofread by various special committees, has to pass three levels of control during the printing process, and every copy of every Arabic Qur'an and translation the Complex prints is stamped and numbered. In addition to this huge technological facility, the Complex also contains housing for workers and visitors, a Department of Academic Affairs with a library, and, finally, the Center for the Translation of the Qur'an (est. 1994), which consists of three units for European, Asian, and African languages. Most of the faculty working in this department are members of the religious elite and are specialised in *tafsīr* or Qur'anic Studies; many are in some way affiliated with the Islamic University of Madinah (IUM). On the structural level, the Complex is directed by the General Secretary, a post held since early 2020 by Shaykh Khālid al-Nafīsī.[10] All major decisions are made by the Academic Council, which also approves or rejects each translation after receiving a special report from the relevant bodies. The General Secretary reports to the Minister of Islamic Affairs of the KSA.

Thus, 'The Complex' is something much more significant that a printing house. Though divided into a number of different units, it carries out all of the necessary processes involved in producing a Qur'an or a Qur'an translation in one place: each text it publishes is written, revised, approved, and finally printed there. Importantly, in 1985, the

9 Ibid., p. 55.
10 Prior to holding this position, he was head of the human resources department at the MOIA.

KFGQPC started to produce its own *Muṣḥaf al-Madīna al-nabawiyya* [Arabic language edition of the Qur'an] with the help of the world-renowned Syrian calligrapher ᶜUthmān Ṭāhā. The project—both to open a printing complex and to accelerate distribution of the Qur'an—has been extremely successful: around 270 million copies of this *Muṣḥaf* had been printed by the KFGQPC before 2013, in almost all the variant readings.[11] As far as I am aware, this is the largest number of Qur'ans printed in any edition in the history of Islam.

With the publication of a new Arabic text of the Qur'an, the KFGQPC became the leading Qur'an printing institution in the Muslim World and also a tourist site (it is often visited by pilgrims who travel to Medina on Hajj). However, its engagement with the question of publishing Qur'an translations was much more complicated. Discussions over the permissibility of translation had already been resolved in favour of scholars who supported the idea, as Chapter Three on the MWL's Qur'an printing project has shown. By the end of the 1970s, some scholars, such as the Egyptian-Qatari Qur'an expert Ḥasan al-Maᵓāyrigī (1927–2008), were even promoting the establishment of a 'World Committee for the Noble Qur'an', a global organisation which would produce, supervise, and publish translations in similar vein to the United Bible Society.[12] Al-Maᵓāyrigī's book on the role of translation in the propagation of Islam, written at the end of the 1980s and introduced by the well-known authority Yūsuf ᶜAbd Allāh al-Qaraḍāwī (1926–2022), suggests that the idea of translation had already become an inherent part of Islamic revivalism, be it in terms of 'translation of the meaning' or some other approach. Even when the KFGQPC was in the very early stages of its activities, al-Maᵓāyrigī praised this institution and its future leadership in the field of Qur'an translation publishing.

Despite the support of many scholars for the KFGQPC project, Saudi domestic religious authorities were concerned enough about the future of the institution to issue a fatwa authorizing the translation of the Qur'an in early 1985. The fatwa, entitled *al-Ḥukm fi qaḍāyā tarjamat maᶜānī*

11 'al-Saᶜūdiyya wazaᶜat 270 milyūn nuskhat al-Qurᵓān al-karīm mundhu 1985', *al-Iqtiṣādiyya*, 27 December 2013. https://www.aleqt.com/2013/12/27/article_810812.html

12 al-Maᵓāyrigī, Ḥasan, *al-Ḥayᵓa al-ᶜalamiyya li-l-Qurᵓān al-karīm: ḍarūrahu li-l-daᶜwa wa-l-tablīgh* (Doha: [n. pub.], 1991).

al-Qurʾān, was published by the General Presidency of Scholarly Research and Ifta of the Kingdom, and its timing was hardly a coincidence: not only was the KFGQPC just about to publish its first ever translation (a revised edition of Abdullah Yusuf Ali's English rendition), but the first Saudi edition of the Hilālī-Khān translation had just appeared, with the official approval of Shaykh Ibn Bāz, the then General President of the institution. This fatwa was decisive, effectively closing the longstanding discussions on the issue while also being a comprehensive apology for the future publication of Qur'an translations.

What does this fatwa actually permit? It is presented as a *ḥukm* [a legal statement] on the translation of the meanings of the Qur'an. The beginning of the fatwa references the permissibility of translating the Qur'an and goes on to mention the 'large demand' for translations in the context of Islamic missionary activity (*daʿwa*). It issues the caveat that any translator should be 'qualified in both languages' as well as knowledgeable in *asbāb al-nuzūl* ['circumstances of revelation']. The authors of the fatwa included this exegetical specification in response to a general insistence that translators have knowledge of the historical context behind the Qur'anic verses.

More surprising is the next section of the statement, which contains a long quotation from Muḥammad b. al-Ḥasan al-Ḥajjawī, 'someone who has discussed the translation of the meanings of the Qur'an'. It reads as follows:

> Translation is one of the desirable deeds (*marghūba*). It is a collective obligation for the Umma to work on it, so if one person produces [a translation], then others do not sin by abstaining from doing so. But if no one produces [a translation], this will be sinful for everyone.[13]

Al-Ḥajjawī (1874–1956) was a famous scholar and reformer from Morocco who held many inspiring positions on a wide variety of topics related to the Muslim world and Muslim minorities. He was a proponent of female education and in many of his writings expressed support for some kind of inculturation, especially at a time that Muslim societies were experiencing major global change with the advent of secularism. For example, al-Ḥajjawī advised believers to use 'foreign dress' so as

13 See 'Tarjamat maʿānī al-Qurʾān bayn al-taʿāyid wa-l-taḥrim', *Majallat al-buḥūth al-Islamiyya*, 12 (1405/1985), 311–25 (p. 311).

not to be excluded from secular circles of power.[14] The source for the quotation cited in the fatwa was a treatise dedicated to the translation of the Qur'an that he had written in early 1931 and published in the journal *al-Maghrib* in 1933.[15] In contrast to many other scholars of his time, al-Ḥajjawī never used the expression 'translation of the meanings' [*tarjamat al-maᶜānī*] when discussing Qur'an translation, instead describing the process as 'translation of the basic apparent meaning (*al-maᶜānī al-aṣlī al-ẓāhir*) of every verse [...] accompanied by the addition of the opinions of the exegetes'.[16] Among the many arguments al-Ḥajjawī puts forward in his treatise (which are mostly textual, and relate to the necessity of conveying the Islamic message to the whole of mankind), he makes the particularly interesting observation that:

> ᶜUmar b. al-Khaṭṭāb, when opening up new lands from the valley of Balkh to Western Tripoli, where people speak Persian and Greek, up to the Egyptian Sudan and Berbers of the Cyrenaica, never ordered people to change their language or to learn Arabic instead.[17]

To this, he adds:

> Islam is the religion of the nations of India, China, the Turks, the Khazars and Persians, the Syrians and Greeks, and the Berbers, and Africans, as well as others, but they do not stop using their [own] languages.[18]

For al-Ḥajjawī, the translation of the Qur'an is clearly not a problem at all, it reflects the 'historical reality' of the Muslim world.[19] The next few pages of the fatwa repeat al-Ḥajjawī's arguments in defence of translation, primarily the example he gives of the preservation of the original languages of various Muslim peoples. The authors of the fatwa draw from this a simple preliminary conclusion: if the Qur'an is being explained in the Arabic language, why not attempt to explain it in another language as well? Of course, in some way this equates

14 Etty Terem, 'Muslim Men, European Hats: A *fatwā* on Cultural Appropriation in a Global Age', *The Journal of North African Studies*, 28.3 (2023), 563–88, https://doi.org/10.1080/13629387.2021.1973246

15 A modern reprint is available: Muḥammad al-Ḥajjawī, *Ḥukm tarjamat al-Qurʾān al-ᶜaẓīm* (Tétouan: [n. pub.], 2011).

16 al-Ḥajjawī, *Ḥukm tarjamat al-Qurʾān*, p. 39.

17 Ibid., p. 46.

18 Ibid., p. 48.

19 Ibid., p. 49.

translation with *tafsīr* (or at least conceptualises translation as a kind of *tafsīr*), which is why, in contrast to al-Ḥajjawī, the fatwa mostly uses the accepted expression 'translation of the meanings' to refer to Qur'an translation. What is innovative here is the way the fatwa takes the idea of historical Qur'an translations into Persian, Urdu, and the other languages of the Islamic world and extrapolates this to justify translations (or interpretations) in European languages. When it comes to directly acknowledging modern translations of the twentieth century, however, the authors of the fatwa mention only those published by 'the Ahmadiyya community' from Lahore and their publication of translations into 'English, Dutch, and German in 1951'.[20]

In their definitive statement on the matter, the Saudi scholars involved in the fatwa regard translation as a 'collective duty' of the Ummah, in exactly the same way that al-Ḥajjawī had proposed years before. The pronouncement, dating to exactly the same year as the KFGQPC started its translation activities, is more favourable towards the general idea of Qur'an translation than any issued before. It situates the undertaking of such projects as the community's responsibility and shows a flexibility that is generally found in Salafi attitudes to legal issues in such cases: whereas the Salafi school had previously relied on legal sources from Hanafi and Shafi'i scholarship to guide their position on the permissibility of the translation of the Qur'an (such as the opinions that had been disseminated from al-Azhar), here the Committee of Fatwas were willing to cite a source from the Maliki tradition that was much more suitable for their purpose.

The First KFGQPC Translations

English Translations: Yusuf Ali's *The Holy Qur'an*

The very first translation published by the KFGQPC was Abdullah Yusuf Ali's English-language work. As the preface to the first edition reveals, the decision to publish this text was made long before the KFGQPC started its activities. Yusuf Ali's translation went through a process of revision and approval prior to publication. In order to produce a reliable English translation that was free from personal bias, a royal

20 'Tarjamat maʿānī al-Qurʾān', p. 315.

decree (No. 19888, dated 16/8/1400 AH [29 June 1980]) was issued by the Custodian of the Two Holy Mosques, King Fahd b. ᶜAbd al-Azīz, at that time deputy prime minister. It authorised the General Presidency of the Departments of Islamic Researches, Ifta, Call, and Guidance to undertake the responsibility for revising and correcting a specific, pre-existing translation which would be selected for this purpose. The resulting text was *The Holy Qur'ān: English Translation of the Meanings, and Commentary by Abdullah Yusuf Ali.*[21]

The establishment of the KFGQPC provided the opportunity to bring this project to fruition and, in 1985, according to Royal Decree No. 12412, the revised translation was approved for printing. Publication of Yusuf Ali's translation was announced only eight months after the project was launched and, given this very short time frame, either the KFGQPC undertook a very speedy revision, or—the more probable explanation—much of the work had already been carried out before the project's official start. The KFGQPC's publication of this new, revised edition of Yusuf Ali's translation marks the first instance of purposeful state-sponsored intervention into the target text by a Middle Eastern state. It is not clear exactly who was involved in the revision process, as neither the Arabic nor the English versions of the preface mention any names. These pages simply refer to the Presidency of Islamic Researches, Ifta, Call, and Guidance, and there were, undoubtedly, many Western-educated Saudi religious scholars with the relevant language skills and religious education to be able to carry out such a task.

The English text was published alongside the Arabic, in verse-to-verse format, and most of the editorial changes appear to fall into the following categories:

1. Formal changes: Yusuf Ali's introduction was removed, as was the poetry with which he had prefaced the translation as a whole and the individual suras;
2. Vocabulary revision: a return to the use of Arabic terms that relate to key concepts of the Qur'an, such as the use of '*zakāt*' instead of 'charity', '*salāt*' rather than 'prayer', etc.;
3. Modernisation of the language used; and

21 Abdullah Yusuf Ali, *The Holy Qurʾān: English Translation of the Meanings, and Commentary by Abdullah Yusuf Ali* (Medina: King Fahd Glorious Qur'an Printing Complex, 1985), p. vi.

4. Reductions to the commentary.

From the first two suras of the Qur'an, one can see that the amendments are not very extensive. The only change to Q. 1, for example, is the replacement of the archaic 'hath' with 'has' to give 'Thou has bestowed Thy Grace', a rendition which still retains the same overall 'King-James-Bible' style. Having said that, the commentary on the *al-ḥurūf al-muqaṭṭaᶜāt* that preface Q. 2 has been changed by the editors. The original 1937 edition provided a few opinions on what the letters *a-l-m* might mean, but the KFGQPC edition only mentions Yusuf Ali's final statement that 'much has been written about the meaning of these letters, but most of it is pure conjecture'.[22] Other changes include, for example, the relatively insignificant change from 'penalty' to 'chastisement' for *ᶜadhāb* in Q. 2:7 and the more meaningful change in Q. 2:10 in which *yakdhibūna* has become 'they lied' instead of 'they are false'. In Q. 2:11, the phrase *nahnu muṣliḥūn* has been changed from 'Why, we only want to make peace' to 'We are only ones that put things right'.

The majority of the changes opt for a more grammatical (or even 'literal') meanings than Yusuf Ali's original, more rhetorical reading. However, theological alterations are also made in some verses. The verb *istawā* in Q. 7:54 reads as 'He settled Himself on the Throne', when the original text provides 'He is firmly established on the Throne (Of authority)'. Crucially for Salafi hermeneutics, with its abhorrence of 'allegorical readings', the KFGQPC edition interprets this verse in an explicitly literal fashion, based on the perspective that we should describe God as He describes Himself and 'without asking how' (*bi-lā kayf*). Moreover, the commentary to this verse has been shortened: the KFGQPC editors have erased the first two sentences of Yusuf Ali's text, notably removing his statement that the 'throne' is a metaphorical symbol of authority. In other instances, the commentary remains untouched even though changes have been made to the translation. For example, in his translation of Q. 103:1, Yusuf Ali has 'By (the Token of) Time (Through the Ages)', which has been changed to 'by the time' in the KFGQPC revision, although the name of the sura is still translated as 'Time (Through the Ages)' and the accompanying commentary has not been touched. This is repeated for Q. 112:1, in which Yusuf Ali's 'The

22 Yusuf Ali, *The Holy Qurʾān* (1985), p. vii.

One and Only' is changed to 'The One', but the commentary on Allāh's qualities faithfully repeats the original 1938 edition.

In 1991, the KFGQPC published Yusuf Ali's translation for a second time, with just a few minor corrections. The text remained one of the institution's most distributed translations until 1997, when it was completely substituted by the Hilālī-Khān translation. The rationale behind the substitution was probably partly an attempt to establish a more 'correct' translation from the Salafi perspective but also to produce one that was more engaged with the *tafsīr* tradition (as Hilālī-Khān cites large blocks of text from classical exegetical works). It may also be that the modern language used by Hilālī and Khān played an important role in the choice to move over to this translation. Despite being replaced, the KFGQPC edition of Yusuf Ali's Qur'an translation has been reprinted by a number of private publishers and translated into other languages such as Russian (in 2008, under the title 'The *Tafsīr* of Abdullah Yusuf Ali').[23] In some ways, the fact that the translation now carries the KFGQPC label has given it more authority: it is now 'approved' by a leading Islamic institution. Furthermore, only a few years after KFGQPC stopped publishing it, another edition of Yusuf Ali's translation was published by the US-based Amana Publications and the International Institute of Islamic Thought (IIIT)—one that has also been republished many times. In 2017, for example, it was printed by the Turkish Directorate of Religious Affairs.[24] None of these editions have changed Yusuf Ali's original language extensively nor interfered with the commentary. Despite not being modernised very much over time, this English translation has been more successful than any published by the KFGQPC.

French Translations: Hamidullah's *Le Saint Coran* and Mohamed El-Moktar Ould Bah's *Le Noble Coran*

The KFGQPC's first French translation, by the Indian scholar of Islam Muhammad Hamidullah (1908–2002), has a similar backstory to the

---

23 *Svyachennyi Koran. Smyslovoi perevod s kommentariyami*, ed. by Damir Mukhetdinov (Moscow: ID Medina, 2015).

24 *The Holy Qur'an. Tr. by Abdullah Yusuf Ali* (Ankara: TDRA, 2018).

one by Yusuf Ali.[25] First published in 1959 in Paris, the translation was well received by a Muslim readership during the 1970s when it was reprinted by a variety of publishers, including a 1973 version printed in Ankara by Hilâl Yayınları (who, as mentioned before, would later publish the Hilālī-Khān translation in 1978). Hamidullah himself, who had a special interest in the history of Qur'anic interpretation in foreign languages, thought his translation was one of the most important works he ever published.[26] In some ways, his text resembled an academic work more than a straightforward translation of a religious text: for instance, Hamidullah used two verse-numbering systems (from the Flügel and Cairo editions of the *muṣḥaf*), cited many Western studies on the Qur'an, and included a preface by the famous Oriental Studies scholar Louis Massignon (1883–1962), who was a Christian rather than a Muslim. However, the edition contained the Arabic text, and thus generally fitted the emerging model of 'Muslim' translations of the Qur'an into Western European languages. The first edition was entitled *Le Saint Coran. Traduction Integrale* [The Holy Qur'an. Complete Translation] and there was no trace of the 'translation of the meanings' theology predominant among Qur'an translations authored by Muslims. Most of the proofreading of the French text was done by Hamidullah's collaborator, the French translator Michel Leturmy (1921–2000), and the editorial work was carried out by Nūr al-Dīn b. Maḥmūd, a journalist from Tunis who had been living in France since 1956.[27] The KFGQPC published its own edition of *Le Saint Coran* in 1989 after a fairly extensive revision process.

First of all, the KFGQPC changed the title to *Le Saint Coran et la traduction en langue française de ses sens* [The Qur'an and a translation of its meanings in the French language]. All the prefaces and introductions originally included by the author were removed, as was much of the commentary. To give an example of how significantly the core text of

25 Muhammad Hamidullah, *Le Saint Coran et la traduction en langue française de ses sens* (Medina: King Fahd Glorious Qur'an Printing Complex, 1989).

26 His general interest in Qur'an translation is demonstrated by the fact that the first edition of his translation contained a pretty comprehensive list of translations into dozens of languages, from Afrikaans to Ukrainian. Present in the 1959 edition (pp. xliii—lxvii), this list is absent from the KFGQPC edition.

27 For more on this figure, see al-Ḥabīb Shaybūb, *al-Ṣiḥāfī al-adīb Nūr al-Dīn b. Maḥmūd: ḥayātuhu wa-mukhtārāt min kitābihi* (Tunis: Wizārat al-Thaqāfa, 2000).

the translation was changed, I compare below the respective renditions of Q. 2:1-5:

Hamidullah (1959)
Au nom de Dieu le Très Miséricordieux, le Tout Miséricordieux. Alif, Lâm, Mîm. Ce Livre, point de doute, voilà une guidée pour les pieux qui croient à l'invisible et établissent l'Office et font largesses de ce que Nous leur avons attribue, et qui croient à ce qu'on a fait descendre vers toi, et à ce qu'on a fait descendre avant toi. Et ceux-là croient ferme à l'au-delà. Eux sont sur la guide de leur Seigneur; et c'est eux les gagnants.

Hamidullah (1989)
Au nom d'Allah, le Très Miséricordieux, le Tout Miséricordieux. C'est le Livre au sujet duquel il n'y a aucun doute, c'est un guide pour les pieux, qui croient à l'invisible et accomplissent come il faut la Ṣalāt et dépensent [dans l'obéissance à Allah], de ce que Nous leur avons attribué. Ceux qui croient à ce qui t'a été descendu (révélé) et à ce qui a été descendu avant toi et qui croient fermement à la vie future. Ceux-là sont sur le bon chemin de leur Seigneur, et ce sont eux qui réussissent (dans cette vie et dans la vie future).

In addition to the omission of commentary, the changes made to the target text are so numerous that accounting for them all would require a separate article, or even monograph. They can be summarised, however, as following the same trajectory as the changes made in the Yusuf Ali translation. For example, 'Dieu' has been changed to 'Allah', basic Qur'anic terms such as '*al-ṣalāt*' are provided in transliteration rather than translation, and some interpretative insertions have been added in brackets. The changes suggest a clear strategy to 'Islamise' the translation, so that it was more appealing to a confessional readership, and to restrict the interpretation of the Arabic text to a more one-dimensional, Salafi, reading. In addition, the KFGQPC attempted to modernise the target text, using vocabulary that makes it more accessible to contemporary readers, especially to French-speaking Muslims living outside France. This shift is not coincidental: Hamidullah's 1950s translation was aimed at a domestic French readership that included a Christian and Secular audience, whereas the KFGQPC's priority was to render his text more 'Muslim-oriented' and broaden its appeal to an international readership.

The committee that carried out the editorial revisions to Hamidullah's translation was entirely of West African origin. Its members included Muhammad Ahmad Lo, a scholar from Senegal who was educated at the IUM; Shaykh Ahmad Al-Chinquity, a representative of the scholarly al-Shinqīṭī family from Mauritania; and, finally, Fode Camara from Guinea, who had been a secretary general for his country's Embassy in KSA. Notably, Hamidullah, who was still alive at this time, was not engaged in the revision process and, in 1989, just after the translation appeared, he published an open letter to King Fahd, objecting to many of the revisions that had been implemented.[28] He disagreed with, among other things, the use of 'Allah' instead of 'Dieu', arguing that this 'correction' would lead non-Muslims to continue to view him as the 'God of Muslims'. Hamidullah's opinion was effectively ignored and, even today, some Saudi scholars defend the revisions that were made, insisting on their necessity on both theological and grammatical grounds.[29] What also usually goes unnoticed is that the KFGQPC edition was based not on Hamidullah's original text but on a previous revision of it undertaken under the aegis of the MWL and prepared by two scholars, Houssein Nahaboo and Maḥmūd Bāballī, some years before. Nahaboo later published his own trilingual translation into French, English, and Creole.[30]

Le Saint Coran remained in print until 2007, when the KFGQPC introduced a new translation by Mohamed El-Moktar Ould Bah (Muḥammad al-Mukhtār Walad Abbāh).[31] Born in 1924 in Mauritania, he obtained a PhD from the Sorbonne in 1975, and worked in many Islamic organisations internationally, including the Organisation of Islamic the Conference (OIC, now the Organisation of Islamic Cooperation). A renowned expert in many fields of Islam, and especially Qur'anic Studies,[32] Ould Bah wrote his translation in line with the KFGQPC

---

28 Muhammad Hamidullah, 'Lettre ouverte du Pr. M. Hamidullah au Roi Fahd de l'Arabie Saoudite', *Le Musulman*, 5.6 (1989), 13–15.

29 al-Traif, Hamad bin Ibrahim, 'Révision de la Traduction Coranique de Hamidullah par le Complexe du Roi Fahd (CRF): (Sourate Al-Hajj en tant que modèle)', *Altralang Journal*, 3.1 (2021), 26–50.

30 Houssein Nahaboo was a Mauritian dentist and scholar, while Maḥmūd Bāballī was a Syrian lawyer and Islamic activist. See Johanna Pink's discovery of this: 'Qur'an Translation of the Week #152: Between Mauritius and Saudi Arabia: The Trilingual Qur'an Translations of Houssein Nahaboo', 14 April 2003, https://gloqur.de/quran-translation-of-the-week-152-between-mauritius-and-saudi-arabia-the-trilingual-quran-translations-of-houssein-nahaboo/

31 Mohamed El-Moktar Ould Bah, *Le Noble Coran et la traduction en langue française de ses sens* (Medina: King Fahd Glorious Qur'an Printing Complex, 2007).

32 See, for example, one of his most popular books on variant readings of the Qur'an: Muḥammad al-Mukhtār Walad Abbāh, *Tārīkh al-qirāʾāt fī al-mashriq wa-l-maghrib* (Sale: ISESCO, 2001).

approach: he presented it as a kind of *tafsīr*. Criticising 'Orientalism' in modern translations, he also made claims for the untranslatability of terms like *ṣalāt* and *zakāt* (although he still translated them it in his work, as, respectively, 'priere rituelle' ['ritual prayer'] and 'le aumône légale' ['legal alms']) and advocated paying particular attention to the rendition of the divine names. A comment comparing the process of translation to 'organ transplantation in surgery' gives an interesting insight into his overall approach.[33] The first edition of Ould Bah's work was published in 2001 by Najah Press in Casablanca under the title *Le Saint Coran*,[34] a second edition, which he prepared for the KFGQPC, was edited by Bello Mana from the Islamic University of Niger. Whereas the first edition was based on the reading of Warsh, the most popular interpretative variant in West Africa, to reflect the religious practices of its main intended readership, the new edition followed the Ḥafṣ reading, although some of the Warsh variant readings are mentioned as well. For example, for Q. 72:20, where the Warsh reading provides *qāla* ('He said') instead of *Qul* ('Say!'), Ould Bah includes a footnote to explain that 'Dis!' ('Say!') does not conform to the Warsh reading. This is interesting because Ould Bah's translation seems to be the only one published by the KFGQPC in which the differences in variant readings are specially addressed. When compared to Hamidullah's translation (even in terms of the KFGQPC edition of this), Ould Bah's translation looks to be more of a literal interpretation, with very little additional commentary. This can be clearly seen in their different renderings of the expression *yawma yukshafu ᶜan sāqin* ['A day on which the shin is shown'] in Q. 68:42:

Hamidullah (KFGQPC edition)
Le jour où ils affronteront les horreurs [du Jugement] et où ils seront appelés à la Prosternation mais ils ne le pourront pas
['The day they face the horrors [of Judgment] and be called to Prostration but they cannot'].

Ould Bah
Le jour où un pied sera découvert, ils seront appelés à se prosterner, mais ils en scont incapables

33 'Tarjamat al-Qurʾān shabīha bi-baᶜḍ ᶜamaliyyāt zaraᶜa al-aᶜḍāʾ', *al-Quds al-ᶜArabī*, 14 June 2006, https://www.alquds.co.uk/ ترجمة-القرآن-شبيهة-ببعض-عمليات-زرع-ال/

34 Ould Bah, Mohamed El-Moktar, *Le Saint Coran, tr. par Mohamed El-Moktar Ould Bah* (Casablanca: Maktabat al-Najah, 2001).

['The day a foot is discovered, they will be called to prostrate, but they are unable to do so'].

Ould Bah opts for a more literal reading that is more in line with Salafi ideas of the *sāq* as a divine attribute and not merely a rhetorical figure. Nevertheless, his translation has never really challenged the established popularity of Muhammad Hamidullah's translation, though it did get some attention in academic circles.[35]

Albanian Translations: Sherif Ahmeti's *Kur'an-i përkthim*

Albanian, one of the 'Islamic languages' of southern Europe, has some eight million native speakers, a predominant share of whom are Muslims, especially in Albania and Kosovo. These two regions are connected by ethnic and cultural ties, however, when it comes to the Islamic religious tradition, the effect of their recent political realities are very different. Kosovo, as a part of socialist Yugoslavia between 1945 and 1992, had at least nominal religious freedom and a basic level of functional religious infrastructure. Communist Albania, by contrast, instigated a Soviet-style total ban on religion in 1967, which was lifted only after 1985. It is, therefore, not surprising that the first modern Qur'an translations into Albanian were primarily produced in Kosovo.

The author of one of these first translations, Sherif Ahmeti (1920–1998), was a national activist, educator, and scholar of religion. After graduating from a local Islamic school, he started out on a career in the state education system as a teacher of Albanian but was later pressured to leave his position because of his religious affiliations because these did not accord with the predominant secular socialist ideology. Ahmeti moved to the Alaudin Islamic school (Medreseja Alaudin) in Prishtina (now the capital of Kosovo), where he embarked on a long-term religious career. By 1968, he had published a short handbook on Islamic religious practices (*ilmihal*) in Albanian, as well as number of articles and translations. By 1985, Ahmeti had been made Mufti of Prishtina. A translation of the Qur'an he had begun to work on in the early 1980s,

35 See, for example: Aicha Bint Mohamed, 'Une traduction mauritanienne du Saint Coran', *al-Mutarǧim*, 10.1 (2010), 27–36.

Kurʾan-i përkthim me komentim në gjuhën shqipe ['The Qur'an and the translation of its meanings into the Albanian language'] was finally published in 1988 by the Kryesia e Bashkësisë Islame (Presidency of the Islamic Community). Soon after that, the second edition was produced by the Libya-based World Islamic Call Society in Tripoli.[36] On the back of growing interest in religion in the Balkans after the fall of the communism and the close attention paid by the Muslim world to the region during the military conflicts it endured in the 1990s, Ahmeti's translation has also been printed by the KFGQPC. Their first edition appeared in 1992[37] and was reprinted in 1994; it was further reissued several times in the 2000s. Typically published under its original name, Ahmeti's translation is based on the Arabic text and informed by plenty of Sunni *tafsīrs*, both classical works such as those by Fakhr al-Dīn al-Rāzī and Ibn Kathīr, and the more modern exegesis of Ṣiddīq Ḥasan Khān al-Qannawjī (1832–1890). It seems that Ahmeti also consulted some Bosnian translations of the Qur'an as well, for example those by Džemaludin Čaušević and Muhammed Pandža (1937) and Bessim Korkut (1977), both of which were quite accessible in Yugoslavia at the time. A 1992 KFGQPC edition of the work includes some extra introductory material, including a history of the Qur'an and a statement by the publisher that the translation was initiated by the MWL—but no further details on that are given. It does name Mansur Halil, an Albanian graduate of the IUM, as having had primary responsibility for revising the original translation for publication by the KFGQPC.

Comparing the first 1988 edition of *Kurʾan-i përkthim* and the 1992 KFGQPC edition, we see that Halil's revisions mostly involved the addition of more explanatory material into the core text and footnotes (including the original Arabic pronunciation of various terms) and a shift from a more literal to a more explanatory style, a trend typical of many KFGQPC translations. The suras are also introduced by short forewords that describe their content, which in some ways is reminiscent of many translations of the Qur'an into Turkish (and their associated

36 For details on his biography and works, see Rajab al-Kūsūfī, *al-Ittijāh al-ʿaqdī li-l-Shaykh Sharīf Aḥmadī min khilāl muʾllafātihi wa-atharihi ʿalā al-wāqiʿ* (Baghdad: Dār al-Māʾmūn li-l-Nashr wa-l-Tawzīʿ, 2010).

37 Sherif Ahmeti, *Kur'an-i përkthim me komentim në gjuhën shqipe* (Medina: King Fahd Glorious Qur'an Printing Complex, 1992).

commentaries). The names of the suras are not translated at all, just given in transliteration. As to language and style, Albanian readers have commented on the use of a 'northern' dialect of their language that is spoken in Kosovo. This is slightly unusual as the modern standard literary language of Albania is based on the so-called 'southern' variant. However, the same approach was taken by two other Albanian Qur'an translations, both of which were also published in Kosovo (Feti Mehdiu, 1985, and Hasan Nahi, 1988).[38] New translations in recent decades, such as those by Emin Emer[39] and Salih Ferhat Hoxha,[40] have challenged the impact of earlier works; however, Sherif Ahmeti's translation and its foreign reprints still remain a very important monument of the post-communist revival of the Muslim tradition in Albania and Kosovo.

Kazakh Translations: Halifa Altay's *Kälam- Şarïf*

With a population of around nineteen million people, Kazakhstan is the largest Central Asian state. Its official language, Kazakh, is the mother tongue of some fifteen million people living both within Kazakhstan and beyond. Kazakh belongs to a Turkic language group of the Kipchak branch and is thus closely related to Kyrgyz, Karakalpak, and Nogai. As is the case with most of the other Turkic languages of the former USSR, Kazakh has moved away from the use of the Arabic script to Cyrillic and is currently undergoing a further transition into using Latin script.

The first printed translation of the Qur'an into the Kazakh language appeared as recently as 1988, with the target text based on the Arabic script. The translator, Halifa Altay (1917–2003), was born in East Turkestan (also known as Altishar) in the south west of Xinjiang and fled China during the Kazakh exodus to take up residence in Turkey (where he lived from 1954 until his move to Khazakstan in 1991). He was known as a writer, scholar, and activist in the Kazakh diaspora movement and produced a lot of material on the history of Kazakhstan and the Kazakh

38 See the short review in Zymer Ramadani, 'Tarihte Yapılmış Arnavutça Kur'an Mealleri', *Marife*, 6.2 (2006), 241–47, https://doi.org/10.5281/zenodo.3343729
39 Emin Emer, *Kurani Me perkthim ne gjuhen shqipe* (Istanbul: Çağrı Yayınları, 2007).
40 Salih Ferhat Hoxha, *Kur'ani me përkthim në gjuhën shqipe nga Ferhat Hoxha* (Skopje: Logos—A, 2016).

people.[41] Having received a traditional Islamic education from religious schools in both Xinjiang and Turkey, Altay had close connections with the Turkish religious establishment. After his move to Kazakhstan in 1991, he was also active there as preacher and national educator, and became a symbol of the Kazakhstan National Revival: one of the biggest mosques in Kazakhstan is named after him—the Halifa Altay Mesheti. Altay was very interested in scholarship on both the Qur'an and Qur'an translations. Qur'an expert Ḥasan al-Maʾāyrigī, in his introduction to the Volga-Ural Tatar translation of the Qur'an by Shaikhalislam Hamidi, *al-Itqān fī tarjamat al-Qurʾān*, mentions meeting a meeting in Istanbul in 1984 with Altay, who introduced him to that translation (which al-Maʾāyrigī later published in Doha, Qatar).[42] Altay also introduced him to many other works published by Russian Muslims towards the end of the imperial era.

The first edition of Altay's Kazakh translation was disseminated among the Kazakh diaspora in Turkey and Iran by the author,[43] while the second, 1990, edition was printed by a local press in Almaty (the capital of the Kazakh Soviet Socialist Republic, or KazSSR, at the time).[44] This second edition was written in the Cyrillic script, on the basis that very few of its target audience were able to read Arabic script. In the same year, Altay visited the KFGQPC, where he stayed for two months to discuss with the academic committee there some of the exegetical choices he had made. This visit was enough to ensure the KFGQPC's approval for his translation, on top of the one he had already received from the MWL, and it prepared a third edition of his translation in 1990 and 1991.[45] Dalilkhān Dzanaltay, a Kazakh diaspora leader from

41 See K. N. Baltabayeva, S. E. Azhigali, S. S. Korabay, G. Gabbassuly, R. S. Kozhakhmetov, K. M. Konyrbayeva, and Abd. H. Altay (eds), *Altay Halifa Gaqypuly: Biobibliographic index* (Almaty: [n. pub.], 2017).

42 See Shaikhalislam Hamidi, *al-Itqān fī tarjamat al-Qurʾān* (Doha: [n. pub.], 1987), p. 2. It is not mentioned in reprints of the Istanbul edition of 1984 (which is also based on the earlier edition from Kazan, 1911).

43 Halifa Altay, *Kälam- Şarïf: tüzetip, tolıqtırıp bastırwsı X. Altay* (Istanbul: Elïf-ofset baspası, 1989).

44 Halifa Altay, *Quran Şarïf* (Almatı: Jazwşı: Sözstan, 1991).

45 Halifa Altay, *Quran Kärim: qazaqs̡a mağına jäne tüsinigi* (Medina: King Fahd Glorious Qur'an Printing Complex, 1991).

Xinjiang who was living in Turkey at the time, is named in this edition as its editor.[46]

The third edition, produced by the KFGQPC, was much like the second. Its text was published in Cyrillic script and was not significantly revised. The volume contains a standard introduction from the Ministry of Islamic Affairs, followed by an introduction by the author, the main text, and finally an index of terms used. A slight deviation from the previous two editions appears on the first page of the introduction. A scene-setting sentence on the place of the Qur'an in Arabic literary tradition that can be found in the 1990 Almaty edition is completely excluded; the paragraph begins with the concept of Qur'anic inimitability. The list of the sources used by the translator, however, has not been changed: in addition to works from the classical *tafsīr* corpus, it includes references to a number of post-classical works, from Ottoman ones, such as *Rūḥ al-bayān* by al-Burūsawī, to various Tatar and Uzbek works produced in the twentieth century. In general, the style of the translation imitates that of a number of Turkish interpretations, for example, the well-known work by Ali Özek and other scholars widely known as 'the Turkish Diyanet translation' [Türkiye Diyanet Vakfı Kur'an Meali], which has been published frequently since 1982. Altay's translation, as well as conforming to the layout used in these Turkish translations, contains the short Arabic introductions to the suras, the actual text of the translation with some insertions and additional commentary, and also notes on places where phrases are repeated in other suras. Reviewers have observed that Altay tends to use vocabulary that would be familiar to members of the Kazakh diaspora, to the extent that there are some parts of the work that might be completely unintelligible to a native speaker of Kazakh born and bred in the former KazSSR. Comparing to Almaty's 1990 edition, the KFGQPC edition contains only a very few insignificant changes to the core text. Even the final 'Amin' that is added to the text after the seventh verse of Q. 1 in his original is faithfully preserved. This is an obvious translatorial addition as it does not exist in the original text of the Qur'an but is recited as part of ritual practice during collective

46 Mykhaylo Yakubovych, 'Qur'an Translations into Central Asian Languages: Exegetical Standards and Translation Processes', *Journal of Qur'anic Studies*, 24.1 (2022), 89–115 (pp.94–97), https://doi.org/10.3366/jqs.2022.0491

prayers. It looks as if the KFGQPC printed this translation 'as is', despite it reflecting the translator's personal reading of the scripture.

When one looks at the text from the perspective of exegetical choices and overall approach, Almaty's translation tends towards an explanatory rather than a very literal reading. For instance, he renders the phrase *hunna ummu-l-kitāb* in Q. 3:7 as 'Solar Kitaptın negizgi irge tası' ['they are the basic meanings of the Book'] instead of 'anası' ['mother meanings'] as is given in some later Kazakh translations. Furthermore, Altay's rather metaphorical understanding of some verses, especially theological ones, differs from the more literal readings found in other KFGQPC translations of the Qur'an. For example, the word *kursī* [literally 'chair', 'throne'] in Q. 2:255 is interpreted by Altay as 'bilimi' ['knowledge']. This has not passed unnoticed by some Salafi readers, and, on the Saudi-run website Qur'anEnc (probably the biggest collection of Qur'an translations available online), the unknown editor of Altay's translation has added another explanation: 'Alla tağalanıñ eki ayağına arnalğan orın' ['This is a place for both of God's feet'], probably based on a *ḥadīth* attributed to Ibn ᶜAbbās and Abū Mūsā al-Ashᶜarī.[47]

Reprinted several times, Altay's translation of the Qur'an has played an important role in the religious revival that has taken place in Kazakshtan. New translations, however, have challenged its authority (especially that prepared by Muhammed Cingiz Qaci and Ermek Muhammed Qali and published by the Turkish Directorate of Religious Affairs in 2015), but it is noteworthy that the KFGQPC has never printed any other Kazakh translation.

Other Early Translations: Turkish, Indonesian, and Bosnian

In 1987, the KFGQPC also published a Turkish translation of the Qur'an, reprinting a text that had been prepared by the Muslim World League. No major changes were introduced into their new edition; the complex just published it 'as is'. They also published a translation into Indonesian, the language with the largest number of Muslim speakers

47 For this verse and correction, see https://quranenc.com/en/browse/kazakh_altai/2. On the tradition see, for instance: al-Qurṭubī, Abū ᶜAbd Allāh, *al-Jāmiᶜ li-aḥkām al-Qurʾān*, 11 vols (Beirut: Dār al-Kutub al-ᶜIlmiyya, 2013), II, p. 180.

after Arabic. In 1990, the KFGQPC published their own new edition of the Indonesian state-commissioned *Al-Qur'an dan Terjemahnya* ['The Qur'an with translation', which was first published between 1965 and 1969 by the Indonesian Ministry of Religious Affairs (MORA) and then subsequently revised and republished. According to a recent, comprehensive study by Fadhli Lukman, MORA and the Saudi authorities established a joint committee to assess the first edition of the translation and to produce recommendations for its revision.[48] Lukman finds that the original *Al-Qur'an dan Terjemahnya* already accorded with Saudi theological ideas, so only minor edits were introduced in the Saudi edition. Nevertheless, some of these interventions were quite challenging, especially the reference to 'Jews and Christians' in Q. 1:7 (for exactly the same reasons as in the first edition of the Hilālī-Khān translation of the Qur'an discussed in Chapter Three). Later, however, the KFGQPC prepared their own, new revision of *Al-Qur'an dan Terjemahnya*, but this happened only after the establishment of the Center for Qur'an Translation inside the KFGQPC.

In 1991, the KFGQPC's Bosnian translation appeared in print. The translator, Besim Korkut (1904–1977), was a scholar of Islamic Studies from Bosnia. After attending Shariah school in Sarajevo in 1925, Korkut continued his religious education at al-Azhar. He graduated in 1931 and returned home to Bosnia, Korkut, where he started working as a lecturer in Arabic, a historian, and a translator. During the era of socialist Yugoslavia (that is, after 1946), Korkut was affiliated with the Philosophical Faculty and Oriental Institute in Sarajevo. Although he completed his Qur'an translation, it was never published during his lifetime. The first edition of *Kur'an: prevod Besim Korkut* appeared in 1977 and included, besides the core text and commentaries, an appendix written by another Bosnian scholar of Islam, Sulejman Grozdanić (1933–96),[49] which outlines typical hermeneutic problems encountered when translating the Qur'an, mostly in relation to its stylistic features. Further editions also include prefaces by other scholars and some specialised supplements (indices, etc.). Korkut's translation is written in very

48 'MORA's decree No. P/15/1989, issued on 4 July 1989, thus established *Tim Penelitian dan Penyempurnaan Al-Qur'an dan Terjemahnya* ("The Committee for Research and Perfection of *Al-Qur'an dan Terjemahnya*")' Fadhli Lukman, *The Official Indonesian Qurʾān Translation* (Cambridge: Open Book Publishers, 2022), p. 79, https://www.openbookpublishers.com/books/10.11647/obp.0289

49 Besim Korkut, *Kur'an: prevod Besim Korkut* (Sarajevo: Orijentalni institut, 1977).

accessible and simple language and is, therefore, suitable for all kinds of readers. It is not overly literal, uses clear idioms, and opts for familiar vocabulary. Only in a few places does the translator employ archaic expressions in order to make his text more impressive and eloquent. New editions (including the revised one prepared and published by the KFGQPC in 1991)[50] contain some minor corrections. Despite being produced in an academic context, Korkut's Qur'an translation uses short but valuable footnotes, plain language, and other features make it popular with even a nonacademic readership. Consequently, around twenty editions have appeared in print up to 2023, and it is available in many bookstores and online. Moreover, it has been used for as the basis for further translations into the Macedonian and Slovakian languages.

Compared to Western European languages, the KFGQPC has been less active in terms of its editorial interventions in translations into 'Muslim' languages such as Bosnian, Kazakh, Turkish, and Indonesian. These translations have not been challenging to Salafi doctrine as, oriented towards Muslim readers, they follow mainstream Sunni readings of the text—with the exception of verses that relate to specific theological issues, such as the divine attributes. However, translations into (European) languages that were intended at least partly to introduce Islam to non-Muslim readers have tended to adopt a more confessional style. This explains why the KFGQPC Turkish translation retains traces of the 'scientific hermeneutics' of the Qur'an and the Kazakh translation allows some 'metaphoric' interpretations of verses relating to God's anthropomorphic attributes when such things have been erased from both the English and French translations.

The KFGQPC Center for Translations: The Production of New Translations[51]

As outlined in the previous section, all of the Qur'an translations published by the KFGQPC prior to 1991 (English, French, Kazakh, Turkish, and Bosnian) were initially published elsewhere and reproduced by the KFGQPC with varying degrees of editorial

50 Besim Korkut, *Kur'an s prevodom* (Medina: King Fahd Glorious Qur'an Printing Complex, 1991).

51 This section is written on the basis of my personal experience while visiting the KFGQPC in April and May 2010 as well as a number of other secondary sources.

intervention. At the beginning of the 1990s, however, there was a shift in policy. The Complex began to develop a framework for not merely revising and publishing pre-existing translations but also for producing new translations in house. The KFGQPC started to publish exclusive works, hiring translators, processing revisions, and undertaking their own publishing and distribution. The following section will address the production processes involved.

Markaz al-Tarjamāt, the Center for Translations, was established in 1994. Its declared remit relates almost entirely to the study of translations and interpretations of the Qur'an in non-Arabic languages. The Center also gathers information on translators of the Qur'an all over the world and publishes bibliographies, dictionaries of the Qur'an, and other auxiliary literature. Initially, the Center consisted of six units: European Languages, African Languages, Asian Languages, the Encyclopedia Unit, the Information Unit and, finally, the Publishing Section. The first head of the Center was a figure who had been associated with the KFGQPC from the very beginning of its activities, Dr ᶜAbd al-Raḥīm al-Vaniyāmbādī, generally known by the name V. Abdur Rahim. Born in India, he attended Presidency College at the University of Madras, where he majored in English Language and Literature, graduating in 1957. He attended al-Azhar in 1964, where he obtained both an M.Phil. and Ph.D. in Arabic Philology. Five years later, he joined the IUM to teach Arabic to students admitted from abroad. Here, he was associated with the TAFL (Teaching Arabic as a Foreign Language) programme; one set of his many Arabic course materials entitled 'Lessons in Arabic for non-Arabic speakers' is still used in Islamic schools around the globe. Abdur Rahim has outstanding skills in a number of foreign languages (it is reported that he is fluent in more than ten languages, both Asian and European), has also authored many books on Qur'anic grammar (including some dedicated to particular suras), and annotated editions of classical works in Qur'anic Studies[52] and basic *tafsīrs*.[53] It is at least partly due to his

52 For example, in 1990, F. Abd al-Rahim published his edition of *Kitāb al-Muᶜarrab* by Abū Manṣūr Mawhūb al-Jawālīqī (Damascus: Dār al-Qalām, 1990). This edition remains one of the most popular for academic usage.

53 See, for example, F. ᶜAbd al-Raḥīm, *Iqsām al-aymān fī aqsām al-Qurᵓān* (Damascus: Dār al-Qalām, 2016).

outstanding intellectual abilities[54] and his broad international contacts that the Center for Translations went on to be such a success.

In the first eight years of its operation, up to 2002, the Center supervised the production of more than ten new translations of the Qur'an, all of which were prepared exclusively for the KFGQPC in accordance with its guidelines for translators. These guidelines were prepared in the 1990s, set out in a document dating from 2002,[55] and updated in the early 2020s. They can be summarised as follows:

The translator should:

- Not inflict his own doctrinal theories, personal interpretations, and philosophical opinions on the translation or his or her[56] commentary on the target text.
- Translate any Qur'anic words that are repeated in the source text consistently, unless their meanings differ according to the context.
- Provide an accurate understanding of the Quranic verses by not departing from the text by adding or removing anything.
- Avoid literal translation.[57]
- Retain Islamic terms that cannot be translated into other languages, such as *zakāt*, *ḥajj*, and *ᶜumra*, presenting them according to their Arabic pronunciation and adding explanations of their meaning in a special appendix.
- Demonstrate commitment to the use of Islamic terms and expressions when translating and avoid the use of words and terms specific to other religions such as Judaism, Christianity, and Buddhism.

54 During the 1980s, he spent time working as a lecturer in Arabic in many countries, from Surinam to Taiwan.

55 *Shurūṭ al-tarjama* (author's personal archive).

56 As of 2023, the only translation to be carried out by a woman is into Polish, a project that is currently in progress but about which no information is currently available.

57 This rule is not really explained, but it seems to refer to the general concept of translation of the Qur'an as 'translation of the meanings' rather than as a word-by-word 'Qur'an in another language' (which is theologically prohibited as the Qur'an is considered to be inimitable).

- Adhere to the 'appropriate' transliteration system when writing Arabic words in other languages.[58]
- Present personal names according to their Arabic pronunciation. Any reference to their pronunciation in the target language should be made in footnotes or in parentheses.
- Use contemporary language that is understood by most of the speakers of the target language, and avoid the use of archaic language.[59]

In addition to these general principles, the KFGQPC developed its own translation strategy, which promoted grammatical rather than interpretative translation. Translators must also preserve the original word order whenever possible and indicate all additions through the use of parenthesis. Many of the rules, such as the requirement to preserve Qur'anic vocabulary and to use modern language, relate to issues of linguistics rather than theology. That is, apart from the edict to 'avoid terms specific to other religions', they are, on the surface, religiously neutral. In their actual contracts with translators, however, the KFGQPC has exerted control over the translators' hermeneutical approach, as they advocate the use of the *tafsīr*s of al-Ṭabarī, al-Baghawī, Ibn Kathīr, and, finally, the twentieth-century Saudi scholar and author of *Taysīr al-karīm al-mannān*, ᶜAbd al-Raḥmān b. Nāṣir al-Saᶜdī (1889–1957). This choice of recommended exegetes is quite understandable: their works all belong to the established Salafi canon. However, the situation is nuanced because, in cases where opinions given in these texts differ, the KFGQPC recommended the use of *al-aqwāl al-rājiḥa*, that is, the meanings that are described in these *tafsīr*s as being most plausible. This leaves quite a lot of room for discussion and variation since, in many cases, exegetes present several different interpretations without giving any final answer as to which meaning they consider to be most applicable. Al-Ṭabarī sometimes uses the expression *fa-ūlū ᶜindī* ('the foremost one for me'), and Ibn Kathīr *aṣaḥḥ qawlan* ('the most correct statement'), but, still, there are many occasions on which they give no clear answers. As a result, this nonspecificity in the *tafsīr* tradition has carried over into

58 No further explanations are given.
59 See the brief official report of activities until 2002: *Taqrīr al-mujammaᶜ* (Medina: King Fahd Glorious Qur'an Printing Complex, 2003).

the many translations published by KFGQPC: for instance, the Russian translation by Elmir Quliyev includes 'alternative' interpretations in parenthesis, even when it comes to theologically loaded phrases, such as 'God rose over the Throne' in Q. 20:5. Nevertheless, most, if not all, of the translations exclusively published by KFGQPC tend to quite openly adopt a Salafi hermeneutical approach, providing the 'correct' interpretation of the Qur'an in terms of the Salafi religious creed. This is a result of not only the translation strategy used by the translators but also the overall editing, revision, and production processes that the translation goes through, which will now be described here in detail, as the impact of these on the final translation cannot be understated.

First of all, there is question of how the KFGQPC chooses in which languages to produce its translations. Predictably, at the very beginning, the major world languages came under focus—which is why English and French translations were published during the Complex's early years. Chinese, Spanish, and Russian translations appeared a little later, meaning that the KFGQPC had already produced translations into several of the most widely-spoken world languages during first ten years of operation. In many other cases, the decision to translate the Qur'an into a particular language was not initiated by the KFGQPC itself. Usually, a translation was the result of an initiative from below: either the translators (or translation teams) themselves or a local Islamic community. This goes some way to explaining why, in the cases of Central Asian languages like Uzbek, Tajik, and Kyrgyz, for example, the KFGQPC only started to develop these translation projects in the late 2000s, when some well-trained individuals appeared on the scene. Those people, who primarily worked on revising existing translations in their own languages, were usually graduates of the IUM or other Saudi institutions of Islamic higher education such as Umm al-Qura in Mecca or Imam Muhammad Ibn Saud Islamic University in Riyadh. Most of the translations produced for the post-Soviet space, for example, took the form of pre-existing translations that were edited by graduates of IUM, and same is true for some of the translations into African languages. These projects were often set in motion when the KFGQPC was contacted by relevant Islamic organisations via the MOIA, sometimes with the help of Saudi embassies, the MWL, or independent Saudi missionary activists. Languages with an indigenous Muslim population of native speakers provide focus: for example, by 2022, the KFGQPC had printed translations into Albanian, Bosnian, Macedonian, Greek, and Hungarian (with the Macedonian and Hungarian translations being produced exclusively for the KFGQPC), whereas it has not pursued many projects in Scandinavian or Baltic languages.[60] Pre-existing Muslim networks have thus played a very important role in the choice of target languages.

Usually, the translator (or whoever proposes the translation) is asked to provide a CV and two references, usually from Saudi-related circles or established Muslim institutions around the world: the latter refers broadly to Muslim-majority regions such as Pakistan, parts of India, Bangladesh, or Sudan, where many Islamic universities have close ties with Saudi Arabia. There are three basic requirements for translators: they should be Muslim, possess a level of religious knowledge (usually demonstrable via a degree from an Islamic university), and have proven expertise in both Arabic and the target language. Once all the documents have been received, these are usually sent on to the academic council of the KFGQPC, which is made up of scholars from its academic department and official representatives of the MOIA. Approval of a translator is followed by the drafting of a contract. This document outlines the terms of reimbursement, the time frame for the project, and the aforementioned translation guidelines.

Around 2020, the KFGQPC updated its translation guidelines to incorporate a few new rules. One introduced a requirement that translators use *al-Tafsīr al-muyassar* (for more on which, see below) to guide their exegetical choices; another asks them to pay special attention to topics such as *jihād*, 'relations with non-Muslims', and 'beating women'.[61] The guidelines also mention a document called *Dalīl al-mutarjim* ('The Translator's Guide') but, as of 2023, this source is still in preparation.

The translation is prepared and submitted in parts, normally between three and six instalments (each containing ten or five parts of the Qur'an, respectively). This explains why some KFGQPC translations, such as the

---

60 The KFGQPC published one work in Swedish (by Abdul-Haleem Joseph) in 2011–2012, and it only comprised the first five parts of the Qur'an. See Abdul-Haleem Joseph, *Den Ädla Koranens fem första delar* (Medina: King Fahd Glorious Qur'an Printing Complex, 2011).

61 *Shurūṭ al-tarjama* (personal archive). The last point clearly refers to the phrase *wa-ḍribūhunna* in Q. 4.34. It translates literally as 'beat them', 'strike them'.

Russian or Azerbaijanian, were first published partially (beginning with the last, thirtieth, part of the Qur'an, from Q. 78 to the end—the part usually used for Qur'an memorisation). After the first part of the work has been submitted, the KFGQPC sends it out for review and revision.

Revision is performed by either an individual or a small team with the same linguistic proficiencies as the translator. Their role is to compare the work to the original Arabic text and to provide the KFGQPC with a report. Most revisers are Saudi Arabian (and usually graduates of IUM) or religious figures from abroad. An example of the first case is the 1997 translation into Greek (discussed below), which was revised by Khalīl Jihād Bilāl, a graduate of Muhammad bin Saud Islamic University. A contrasting example is the Spanish translation by Abdel Ghani Melara Navio, also published in 1997. It was revised by Omar Kaddoura, the imam of a mosque in Venezuela, and Isa Amer Quevedo, the head of the Islamic Centre in Bolivia.[62] The latter was also the editor of another translation into Spanish by an Argentinian convert and graduate of Umm al-Qura University in Mecca, Isa Garcia.[63] For some languages, the selection of the reviser seems not to have been an easy task: a few translations do not mention a reviser but an oversight committee, suggesting that responsibilities were divided across a number of individuals. An example is the Macedonian translation by Hasan Dzilo that appeared in 1998.[64] For the Korean translation by Hamid Choi (1997), no reviser mentioned at all.[65]

However, greater emphasis seems to have been placed on revision in recent years as all translations published since 2015 provide the names of at least two revisers.

---

62 *El Noble Coran y Su Traduccion Comentario En Lengua Española* (Medina: King Fahd Glorious Qur'an Printing Complex, 1997).

63 See Isa Garcia, *El Corán. Traducción Comentada. Traducción Isa Garcia* (Bogota: [n. pub.], 2013).

64 *Kur'an so Prevod* (Medina: King Fahd Glorious Qur'an Printing Complex, 1997).

65 *Seong kkulan uimiui hangug-eo beon-yeog* (Medina: King Fahd Glorious Qur'an Printing Complex, 1997). Still, his work (mostly based on A.Y. Ali's English translation) has been edited by some local proofreaders consisting of Korean Muslim scholars of Arab origin. See: Hamid Choi, 'Tajrībatī fī tarjama maᶜānī al-Qurᵓān ilā al-Lughah al-Kūriyya', in *Abḥāth al-nadwa tarjamat maᶜānī al-Qurᵓān: taqwīm li-l-māḍī wa-takhṭīṭ li-l-mustaqbal*, 2 vols (Medina: King Fahd Glorious Qur'an Printing Complex, 2002), II, p. 270.

Sometimes the translations are reviewed by the experts from within the KFGQPC itself, as was the case with the Persian translation by Walī Allāh al-Dahlawī (1703–1762) that was published by the KFGQPC in 1997.[66] On this translation, the revisions were carried out by ᶜAbd al-Gafūr al-Bulūshī, one of the KFGQPC's leading scholars, and another Saudi scholar, Muḥammad ᶜAlī Dārī.[67] The KFGQPC's edition of al-Dahlawī's translation met with some criticism, as the changes that had been made to the original text were not always marked clearly as interventions.[68] Thus, the revisers seem to have generally followed the same practice as was used by the KFGQPC in its earlier versions of the English translations of Yusuf Ali and Muhammad Hamidullah: prioritising the 'usability' of the translation as a more or less approximate 'meaning' of the Qur'an over protecting the original translator's intellectual rights, and thereby treating the translation as no more than a kind of auxiliary text. These interventions also reflect an attempt to strengthen the Sunni discourse in the translation, which is used mostly by Shii speakers of Persian. The official Saudi religious elite has always been extremely critical of Shi'ism, especially in the late 1980s and 1990s, before the reign of King Abdullah.[69]

The report submitted by the reviser consists of a spreadsheet with a list of 'errors' (*akhṭāʾ*), divided into mistakes of four kinds:

1. *lughawī*—'language errors'. These include typos, the usage of incorrect words, etc;
2. *ᶜaqīdī*—'dogmatic errors'. This refers to things that arise from theological issues, such as 'misinterpreting' the divine attributes;

---

66 According to al-Bulūshī, the KFGQPC considered publishing various other Persian translations, in particular one by Elahi Ghomshei, but the committee found it 'weak when compared to the Arabic original'. See ᶜAbd al-Gafūr al-Bulūshī, 'Tārīkh taṭwīr tarjamāt maᶜānī al-Qurʾān ilā al-Fārisiyya', in *Abḥāth al-nadwa tarjamat maᶜānī al-Qurʾān: taqwīm li-l-māḍī wa-takhṭīṭ li-l-mustaqbal*, 2 vols (Medina: King Fahd Glorious Qur'an Printing Complex, 2002), I, p. 145.

67 ᶜAbd al-Gafūr al-Bulūshī, *Tafsīr Qurʾāni Karīm* (*Lahore: Dawᶜ*atu l-Ḥaqq), 1433/2011. Al-Bulūshī also authored his own translation of the Qur'an into his native Balochi, which was published in Pakistan.

68 See, for example, Bahāᶜ al-Dīn Khurramshāhī, *Terjume Shāh Weli Allah Dehlawi*. Terjuman e-Wahy, 9 (Shahriyār 1380), 61–71.

69 Ismail, *Saudi Clerics*, pp. 105–07.

3. *sharʿiyya*—'legal errors'. These are usually related to legal issues mentioned in the Qur'an; and
4. *minhajī*—'methodological errors', such as ignorance of the context of the revelation for a particular verse.

Once the revision on all parts is complete and positive reports have been handed over to the KFGQPC, the translator is usually invited to Saudi Arabia to visit the KFGQPC, if possible. A special committee is convened during this visit to discuss any final matters. This stage of the process usually relates to issues to do with the commentary and additions to the text. Special attention is also given to questions relating the treatment of verses that deal with the divine attributes and legal rules and to those that contain special vocabulary. This might also involve discussing the rendition of verses for which a literal translation is considered 'misleading', for instance how to translate *inna-llahu maʿanā* ('God with us' Q. 9:40). As any implication of 'physical presence' is completely unacceptable to Sunni Islam, a comment might be added to explain that this 'presence' relates to God's power and knowledge only. Another example of this kind of verse can be seen in Q. 4:93, *man yaqtul muʾminan muʿtamidan fa-jazāʿūhu jahannam khālidan fīhā*. The literal translation—'But anyone who kills a believer deliberately, his punishment will be Hell, abiding therein forever'—must be amended to make it compatible with a doctrine of final salvation from hellfire for every believer.[70]

After final approval has been given, the translation then goes through one more proofread. A special committee checks the Arabic text, and the translator re-reads his text one more time. Finally, a formal introduction by the head of the MOIA is added in and, often, also a statement by the translator or reviser. Just before 2020, the KFGQPC also started to include an additional introduction in Arabic to its new translations.[71] This outlines the divine origin and earthly history of the *muṣḥaf* [the Arabic text] and what translation actually is, equating 'explanatory

70 In the Sunni tradition, this verse is interpreted as *waʿīd*, that is, 'threatening', as the Saudi exegete al-Saʿdī explains in his *tafsīr*. See Nāṣir b. ʿAbd Allāh al-Saʿdī, *Taysīr al-Karīm al-Raḥmān fī tafsīr kalām al-mannān* (Riyadh: Darussalam, 2002), pp. 209–10.

71 *Muqaddimat tarjamāt al-Qurʾān al-karīm* (Medina: King Fahd Glorious Qur'an Printing Complex, 2019).

translation' to *tafsīr*. The premise upon which the permissibility of translation is built in this, not surprisingly, is Ibn Taymiyya's statement about the 'obligation to convey the Qur'an' [*ḍarūrat tablīgh al-Qurʾān*].[72] This introduction has already appeared in a number of translations, for example, the 2020 translation into the Kurmanchi dialect of Kurdish by Ali Ismail Taha.[73]

Once the translation has been printed and passed through three levels of quality control, it is sent out for distribution. Copies are provided as gifts to pilgrims visiting Medina, and all translations are available in Saudi Arabia's two main mosques, the Holy Mosque in Mecca and the Prophet's Mosque in Medina. At an international level, the KFGQPC also distributes translations via Saudi embassies worldwide, and these are, again, mostly distributed gratis. In addition, the KFGQPC is also active in some bookfairs, mostly in the Gulf region. These activities, together with the digital availability of recently published works via the qurancomplex.gov.sa website, makes any newly issued translations easily accessible. Statistics about how many copies of each translation are printed are not openly available, but the decision seems to depend on the number of native speakers of each language. For languages such as Indonesian, the initial print run could come to over 100,000 copies; for others the number is much smaller, often between 10,000 and 20,000 copies. According to the Saudi database 'Open Data', during 2016–2017, the total number of Qur'an translations distributed by the KFGQPC was as follows:[74]

Asia: 334,280

Australia: 1,810

Africa: 25,750

South America: 3,780

North America: 1,080

Europe: 21,020

---

72 Ibid., p. 16.
73 *Qurʾānī Pīrūz* (Medina: King Fahd Glorious Qur'an Printing Complex, 2020).
74 MOIA statistics, https://data.gov.sa/Data/ar/dataset/holy-quran/resource/7e7664db-3793-49a1-9a58-544b9c8aad9f

These figures show that a much larger number of translations was distributed in Asia than in all other regions. This distribution pattern correlates with the languages of translations. As of 2022, the KFGQPC had produced Qur'an translations in thirty-nine Asian languages, nineteen African languages, and only sixteen European languages, including English, French, Spanish, and Portuguese which have many speakers outside Europe. Of course, these figures should be approached with the caveat that they only pertain to one year and thus may not be particularly representative, especially given that most of the KFGQPC's translations into European languages mainly date from the late 1980s to the early 2000s.

Al-Tafsīr al-muyassar: The First Exegesis Designed for Use in Translation Projects

In 1998, the KFGQPC published a Qur'an commentary entitled *al-Tafsīr al-muyassar* ['The simplified *tafsīr*']. This work continues a long tradition of exegetical publications that are intended to provide a 'simple' and 'accessible' explanation of the Qur'anic verses. Although some works of this sub-genre were written in the premodern period of Islamic history,[75] most 'simplified' commentaries were written in the twentieth century and grew out of the Islamic reformist movement and the idea of propagating religious knowledge to the masses. An early example of this kind of *tafsīr* is the Ibadi work *Taysīr al-tafsīr* ['The simplification of the *tafsīr*'] by Muḥammad Aṭfayyash, which was written around 1910.[76] Later on, Salafi scholars in particular contributed to this field, perhaps most notably in terms of ᶜAbd Allāh Khiyāṭ's *al-Tafsīr al-muyassar: khulāṣat muqtabasa min ashhār al-tafāsir al-muᶜtabara* ['The simplified *tafsīr*: short extracts from the most authoritative *tafsīr*'],[77] ᶜAbd al-Raḥmān al-Saᶜdī's aforementioned *Taysīr al-laṭīf al-mannān fī khulāṣat tafsīr al-Qurʾān* ['A facilitation from the Sublime, the Generous: a digest of Qur'anic exegesis'], and Abū Bakr al-Jazaʾīrī's *Aysar al-tafāsir li-l-kalām al-ᶜālī*

75 For example, *al-Taysīr fī al-tafsīr* by Najm al-Dīn al-Nasafī, who died in 1143.

76 Muḥammad Aṭfayyash, *Taysīr at-tafsīr (Muscat: Wizārat at-Turāth wa-l-Thaqāfa, 2004)*.

77 ᶜAbd Allāh Khiyāṭ, *al-Tafsīr al-muyassar: khulāṣat muqtabasa min ashhār al-tafāsīr al-muᶜtabara* (Jeddah: Maktabat al-Najāḥ, 1377/1958).

al-kabīr ['The simplest explanation of the speech of [God] the Exalted, the Great'].[78] The introductions to these *tafsīrs* express a common aim: the authors' desire to make their interpretations as broadly accessible as possible. For instance, al-Jazāʾirī (who was a preacher at the Prophet's Mosque in Medina), writes:

> I am often asked by those attending my *tafsīr* classes if I could write a *tafsīr* for Muslims that was written in a simple style, with easily understandable interpretations, that would help [the reader] to understand the words of God the Almighty.[79]

This trend for 'simplified' *tafsīrs* reflects the Salafi perspective that making religious knowledge available for every Muslim is a requirement, above all because it is imperative that believers understand the reality of Islamic monotheism, *tawḥīd*. For this reason, religious writing and publishing in the Saudi context focuses on the popularisation of religious knowledge and the propagation of Salafi doctrine rather than taking a more encyclopaedic approach. The KFGQPC's production of *al-Tafsīr al-muyassar* seems a deliberate attempt to propose a more standardised approach to Qur'anic hermeneutics. On one hand, we can see in this text the idea of Qur'an translation as the delivery of the 'approximate' basic meaning of the divine word at work. On the other, the KFGQPC's *tafsīr* introduces an approach to exegesis that prevents any 'distortions' from the ideal of 'the correct creed' [*al-ʿaqīda al-ṣaḥīḥa*], which, for Salafi scholarship, equates to 'belief of the early Muslims' [*al-salaf al-ṣāliḥ*]. Thus, the appearance of *al-Tafsīr al-muyassar* and its growing influence on KFGQPC translations (as well as the official requirement that it is used in the preparation of these) is an important step towards the development of a specifically Salafi approach to both Qur'an interpretation and translation.

Given the growing significance of *al-Tafsīr al-muyassar*, one has to ask: why is this exegesis regarded as a 'better' reference work for those undertaking Qur'an translation than other *tafsīrs*? How can one *tafsīr*, written in Arabic, be useful for conveying the meanings of the Qur'an

78 Abū Bakr al-Jazāʾirī, *Aysar al-tafāsīr li-l-kalām al-ʿalī al-kabīr*, 2 vols (Jeddah: Rāsim, 1990).

79 Al-Jazāʾirī, *Aysar al-tafāsir*, I, p. 5.

into other languages, taking into consideration all the differences in syntax and grammar that can occur between languages?

Written in the mid-1990s, *al-Tafsīr al-muyassa*r appeared in print in 1998 with an enigmatic authorship: the title page credits *nukhba min al-ulamāʾ* ['an elite group of scholars']. No more information is provided in either this or any subsequent editions (the second edition came out in 2008) about the identity of these scholars. This anonymity is extremely unusual in contemporary Islamic religious scholarship, especially when it comes to Qur'anic Studies, as the name of the author often conveys authority (as do the names of the previous authorities cited who 'transmit' knowledge from earlier generations). To provide some comparison with other collaborative tafsīr projects, the voluminous *al-Tafsīr al-mawḍūʿī* ['The thematical commentary'], for example, which was first published by the University of Sharjah in 2010, lists on its initial pages all of the scholars who worked on it.[80] Likewise, *al-Mukhtaṣar fī tafsīr al-Qurʾān* ['A short commentary on the Qur'an'], published in 2014 by the Markaz al-Tafsīr li-l-Dirāsāt al-Qurʾāniyya [The Tafsīr Centre for Qur'anic Studies] in Riyadh, lists all the contributing authors and editors by name.[81]

Al-Tafsīr al-muyassar thus demonstrates a new approach to exegesis. The institution that produces the exegetical works is the authority: here is a *tafsīr* 'by the KFGQPC'. This impression is reinforced by references in the introduction that identify the KFGQPC as the initiating force behind the work: '*raʾā al-mujammaʿ an yuṣdira tafsīran muyassaran*' ['the Complex decided to publish a simplified commentary'].[82] They position this *tafsīr* as the product of a collective effort by an institution that has already gained perceived authority in the field of Qur'an printing due to the global popularity of its Arabic 'Medinan Qur'an', the *Muṣḥaf al-Madīna al-nabawwiya*. The fact that KFGQPC's Arabic *muṣḥaf* is the most widely distributed Arabic Qur'an in the world[83] would lend authority to any *tafsīr* it produced.

80 *al-Tafsīr al-mawḍūʿī li-l-suwar al-Qurʾān al-karīm* (Sharjah: Jāmiʿa al-Shāriqa, 2010).

81 *al-Mukhtaṣar fī tafsīr al-Qurʾān* (Riyadh: Markaz al-Tafsīr li-l-Dirāsāt al-Qurʾāniyya, 1436/2014).

82 *al-Tafsīr al-muyassar* (Medina: King Fahd Glorious Qur'an Printing Complex, 2019), p. ḥ.

83 By 2007, that is, in the first twenty-three years of its operation, the KFGQPC had printed 127,420,423 copies of the holy book of Islam.

However, despite efforts to anonymise the authors of the *al-Tafsīr al-muyassar*, a few of the individuals who worked on the project have been named subsequently by other sources. One member of the editorial board has been identified as Shaykh Ḥāzim Ḥaydar al-Karmī, a Palestinian graduate of the Islamic University of Madinah.[84] Al-Karmī has received numerous testimonials from many twentieth-century authorities in *tafsīr*, including ᶜAbd Allāh al-Shinqīṭī, the son of Muḥammad al-Mukhtār al-Shinqīṭī, who wrote the popular *tafsīr Aḍwāḥ al-bayān fī iḍāḥ al-Qurᵓān bi-l-Qurᵓān* ['Lights of Clarity in the Explanation of the Qur'an by the Qur'an'].[85] Another contributor to *al-Tafsīr al-muyassar was* ᶜAbd al-Azīz Ismaᶜīl (1942–2010), a scholar of Qur'anic Studies from Egypt (and a graduate of al-Azhar) who has taught at Muhamamad bin Saud Islamic University and also worked for the MOIA and the Saudi broadcast company Al-Qurᵓān.[86] His involvement, alongside other scholars from Saudi Arabia, Egypt, Syria, and Jordan, was confirmed in an obituary published by the Rābiṭat al-ᶜUlamāᵓ al-Sūriyyūn [*'League of Syrian Scholars'*].[87] Thus, it appears that an international team worked on the project, while the final copyright belongs completely to one institution, the KFGQPC.

What approach does this *tafsīr* adopt? From its several introductions—two official ones (provided by the heads of the MOIA and the KFGQPC) as well as a more substantial general one—we learn that the work follows the tradition of *al-tafsīr bi-l-maᵓthūr*, that is, 'transmitted *tafsīr*' (as opposed to *al-tafsīr bi-l-raᵓy* ['*tafsīr* based on reason']). The anonymous KFGQPC authors reference and thereby invoke the authority of the 'classical' Salafi canonical commentaries of al-Ṭabarī, al-Baghawī, and Ibn Kathīr, then describe the main aim of their project in the following terms: 'There is a strong need in this era to produce a short commentary, which observes the principles of *tafsīr* and its sources in accordance with

https://web.archive.org/web/20110715141722/http://www.qurancomplex.com/Display.asp?section=7&l=arb&f=nobza05&trans=

84 For more on Shaykh Ḥāzim Ḥaydar (in Arabic), see https://areq.net/m/حازم_حيدر_الكرمي.html

85 Īlyās al-Birmāwī, *Imtāᶜa al-fuḍalāᵓ bi-tarājim al-qurāᵓa fīmā baᶜd al-qarn al-thāmin al-hijri*, 2 vols (Riyadh: Dār al-Nadwa al-ᶜĀlamiyya, 2000), I, p. 78.

86 'Rāḥil al-ᶜAllāma ᶜAbd al-Azīz Ismāᶜīl, ṣāḥib *al-Tafsīr al-muyassar*', https://al-maktaba.org/book/31617/71606.

87 Majd al-Makkī, 'Rāḥil al-ᶜAllāma al-Duktūr ᶜAbd al-Azīz Ismāᶜīl', https://islamsyria.com/ar/التراجم/المترجمين/جمع-وترتيب-مجد-مكي

the method of the righteous predecessors (*al-salaf al-ṣāliḥ*).'[88] Next, the KFGQPC's introduction relates their commentary to their translation activities:

> After detailed study, the Complex decided to publish a simplified commentary to the Glorious Qur'an, which will summarise the principles of *tafsīr* and its original sources, so that it can form the basis for translations of the Qur'an into the languages of Muslim and non-Muslim nations [produced] by the Complex.[89]

The introduction goes on to give more detailed explanations of the methodological principles that guided the writing of the *tafsīr*. The primary aim of the *tafsīr*, as cited above, confirms the KFGQPC's commitment to 'the *madhhab* of the righteous ancestors (*al-salaf al-ṣāliḥ*)'; other stated exegetical principles mainly relate to fairly standard ideas about 'simplification' (presenting one, the 'predominant', opinion only) and the provision of explanations for unusual or rare words (*gharīb*). However, the authors' final point is very definitely innovative: 'The exegete should be mindful of the fact that this *tafsīr* will be translated into various languages, thus [the use of] any terms that cannot be translated should be avoided.'[90]

How are those principles realised in practice, especially when it comes to languages from different families? To address this question, I will discuss four translations of this *tafsīr*, two published by the KFGQPC (a complete Tajik translation dating to 2014 and the Swahili translation of 2019), and two partial ones, in English and Ukrainian, that were printed by Maktab al-Taᶜāwunī li-Tawᶜiyyat al-Jāliyāt (the Communities Awareness Bureau in the Old Industrial City), an Islamic NGO based in Riyadh. The latter two translations comprise suras 1 and 58–114, known as *al-ᶜushr al-akhīr*, or the 'final tenth' of the Qur'an. Thus, the sample texts include translations into both 'Islamic' (Tajik and Swahili) and 'non-Islamic' (English and Ukrainian) languages.

Before embarking on this comparison, it is necessary to address the style of the commentary in the original Arabic. The *tafsīr* takes an extremely literal approach to textual reasoning, and many words

88 *al-Tafsīr al-muyassar*, p. ḥ.
89 Ibid.
90 Ibid., p. ṭ.

are simply explained through the use of more popular synonyms in Modern Standard Arabic. On other occasions, mainstream explanations are provided in quite a concise way. A good example of this can be seen in its treatment of the story of the people who are described as being *ummatan wāḥidatan* ['one community'] in Q. 2:213 and Q. 13:19. For both verses, *al-Tafsīr al-muyassar* provides the simple explanation that the story refers to 'one religion which is Islam'.[91] This appears to be based on al-Ṭabarī's interpretation of this phrase, which, he argued is 'the most correct', above the two others he cites.[92]

Some parts of the *tafsīr* look as if they would present more challenges for translators than others. For example, the phrase *innā makkannā lahu fī-l-arḍ* occurs in Q. 18:84, at the beginning of the story of Dhū-l-Qarnayn that is related in this sura. The verb *makkannā* here is generally translated into English in one of three ways: 'Indeed We **established him** upon the earth: (Saheeh International); 'We **made him strong** in the land' (Yusuf Ali); and 'We **established his power** in the land' (Abdel Haleem). However, the commentary in *al-Tafsīr al-muyassar* reads exactly the same as the Qur'anic text itself, with no further explanation or use of synonyms. The same expression occurs again in Q. 12:21 (*makkannā li-Yūsuf fī-l-arḍ*), and it is again reproduced in *al-Tafsīr al-muyassar*. Explanation of *makkana* is provided only on the first instance of its use, in Q. 7:10, *makkannākum fī-l-arḍ* ['We **established them** on the earth], where it is glossed with the addition *jaᶜalnāhā qirāran lakum* [literally 'We made it [the earth] a place for them']. To the authors of the original Arabic *al-Tafsīr al-muyassar*, it seems the meaning of the verse was self-evident. However, this is not necessarily the case for those translating *al-Tafsīr al-muyassar* into other languages. The Tajik translation renders the relevant phrase in Q. 7:10 as *hamono -ej mardum-dar zamin çojgohaton dodem'* ['We have given you a place on the earth, O people'], but in Q. 18:84 it is translated differently, as *hamono Mo ūro dar zamin qudrat dodem* ['We gave him power on earth']. This is just one example, but it illustrates clearly that the exegesis presented in *al-Tafsīr al-muyassar* is not clear enough to provide a strong basis for a monolithic translation, as it was intended to be.

91 Ibid., p. 210.

92 The alternatives he rejects understand the verse to refer to Adam as the father of humanity. See al-Ṭabarī, *Jāmiᶜ al-bayān ᶜan tāᶜwīl āy al-Qurʾān*, 16 vols (Cairo: Dār Hijr, 2001), III, p. 625.

In other cases, the exegesis presented in *al-Tafsīr al-muyassar* gives rise to even greater variation in translation. A very interesting example is an extra-Qur'anic term *karāmāt*, which *al-Tafsīr al-muyassar* uses in its commentary on Q. 58:22 with reference to the phrase *raḍiya-llahu ᶜanhum wa-raḍū ᶜanhu* ['God is well pleased with them, and they with Him']. The verse itself generally describes the reward that awaits believers:

> [Prophet], you will not find people who truly believe in God and the Last Day giving their loyalty to those who oppose God and His Messenger, even though they may be their fathers, sons, brothers, or other relations: these are the people in whose hearts God has inscribed faith, and whom He has strengthened with His spirit. He will let them enter Gardens graced with flowing streams, where they will stay: God is well pleased with them, and they with Him. They are on God's side, and God's side will be the one to prosper.[93]

The original Arabic *al-Tafsīr al-muyassar* provides the following commentary on the phrase *raḍiya-llahu ᶜanhum wa-raḍū ᶜanhu: 'raḍū ᶜan rabbihim bimā aᶜṭāhum min al-karāmāt wa-rafīᶜa al-darajāt'*, which means 'And they are pleased with their Lord for the *karāmāt* and high levels He gave them'. This raises the question of what the word *al-karāmāt* really means.

The authors of *al-Tafsīr al-muyassar* seem to follow al-Saᶜdī's interpretation of the verse, since he also mentions *anwāᶜ al-karāmāt* ['various *al-karāmāt*'].[94] In the Islamic tradition more generally (especially Sufism), *karāmāt* is used to denote the 'blessings' or miraculous wonders performed by the *awliyāʾ* ['friends of God'], which God grants them the power to bring about.[95] However, the Salafi perspective does not consider *karāmāt* to denote supernatural powers. This can be seen in the commentary of Saudi authority Shaykh Ṣāliḥ b. Fawzān al-Fawzān on Muḥammad b. ᶜAbd al-Wahhāb's treatise on belief. Al-Fawzān writes, 'People of Sunna and community recognise true *karāmāt* [...] still, it is necessary to be careful in those issues, neither denying it fully nor accepting it absolutely.'[96] His words imply that Salafis do not deny

93 The translation here is by Abdel Haleem.

94 al-Saᶜdī, *Taysīr al-Karīm*, p. 1000.

95 L. Gardet, 'Karāma' in *Encyclopaedia of Islam, Second Edition*, ed. by P. Bearman, Th. Bianquis, C. E. Bosworth, E. van Donzel, and W. P. Heinrichs (Leiden: Brill, 2012), http://dx.doi.org/10.1163/1573-3912_islam_COM_0445

96 Ṣāliḥ b. Fawzān al-Fawzān, *Sharḥ ᶜaqīdat al-Imām Muḥammad b. ᶜAbd al-Wahhāb* (Riyadh: Maktabat al-Minhāj, 1436/2011), p. 113.

the existence of supernatural powers (especially those given by God to 'righteous people', *awliyāʾ*), but recommend against calling them *karāmāt*. In the same text, al-Fawzān also warns against believing in any sorcery that could come 'from *shayṭān*' [an evil spirit].[97] The concept of *karāmāt* is a major tenet of some Sufi brotherhood and is closely linked to the veneration of *awliyāʾ*, both of which are heavily criticised by Salafi scholarship, which makes it surprising that this term appears in a Salafi commentary, especially given that Sufi exegesis on this verse explicitly link it with *awliyāʾ* and their *karāmāt*.[98] Given this, it is not entirely clear why the authors of *al-Tafsīr al-muyassar* chose to use this term.

The way the word is treated in the different language versions of *al-Tafsīr al-muyassar* indicates that the translators were not expecting to come across any language with Sufi connotations.[99] The anonymous English translation uses the term 'noble things', so the text reads as 'And they are pleased with their Lord for the noble things and high levels He gave them'. This might, in some way, reflect an attempt to provide a literal translation for *karāmā*t, on the basis that it is a plural of the singular *kirāma* ['dignity', something 'noble'] but, in reality, the use of 'noble things' here is not clear and comprehensible to the reader. The Ukrainian translation renders it as 'dana jim poshana' ['the respect they have'], which could be said to be 'correct' if one understands *karāmāt* to denote a divine gift [*ikrām*], but this is unrelated to the concept of *karāmāt* outlined above. The Tajik translation opts to completely omit this expression. Since most of the text is rendered in a very faithful way, this omission was probably intentional, a way of avoiding the need to explain a Sufi concept in the context of a Sunni-Salafi translation. Finally, the Swahili version interprets *karāmāt* using the single word 'utukufu', which generally means 'glory'. This one example shows the level of variation that can arise from even a serious attempt to write a 'standard' interpretation for many languages at once, and it demonstrates the difficulties that can arise with the re-translation of the meaning of individual words and terminology.

---

97 al-Fawzān, *Sharḥ*, p. 281.

98 See, for example, Ismāʿīl Ḥaqqī Afandī, *Rūḥ al-bayān*, 10 vols (Beirut: Dār Iḥyāʾ al-Turāth al-ʿArabī, 1985), IX, p. 414–15.

99 All the versions compared here are available online on the multi-language website https://tafseer.info/

A few more examples illustrate other translation-related differences that appear in the various language versions of *al-Tafsīr al-muyassar*. The difficulties presented by culturally specific terminology direct the various treatments of the *ẓihār* formula ['You are to me like the back of my mother'] that is referenced in Q. 58:2. This expression is described in *al-Tafsīr al-muyassar* as 'used by "someone"', but there is no explanation that it was a declaration of divorce used in pre-Islamic times. This absence led the Tajik translator to break from a literal translation and add in an explanatory footnote. Also challenging for translators are the historical 'facts' included in the original text of KFGQPC's *tafsīr* about believers of other religions that are not entirely clear. An example is its exegesis on the following verse:

> Indeed, those who have believed and those who were Jews and the Sabeans [*al-ṣābiʾūn*] and the Christians and the Magians and those who associated with Allah—Allah will judge between them on the Day of Resurrection. Indeed Allah is, over all things, Witness (Q. 22:17)

Al-Tafsīr al-muyassar gives a fairly atypical explanation of *al-ṣābiʾūn*, describing the community as 'those people [who] remain in their inborn nature with no religion to follow'. This is quite strange because all of the other communities mentioned in the verse are interpreted in a historical sense: apart from 'believers in God and His Messenger', there are Jews, Christians, 'fire-worshippers' [*majūsīyūn*], and, finally, 'polytheists'. The same explanation is given at Q. 2:62 ('The [Muslim] believers, the Jews, the Christians, and the Sabians—all those who believe in God and the Last Day and do good—will have their rewards with their Lord. No fear for them, nor will they grieve'), in which *al-ṣābiʾūn* are also mentioned. The identity of this group is a subject of debate in modern discourse (whether they are followers of some ancient cult from Harran or Mandeans), and medieval Islamic scholars also proposed different options, ranging from their being adherents of a particular monotheistic religion to their being people who shift from one belief to another. Muslims jurists have also debated their status as *ahl al-kitāb* ['People of the Book']: Hanafis include them in the ahl al-kitāb along with Jews and Christians, the Malikis generally do not, and the Shafiis and Hanbalis have not historically had a shared consensus.[100] *Al-Tafsīr al-muyassar*'s

100 For a general outline of exegetical opinions on this community, see Muhammad Azizan Sabjan, 'The Al-Sābiʾūn (the Sabians) in the Quran: An Overview from the

treatment of *al-ṣābiʾūn* follows the opinion of Ibn Kathīr on this issue, although some nuance still exists. When the medieval scholar Ibn Kathīr uses the expression *lā dīn muqarrar lahum* ['they have no established religion'], he means the word *dīn* to carry a sense of 'monotheistic belief', rather than the sense of 'religion' that it carries in contemporary Arabic.[101] That is why, for example, the Tajik translator adds a footnote explaining 'Совijon' as a monotheistic group that existed from the times of the prophet Ibrahim or, 'as al-Saᶜdī suggests, a group of Christians'. In contrast, the Swahili version faithfully repeats the wording of *al-Tafsīr al-muyassar* verbatim. This example is further evidence that the basic claim that *al-Tafsīr al-muyassar* can serve as an auxiliary tool to simplify and clarify the process of Qur'an translation is untenable: the Arabic source text gives rise to differences in translation, even in what seem to be the most easily interpreted verses.

To conclude this general overview of *al-Tafsīr al-muyassar*, it can be said that the main priorities of the authors relate to issues of doctrine, especially when it comes to the divine attributes and other important points of Salafi theology. The *tafsīr* tends to preserve these topics in the most literal way, even in cases such as Q. 68:42, 'The Day the shin will be uncovered' (Saheeh International), when the verse is interpreted in such a way that it is understood to mean 'the noble shin of God, which is not similar to any other thing'. There is one final aspect of the exegetical approach taken in *al-Tafsīr al-muyassar* that is worth mentioning, and this relates to the treatment of Q. 1:7, *ṣirāṭa-lladhīna anᶜamta ᶜalayhim ghayri-l-maghḍūbi ᶜalayhum wa-la al-ḍāllīn* ('[Guide us to] the way of those on whom You have bestowed Your grace, those who do not feel God's anger and who are not in error'), which is often read as referring to Jews and Christians. Like the Hilālī-Khān (see Chapter Three), which is the only English translation to explicitly name these two religions in the target text, *al-Tafsīr al-muyassar* refers to them directly. Both the Tajik and Swahili translations of the *tafsīr* replicate this exegesis exactly as it is presented in the Arabic original: 'those who felt God's anger' are

Quranic Commentators, Theologians, and Jurists', *Journal of Religious & Theological Information*, 13 (2014), 79–87.

101 For more on this term in classical Islam, see Ahmet T. Karamustafa, 'Islamic Dīn as an Alternative to Western Models of "Religion"', in *Religion, Theory, Critique*, ed. by Richard King (New York: New York Columbia University Press, 2017), pp. 163–72.

the Jews, and 'those in error' are the Christians. In contrast to the later editions of the Hilālī-Khān translation printed by the KFGQPC, where this controversial reading was erased from the text, the most recent printing of *al-Tafsīr al-muyassar* (2019) still retains it.

The *al-Tafsīr al-muyassar* has been followed by translators of the Qur'an; it certainly seems to have been a key source for those producing recent KFGQPC translations. However, it is unrealistic to expect it to replace all other exegetical approaches and interpretations that are used to understand and translate the Qur'an, especially by non-Muslim audiences. Above and beyond this, the brief discussion above demonstrates that any translators undertaking an uncritical reproduction of the *tafsīr* will be unable to prevent questions concerning the text and its meaning. This is partly because *al-Tafsīr al-muyassar* concentrates on theological issues of belief and, so, covers others only briefly, sometimes insufficiently. It was written in line with the inherent Salafi approach to Qur'an translations as texts intended to introduce the basic idea of *tawḥīd*, the concept of Divine Oneness, while all but ignoring the Qur'an's eloquence, style, historical realities, and even legal rules.

Newly Standardised Editions: Qur'an Translations Published After the Mid-1990s

The establishment of the Center for Translations of the Qur'an in 1994 opened KFGQPC operations to new opportunities. From the mid-1990s onwards, new editions that had been subject to very thorough review began to appear in print. In the following sections, I will explore some examples of both new commissions by the Complex and its revised editions of previously published works to assess how successful they were and why.

Greek Translations: *Το Ιερό Κοράνιο*

In 1978, one of the first 'Muslim' renditions of the Qur'an into Greek was produced under the aegis of al-Azhar, from the original Arabic.[102]

102 *To Iero Koranio* (Athens: Marianna Latsis, 1978).

Financed by Yiannis Latsis (1910–2003), a Greek shipping tycoon, the first edition of this translation was prepared by a group of academics that consisted of both scholars from al-Azhar and experts in the Greek language. This version was edited and published by the KFGQPC in 1997.

Among the eight Egyptian members of the committee listed in the introduction to the translation are such notable religious authorities as ᶜAbd al-Jalīl al-Shilbī, the general secretary of the Islamic Research Academy in al-Azhar University, and ᶜAbd al-Muhaymin al-Fiqī (see Chapter One). The Greek translation was published alongside the original Arabic text (following the standard Cairo edition) in verse-by-verse format and also contained a small preface and two pages of commentary. Entitled *al-Qurʾān al-karīm* in Arabic and *Το Ιερό Κοράνιο* in Greek (both of which can be translated as 'The Holy Qur'an'), it features a verse from the Qur'an in a header above the Arabic title: 'God is in command, first and last. On that day, the believers will rejoice at God's help' (Q. 30:4–5). A second edition of this translation appeared in 1987, thanks to the support of Latsis's daughter Marianna. According to the publishing information on the back cover, this second edition was published 'for the sake of Arab-Greek friendship before God' [*'iḥtisāban ᶜalā al-ṣadāqa al-ᶜArabiyya al-Yunāniyya li-wajh Allāh'*].

Το Ιερό Κοράνιο was one of two Muslim-authored translations of the Qur'an into Greek that were available in the early 1990s (the second was published by the Ahmadi community in 1989). It attracted interest from the KFGQPC, who published a third edition in 1997 with the permission of the copyright holder Marianna Latsis. The new edition refers to its original translators simply as a 'group of al-Azhar scholars' but names Shaykh Jihād Bilāl Khalīl as its most recent reviser. He is a Saudi scholar with a high level of expertise in both Arabic and Greek. Originally from the Turkish-speaking Muslim minority area of Thrace in Greece, Jihād Bilāl Khalīl graduated from the Imam Muhammad ibn Saud Islamic University in Riyadh and went on to obtain a PhD on nineteenth- and twentieth-century Greek Orientalism in 2000.

Jihād Bilāl Khalīl's revisions are significant: the KFGQPC edition of *Το Ιερό Κοράνιο* greatly diverges from the previous edition. For instance, the translation of the *bismillah* (*bi-smi-llāhi-l-raḥmāni-l-raḥīm*) was changed from 'Στό όνομα του ΑΛΛΑΧ Ελεήμονα, Φιλάνθρωπου'

['In the name of Allah, the Merciful, the Human-loving'] to 'Στο όνομα το ΑΛΛΑΧ του Παντελεήμονα, του Πολυεύσλαχνου' ['In the name of Allah, the All-Merciful, the All-Gracious'], probably because the basic meaning of 'Φιλάνθρωπου' as 'Human-loving' too closely echoed terminology used in Greek Christian texts.

Some of the sura names were changed. Οικογενεια Ιμραν ['The family of Imran', Q. 3] was modified to η Οικος Ιμραν ['The household of Imran'] and Τραπεζα ['The table', Q. 5] became Το Στρωμενο Τραπεζα ['The table set']. To those that include the names of prophets (Q. 10, 11, 12, and others), Ο Προφέτης ['The prophet'] has been added. Some of the basic vocabulary that appears throughout the text has also been altered—but not consistently. For example, the first/second edition uses Κύριος for the Arabic *rabb* ['Lord'] throughout, while the KFGQPC's third has Αρχοντας in Q. 1:2 but retains Κύριος in other instances, such as Q. 113:1 and Q. 114:1. Most of the Islamic religious terms used in the earlier editions were retained in this one.

Although the KFGQPC usually attends specifically to the use of 'Shariatic terms', its *Το Ιερό Κοράνιο* treats these with some variation. *Zakāt*, for example, is rendered as Ελεημοσυνη (Ελεημοσυνη ['alms'] is used in Q. 7:156 and Q. 9:5 in both versions, while sometimes other expressions are used). The same word, Ελεημοσυνη, is used to translate *ṣadaqa* in Q. 2:263, where the original Arabic term means 'charity' in a broad sense rather than the obligatory *zakāt*. However, at the first usage (in Q. 2:43), both versions provide transliteration of the Arabic term (Ζακατ in the al-Azhar edition, and Ζεκατ in the KFGQPC edition) and both give a rather general explanation about this referring to one-fortieth of income received. Interventions in the KFGQPC edition are also evident in some—but not all—verses of particular theological import. For example, for Q. 7:54, both versions provide 'κι επειτα μονιμα εγκατασταθηκε πανο οτο Θρονο (τησ εξουσιας)' ['and then He established Himself on the Throne [of power] firmly']. Contrast, however, Q. 20:5, where one finds εχει επικρατησει πανο οτο Θρονο ['He ruled over the Throne [of power]'] in the first/second edition and 'εγκατασταθηκε οτο Θρονο' ['He established Himself on the Throne'] in the KFGQPC's third.

The issue of style presents quite a challenge to anyone translating the Qur'an into Greek, specifically whether or not to echo Biblical language and style (notably that of the Greek New Testament). Many translations of the Qur'an, including into Russian and Romanian languages, have tended to reflect the religious discourse of the Eastern Orthodox Church. However, in contrast to the earlier 1886 Pentakos translation into Greek, the KFGQPC's Muslim-authored edition has very few parallels with the wording of the Greek New Testament. A recent study by Sofia Koutlaki and Hekmatollah Salehi comparing the translation of Q. 13:24 in the three editions of *Το Ιερό Κοράνιο* with that in Luke 20.19 identifies the shared usage of the expression Εἰρήνη ὑμῖν ['Peace be with you'] for salāmun ᶜalaykum.[103] Apart from this and the usage of Greek Bible variants for personal names, though, the language of the two texts is not similar. This is also true of the commentary, which consists of fifty-four short remarks with no mention of any sources such as *tafsīr*s. Some stylistic heterogeneity, likely the result of collective team work, is present in the KFGQPC's edition, but the complex seems to be generally successful in its goal of representing a 'Muslim' rendition of the text.

In the 1990s and 2000s, *Το Ιερό Κοράνιο* was one of the most commonly used texts for referencing the Qur'an in Greek, but new translations have since overshadowed its popularity. It is also rumoured that a team of Greek Salafi Muslims (drawn from both the Arab diaspora and Greek converts) are currently discussing the production of a completely new Muslim-authored translation into Greek. The realisation of such a work may further erode usage of this edition.

Italian Translations: Hamza Roberto Piccardo's *Il Nobile Corano*

One of nearly a dozen modern translations of the Qur'an into Italian, Hamza Roberto Piccardo's rendition plays an important role for the Islamic community in Italy. First of all, his seems to be the first complete Muslim-authored translation of the Qur'an from Arabic. Secondly, Piccardo's translation has been widely promoted through different Muslim organisations in Italy, such as the Unione delle Comunità e Organizzazioni Islamiche in Italia (UCOII), as well as various

103 Sofia Koutlaki and Hekmatollah Salehi, 'Quranic Translation in Greek: Challenges and Opportunities', in *International Conference for Quranic Translation* (Tehran: Allameh Tabataba'i University, 2014), pp. 125–34.

authoritative institutions in the wider Islamic world: not only the KFGQPC but also the TDRA.

Piccardo converted to Islam in the mid-1970s and became a religious activist, authoring books on Islamic topics that were most often printed by the Al Hikma publishing house. The first edition of his translation was printed in 1994,[104] while the 'revised' version (modified with the help of the editorial committee of the Union of Islamic Communities and Organisations of Italy, UCOII) appeared in 1996.[105] The latter garnered a great deal of attention for being 'carried out under the doctrinal control of the UCOII' and was selected for revision and reprinting by the KFGQPC in 1432 (2010/2011). In contrast to previous editions in Italy, which had simply been called *Il Corano*, the complex's translation took the title *Il Nobile Corano e la tradizione dei suoi significati in lingua Italiana* to accord with the common, modern Sunni concept of translation as merely 'translation of the meanings'.[106] Other changes include updates to some of the footnotes and the addition of short introductions to the suras. The text of the translation was also slightly changed. For example, the Italian edition has '*il sangue*' for the Arabic *damm* ['blood'] in Q. 5:3, but the KFGQPC edition has '*il sangue effuso*' ['flowing blood'], that is, that which comes out of an animal's body. This change seems to have been implemented on the basis of *tafsīr*s: for example, *al-Tafsīr al-muyassar* interprets the term as '*al-damm al-sāʾil al-murāq*', which corresponds with the revised translation. Another change can be seen in Q. 5:6, where the Saudi edition provides '*mani*' ['hands'] in place of '*avambracci*' ['forearms'] in the Italian one. The Saudi edition also better conveys the sense of Arabic *aydiyakum* ['hands']. More significant changes can be seen in some footnotes in the KFGQPC edition. Most of the 'anti-Christian' and 'anti-Western' objections in the Italian edition have been completely removed; instead, there are rather traditional notes regarding parallels, explained terms, and quotations from *tafsīr*s (mostly al-Ṭabarī's).

104 Hamza Roberto Piccardo, *Il Corano* ([n. p.]: Newton & Compton, 1994).

105 Hamza Roberto Piccardo, Pino Blasone, and Grandi tascabili economici Newton, *Il Corano* (Rome: Grandi tascabili economici Newton, 1996).

106 Hamza Roberto Piccardo, *Il Nobile Corano e la tradizione dei suoi significati in lingua Italiana* (Medina: King Fahd Glorious Qur'an Printing Complex, 2011).

The second edition of Piccardo's translation was also revised by the Turkish company TDRA and republished by them in 2015. Many more changes were introduced, including some prefatory statements and appendices that discuss the basics of Islam. The title was modified, too, to *Il Sacro Corano: traduzione interpretativa in italiano* ['The Sacred Qur'an: an interpretative translation into Italian'].[107] However, both the KFGQPC and TDRA preserved some of the core lexical features from the earlier editions produced in Italy. For the Qur'anic *al-naṣārā*, which is usually translated as 'Christians', for example, Piccardo used '*nazareni*' and described his choice as a faithful reflection of the Arabic text: '*Per ragioni di fedeltà al testo coranico* [...] *"nazareni" deriva da Nasira* (*Nazareth*) *la città natale di Gesù*' ['For reasons of fidelity to the Qur'anic text [...] "nazareni" is derived from Nasira [Nazareth], the city where Jesus was born']. All other Qur'an translations into Italian use the more conventional 'cristiani', so the question arises: did the TDRA and KFGQPC revisers intend to distinguish between seventh-century and present-day Christians, or were there other reasons for that choice?

The different editions of Piccardo's translation illustrate various contemporary translation strategies, mostly implemented through footnotes. The first edition, issued in Italy over twenty times, shows a kind of ideological, missionary approach targeting in a predominantly Christian society. The KFGQPC edition pays more attention to the historical, theological, and ritualistic discourse of the Qur'an; while recent editions from Turkey attempt to produce a comprehensive manual that introduces the holy book of Islam using plenty of extra-Qur'anic material. Today, Piccardo's translation (in its many versions) is a major domestic reference for Italian-speaking Muslims, despite the many other translations available on the market.

Macedonian Translations: Hasan Dzilo's Work

The 1997 translation of the Qur'an into Macedonian (since republished twice) comprises the first, and so far only, full translation of the Qur'an into a Balkan language to be produced by the KFGQPC (two others, into Bosnian and Albanian, were published independently before).

107 Hamza Roberto Piccardo, *Il Sacro Corano: traduzione interpretativa in italiano* (Ankara: TDRA, 2015).

Its author, Dr Hasan Dzilo, is a leading North Macedonian scholar of Islamic and Qur'anic Studies who graduated first from the Gazi Husrev Beg medrese and then from the Faculty of Islamic Studies in Sarajevo. Dzilo has authored numerous books and articles on the history of Islamic philosophy, Islam in North Macedonia, and Islam and modernity. He is currently affiliated with the Faculty of Islamic Studies of the Islamic Religious Union in Skopje, North Macedonia.

Dzilo's translation contains, in addition to a translation of the entire Qur'anic text, a short dictionary of Arabic terms and names and a thematic index. The translation itself is more literal than explanatory, and Dzilo replicates Qur'anic ellipses and favours the use of short sentences. Dzilo's approach is successful when it comes to conveying the style of the Qur'an: his translation often delivers not only the meaning but also the emotional impact of the Qur'anic verses.

Regarding the more linguistic aspects of his translation, Dzilo adopts the full spectrum of Islamic terms of Arabic and Turkish origin that are used in the religious practice of Macedonian Muslims (some of the Divine Names are transliterated rather than translated—such as *al-Qadīr*, for example). He shows a preference in places for the Western dialects of the Macedonian language, which is widely spoken by the Slavic Muslims of Macedonia (the Torbesh). There is no commentary or exegetical appendices in this translation; however, it is obvious that the author has worked with the most authoritative Sunni *tafsīrs*, especially when it comes to his handling of doctrinal issues. This can be seen in the way many words are rendered into through transliteration rather than translation, for example the Macedonian 'halal' is used for the Arabic *ḥalāl*. Other examples include *'haram'* (*ḥarām*), *'hasret'* (*ḥasra*), *'selam'* (*salām*), *'zekat'* (*zakāt*), *'sadaka'* (*ṣadaqa*), *'rsk'* (*rizq*), *'mihrab'* (*miḥrāb*), and *'miraz'* (*mīrāth*). Dzilo chose to explain these terms, instead, in his included dictionary, which helps to make the translation accessible for a non-Muslim audience. Likewise, the names of the prophets and other individuals are rendered in accordance with Arabic pronunciation, though the later editions provide a table with the corresponding Christian names. Dzilo is not entirely consistent in this, however, as some key concepts are given in translation (the Arabic word *muslimūn*, for example, is translated as *'Poslušni'* ['the obedient ones'] and *rasūl* is translated using the Turkish loan-word *'Pejgamber'*, which is widely used by Bosnian, Macedonian, and Bulgarian Muslims. Some purely stylistic features are preserved in the translation as well. For example, in some Meccan suras, Dzilo uses end rhyme to reflect the style of the original. Thus, in *Sūrat al-ᶜĀdiyāt*, he opts for the ending *–at*: the Macedonian *'ržat'* is used for the Arabic *ḍabḥā* and, likewise, he uses *'iskrat'* (*qadḥā*), 'napagaat' (*ṣubḥā*), 'digaat' (*naqᶜā*), 'vleguvaat' (*jamᶜā*):

> *Se kolnam vo trkačkite konji koi 'ržat, pa, so nozete svoi po kamenjata iskri iskrat, i koi vo utrinsite časovi napağaat, i koi, trčajḱi, prašina digaat, i, taka, vo mestoto zaednički vleguvaat! Da, čovekot e neblagodaren kon Gospodarot svoj, toj za toa, navistina, e svedok, i toj, navistina, e cvrst vo ljubovta kon imotot, dobroto. Ne znae li deka koga ḱe bide oživeano ona što e vo mezarite, i koga ḱe izleze ona što e vo gradite* (Q. 100:1–10).

The first (1997) edition of this translation was published in Medina. Since then, it has been reprinted twice (most recently in 2011) in North Macedonia with the addition of an introduction and short commentaries. As well as in these three print editions, the text is accessible online via many Islamic websites and a standalone app. Both of the locally printed editions are available in larger Macedonian libraries and are widely used by local Muslim communities. The translation is also widely referenced in Islamic books and academic studies in the Macedonian language.

Azerbaijanian Translations: Alikhan Musayev's *Qurani kerim* and *Qurani-Kərim*

There is a rich Azerbaijan Islamic tradition and, consequently, there are a number of modern translations of the Qur'an in Azerbaijanian—a language spoken by twenty-five million people. For example, translations by Ziya Bunyadov and Vasim Mammadaliyev (1991), Nariman Gasimzade (1994), Memmedhasan Ganioğlu and Tariyel Bilaloğlu (2000), and Aladdin Sultanov (2011) were all made directly from the Arabic text.[108] Unlike other post-Soviet regions, Azerbaijan has

108 The first of these was commissioned by the centralised Islamic religious board in Baku, Qafqaz Müsəlmanları İdarəsi. For the older translations, see Mykhaylo Yakubovych, 'The First Vernacular Tafsir in the Caucasus: The Legacy of Two 20th Century Azerbaijani Qurʾān Commentaries', *Australian Journal of Islamic Studies*, 7.1 (2022), 72–95, https://doi.org/10.55831/ajis.v7i1.457. For the newer ones, see

a predominantly Shii population (of around sixty percent). However, the state promotes a multicultural ideology that prevents any direct criticism of Sunni or Shii beliefs in religious discourse. This has affected the field of Qur'an translation there somewhat: it is usually hard to tell from an Azerbaijanian text whether the translator has a Shii or Sunni background.

The KFGQPC has published two Azerbaijanian translations. In 2004 it brought out a partial translation of the *Fātiḥa* and the *juzᵓ ᶜamma* (suras 1 and 78–114); and, in 2013, they published a complete translation.[109] The earlier edition does not name the translator, but it was the work of Alikhan Musayev. We can be sure of this as his translation of the entire Qur'an was published in Baku by the KFGQPC later in the same year under the title *Qurani-Kərim və Azərbaycan dilinə mənaca tərcüməsi.* Musayev was a graduate of the Islamic University of Madinah who returned to Azerbaijan to pursue a career as a preacher and translator of Islamic literature. His published translations include large parts of the *ḥadīth* corpus, such as the *Ṣaḥīḥ* of al-Bukhārī. As with the 2004 partial translation, the KFGQPC's 2013 complete translation of the Qur'an into Azerbaijanian does not include much introductory information. It does include a short statement from the (anonymous) translator, but this consists mostly of Qur'anic verses selected to emphasise the divine origin of the Qur'an and the importance of following its teachings. In contrast to most other translations produced by the KFGQPC, this rendition does not include any commentary apart from some minor interpolations in italics (mainly relating to the referents of Arabic pronouns such as *-hu, -hā, -hum*).

The Azerbaijanian language is abundant in Arabic loan words (much more so than modern Turkish, for example), which makes it possible to preserve almost all of the Qur'an's basic religious vocabulary. Thus, for example, Musayev renders Q. 2:2-4 as follows:

Erdoğan Pazarbaşı, 'Kur'an'ın Azerbaycan'da Yaygın Tefsir ve Tercümeleri', *Bilig*, 25 (2003), 73–97.

109 *Qurani kerim ve Azerbaycan dilinde manaca tercümesi* (Medina: King Fahd Glorious Qur'an Printing Complex, 2013). The decision to initially publish a partial translation is typical of the KFGQPC: the complex's first publication of translations in Tamazight, Swedish, and Russian consisted solely of the *juzᵓ ᶜamma.*

> *Bu, qətiyyən şübhə doğurmayan, müttəqilərə doğru yol göstərən bir Kitabdır. O kəslər ki, qeybə iman gətirir, namaz qılır və Bizim onlara verdiyimiz ruzidən Allah yolunda xərcləyirlər. O kəslər ki, sənə nazil olana və səndən əvvəl nazil olanlara iman gətirir, axirətə də yəqinliklə inanırlar.*
>
> [This is the Scripture in which there is no doubt, containing guidance for those who are mindful of God, who believe in the unseen, keep up the prayer, a and give out of what We have provided for them; those who believe in the revelation sent down to you [Muhammad], and in what was sent before you, those who have firm faith in the Hereafter' (Abdel Haleem).]

Many of the Azerbaijani words used in the translation of this verse correspond to Arabic concepts ('müttəqilər' for *muttaqīn* [those who are mindful of God], 'qeybə' for *ghayb* [unseen], 'axirətə' for *akhīra* [Hereafter], in addition to widely used words like *imān* [faith].

No *tafsīr*s are mentioned in either the introduction or the actual text, but, on the basis of the translation itself, contemporary Salafi theology seems to be the primary lens through which at least some verses are interpreted. Musayev translates the beginning of Q. 2:255 as: '*Allah Özündən başqa haqq məbud olmayandır*' ['He is Allah! There is no object of worship but Him']. Compare this to Aladdin Sultanov's 2011 Azerbajiani translation: '*Allah! Ondan başqa tanrı yoxdur*' ['Allah! There is no god but He alone']). In Musayev's rendition, his choice of '*məbud*' ['object of worship'] rather then '*tanrı*' ['deity'] suggests adherence to the Salafi concept of godhood [*ulūhiyya*] as 'oneness of God in worship'. His translation, largely because of its Salafi leanings, quickly became popular on Islamic websites and mobile apps, and it went on to be published by a Baku publishing house independently of the KFGQPC. At least among Sunni Muslims (especially Salafis), Musayev's translation is nowadays one of the most used and cited translations of the Qur'an in Azerbaijanian.

Portuguese Translations: Helmi Nasr's *Nobre Alcorão*

The history of the KFGQPC's Portuguese Qur'an translation, *Nobre Alcorão*, which was printed in 2006 and widely distributed all over

Brazil, begins in the mid-1980s.[110] In 1984, the MWL contracted Helmi Nasr (1922–2019) to carry out this project.[111] Nasr is a particularly interesting character. Not a native speaker of Portuguese, he was born in Egypt, where he pursued an education in Arabic and, later, French. He moved to Brazil in 1962 with the mission of establishing a chair of Arabic studies at a university in São Paolo. For many years, he was one of the most active members of the growing Arabic community in Latin America and had close ties with the Muslim World League. Nasr began work on his translation in 1984 and completed it in 1988. He himself has explained that the translation was never published by the MWL because it lacked an appropriate committee to review the translation: quite simply, no one had the required linguistic skills in Arabic and Portuguese combined with a basic knowledge of the Qur'an and Islam. Only in the early 2000s, when the file was transferred to the KFGQPC, was the draft translation reviewed and published. Two reviewers are named as the reviewers of this edition, Shaykh Muhammad Kassim Gifa and Shaykh Yunus Zacaria Hamid, but I have been unable to trace information about either of them. They were probably members of local Muslim communities in Brazil.

The *Nobre Alcorão* is usually promoted as the first Muslim translation of the Qur'an into Portuguese (by those who do not count the Ahmadiyya translation that came out in 1988[112]). It was published with a parallel Arabic text in a standard KFGQPC print edition. Nasr's translation contains a great deal of commentary, especially when it comes to the first few suras, and this is oriented towards both Muslim and non-Muslim audiences. The language used is described by some reviewers as Brazilian Portuguese ('português brasileiro'), which differs from that spoken in Portugal in both phonology and prosody. In addition, Nasr makes recourse to some specifically Brazilian domestic sources to provide some of his religious vocabulary. For example, when explaining his translation of the *bismillah* formula, he compares different terms to phrases used in Christian sermons in the local form of Portuguese.

110 Helmi Nasr, *Nobre Alcorão: para a língua portuguesa* (Medina: King Fahd Glorious Qur'an Printing Complex, 2006).

111 Aida Hanania and Jean Lauand, *O diplomata da língua e cultura árabes—estudos em homenagem a Helmi Nasr* (São Paulo: Factash Editora, 2015), pp. 39–40.

112 *O Sagrado Alcorao* (Tilford: Islam International Publications, 1988).

Nasr's use of Christian vocabulary and avoidance of Arabic-specific vocabulary makes his translation easily accessible for a non-Muslim audience. For example, in the commentary provided at the beginning of Q. 2, Ibrāhīm is named 'Patriarca Abraão' ['Patriarch Abraham'], which seems to be an exclusively Christian term used to refer to Biblical prophets. The text is mainly literal in its style of translation, although it does include some insertions, which are emphasised in bold. This, again, is a stylistic device found in many Bible translations. Nasr also provides quite long introductions to the suras, located in footnotes, mostly covering the history of the events mentioned in the text. Generally, there is no direct reference to any specialist *tafsīr* literature, but it does seem that the translator did consult *tafsīr* works. For example, Q. 8:5 reads as follows:

> **A situação de desagrado, acerca da distribuição de espólios,** é como **aquela havida, quando** teu Senhor, em nome da verdade, te fez sair de tua casa **para combateres**, enquanto um grupo de crentes, o estava odiando.
>
> [**The situation of displeasure, concerning the distribution of spoils, is like that which took place, when your** Lord, in the name of truth, made you go out of your house **to fight, while a group of believers, were hating this.**]

The text presented in bold denotes insertions from exegetical sources, without which the literal meaning of the Qur'anic text would be not clear to the reader. Even in the most literal translations of this verse (such as Yusuf Ali's rendition 'Just as thy Lord ordered thee out of thy house in truth, even though a party among the Believers disliked it'), additional commentary is supplied. Nasr follows this approach, providing a few footnotes specifically for this verse. His choice to indicate insertions by using bold text (rather than brackets, as is the format in almost all other KFGQPC editions) has clearly posed some challenges to later editors. For example, the 2020 edition of this work published in Brazil (which contains no Arabic text or commentary) presents all the text in the same format, so it is completely impossible to distinguish the actual translation from Nasr's explanatory interventions.

Although a few other Muslim translations into Portuguese are available, such as the 1975 text by Samir El Hayek, Nasr's work seems to be the most popular source of reference for Muslims living in Brazil (a minority constituting an uncertain number somewhere between 20,000 and 200,000 people out of a total population of some 214 million[113]) as well as for domestically produced academic studies on Islam.

The KFGQPC's Status as the Largest Producer of Qur'an Translations

Before coming to any general conclusions about how the KFGQPC emerged as a global actor in Qur'an publishing and translation, a few more specific examples of translations that have been published should be briefly mentioned. The use of special hermeneutical approaches (above all, Salafi ones) is mostly found in the newly-produced translations like the Russian *Sviashchennyĭ Koran* by Elmir Quliyev (2002).[114] This work is a literal, but still readable, translation and includes plenty of commentary, primarily from the Sunni corpus. It has enjoyed enormous success in Russia and beyond, having been published in other post-Soviet countries, such as Ukraine and Moldova, and, even further afield, in Gemany. Published at a time of growing interest in primary Muslim sources and, of course, the Salafi movement, the *Sviashchennyĭ Koran* has been printed by dozens of publishers and is widely available online. Numerous copies have also been distributed gratis.[115] Despite this success, a ban on this translation (for being an 'extremist work') was imposed by a Russian court in 2013—although, later, this was lifted.[116] *Sviashchennyĭ Koran* may have run into opposition because it was perceived as being an especially 'Muslim', tafsīr-based interpretation, in contrast to other Russian translations produced in academic context or not so deeply rooted in Qur'anic exegesis.

The case of the KFGQPC's Ukrainian translation, *Preslavnyi Koran. Pereklad smysliv Ukrainskoju movoju* (produced in 2013 by the author of

113 Vitória Peres de Oliveira, 'Islam in Brazil or the Islam of Brazil?', *Religião & Sociedade*, 2 (2006), 1–20 (p. 4).

114 Elmir Quliyev, *Sviashchennyĭ Koran: Smyslovoi perevod na russkij jazyk* (Medina: King Fahd Glorious Qur'an Printing Complex, 2002).

115 Like the German Salafi-run 'Lies!' project, or the Ukrainian 'Chytai' ['Read!'].

116 The story gained some coverage in world media. See, for example, Alissa de Carbonnel, 'Russian Muslim Clerics Warn of Unrest over Ban of Translation of Koran', 20 September 2013, https://www.reuters.com/article/us-russia-koran-idUSBRE98J0YW20130920

this volume)[117] is a similar story. This was not only the first 'Muslim' translation of the Qur'an into Ukrainian but also the first-ever complete translation of the Qur'an from Arabic into this language. *Preslavnyi Koran* has been reprinted fourteen times, including once by the official press of the TDRA in Turkey. In contrast, the Kyrgyz translation (by Shamsuddin Hakimov) has only been reprinted once after its initial publication in 2013 and has not made much headway with readers. There are several possible reasons for this, but it seems to be primarily due to the fact that Salafi influence in the Kyrgyz Republic has been limited due to tight levels of state control.[118]

These and other cases generally show that the success of translations published by the KFGQPC so far has been due primarily to factors other than its institutional authority. Editions' popularity depends, rather, on market demand, whether similar products in the target language are already being promoted, how active the translator is in pursuing publication of his work with different publishers, and so on. As with many other translations of sacred texts, it is quite hard to find an exemplary 'success story'. What is obvious is that a particular translation can become popular only when it is reprinted by other printing houses, since the print runs of the KFGQPC are limited by design. The copies it produces are intended for free distribution, they are almost never available in bookstores, and those provided for pilgrims visiting the KFGQPC have had quite a small impact on demand. Nevertheless, whether or not its translations have been used on a large scale, the Arabic Qur'an published by the KFGQPC, in almost all the common variant readings, has remained one of the most published religious books in the world. Theirs has become the gold standard source text for use in the production of Qur'an translations.

In conclusion, it can be said that the establishment of the KFGQPC is one of the most significant events in the modern Qur'an translation movement, not only for the KSA but for the entire Muslim world. Although it is not the first institution to supervise the production of its own translations (a few projects were earlier undertaken by WICS in Libya and the Turkish TDRA, not to mention the Ahmadis), the

117 Mykhaylo Yakubovych, *Preslavnyi Koran. Pereklad smysliv Ukrainskoju movoju* (Medina: King Fahd Glorious Qur'an Printing Complex, 2013).
118 See Yakubovych, 'Qur'an Translations into Central Asian Languages'.

KFGQPC succeeded the MWL in creating 'official', 'state-authorised', and 'Muslim-approved' translations of the Qur'an. The Complex introduced the concept of the publishing institution acting as an authoritative mediator between the reader and the translator, which is why its translations are often referred to merely as 'the Saudi translation' or 'the King Fahd translation'. This perception is underlined through the design and format of the translations it publishes, not least by the inclusion of text on the cover page of every edition that explicitly names the ruling king as the royal authority who distributes the translation as a gift. The KFGQPC translations also make a point of making visible the Arabic text or, rather, textuality: every translation opens with an introduction provided by the current head of the MOIA in Arabic then, secondarily, in translation. Many later reprints of KFGQPC translations by other printers and publishers still carry the KFGQPC label (even if they have been edited by the 'new' publisher) as, for many Muslims, this has become a mark of quality assurance. For those who are critical of Salafism, the opposite may be the case; however, as this and previous chapters have demonstrated, Salafi hermeneutics has had only a limited impact on the actual translations produced, the most obvious example being that of the Hilālī-Khān translation (see Chapter Three). Even recent efforts to ensure all the KFGQPC translations conform to a particular theology and format—as prescribed by its own *al-Tafsīr al-muyassar*—have not prevented variation in the target texts. The translations take diverse approaches to the most crucial theological issues in their interpretations of the Qur'anic verses. This is especially apparent when one compares those the KFGQPC merely revised to those it specifically commissioned or fully produced.

Of the sixteen translations into European languages the KFGQPC has published, only seven were prepared specifically for (or by) the institution.[119] The proportion is higher for translations into non-European languages: fifty percent of the nineteen 'African' and thirty-nine 'Asian' translations are 'exclusive works'. The reasons for this discrepancy relate to the KFGQPC's strict requirements for translators and revisers. Because the institution requires them to have knowledge

119 This number includes the Portuguese translation that was prepared in collaboration with the MWL but only published after the KFGQPC had taken over responsibility for it.

of the source and target languages as well as a reasonably advanced level of Islamic education, it is not always easy for them to find two (or two sets of) people with such skills in languages that have fewer Muslim native speakers. In such cases, a text may be approved without subsequent revision if members of the 'Academic Affairs Division' are satisfied with the exegetical choices explained by the translator(s) during their in-person conversations (which are conducted in Arabic).

The KFGQPC has developed a network—with the help of the Muslim World League and several Saudi Institutions of higher Islamic education operating within the Kingdom—that has allowed it to become a global institution. Over the last thirty years, it has had a significant impact on the understanding of both the function of translation and the meaning of the Qur'anic text all over the Muslim world. The policies and publications of the KFGQPC both reflect and have influenced the changing strategies of Islamic missionary activities in recent decades, in which the Qur'an in translation has come to play a decisive role.

5. Translation for Everyone: Collaborative Saudi Publishing Projects in Foreign Languages

As discussed in previous chapters, Qur'an translations were introduced into the general Islamic religious discourse 'from above', as a result of an alliance between the Saudi government and 'established' ulema. However, in addition to officially approved systems of Islamic learning and missionary activism, many private and non-government initiatives in the country also include publishing projects. This kind of 'unofficial' Islam is not necessarily 'oppositional' to the government (in the way, for example, many radical jihadist movements have been); it should instead be understood as a parallel religious framework that is similarly oriented towards the propagation of Sunni-Salafi Islamic learning. These 'unofficial' initiatives have often originated from non-Arab Islamic communities: this was the case during the formative period of the modern Saudi state (that is, prior to the reforms implemented by King Faisal) and has not changed in recent times. During the 1980s and, especially, the 1990s, when publishing 'new' translations of the Qur'an became a mainstream activity in Saudi Arabia, many private commercial presses also became involved. Furthermore, the influx of foreign workers into Saudi led many local religious organisations, which had previously been oriented primarily towards Arabic speakers, to begin publishing books in foreign languages. These publications included translations of the Qur'an.

It is hard to outline all of these endeavours in a systematic way. Some projects were run independently, some emerged from collective efforts and initiatives spearheaded by local scholars, yet others involved no

©2024 Mykhaylo Yakubovych, CC BY-ND 4.0 https://doi.org/10.11647/OBP.0381.05

more than the commercial reproduction of previously published works. Increases in Saudi missionary activities during the 1980s and 1990s opened the way for translations to be published abroad but, as has been addressed in previous chapters, these were always produced under some degree of supervision by Saudi-based religious foundations. This raises the questions of how and to what degree non-governmental Islamic institutions from the Kingdom have contributed to the Saudi Qur'an translation industry.

The Qur'an in 'Turkistani': The First Foreign-Language Translation Produced in Saudi Arabia

If al-Hilālī and Khān were the first Saudi-based scholars to produce a translation into English in the early 1970s, translations into a number of 'Muslim' languages had already been the subject of interest some years before, in the 1950s.[1] One such example is the first translation of the Qur'an into Uzbek, by Maḥmūd al-Ṭarāzī (1895–1991), an emigrant from Soviet Central Asia who settled in Medina in the late 1940s.[2] Before moving to Saudi Arabia, he received a religious education in Tashkent and Bukhara and taught in a *medrese*, but he had to leave his homeland forever to avoid persecution by the Soviet authorities.[3] Al-Ṭarāzī's translation, first published as a lithograph in Bombay in 1955–56, was sponsored by the Nūr al-Dīn family from the Saudi city of Taif, also expats from Central Asia; it was mainly distributed by a judge based in Taif—one Mīrzā ᶜAbd al-Karīm Khān. The translation was reprinted in Medina in 1975–76 (where the author lived until his death) and Jeddah in 1980–81. Some copies made their way to the Soviet Union in the late 1980s, where they were sold illegally, since suthorities there considered al-Ṭarāzī a dangerous Islamic threat to state-supported

1 This is true of Khān, at least, as he worked in Saudi Arabia until his death.

2 Fillip Khustuntdinov, 'Turkestani Muslim Communities ... Have Been Deprived of this Happiness: The Dissemination of Tarazi's Qur'an Translation and Exegesis in Soviet Uzbekistan', *Islamology*, 11.1 (2021), 84–103, http://dx.doi.org/10.24848/islmlg.11.1.07

3 Vahrom Muminov and Valihan Alihanov, 'Prosvetitel iz Taraza', *Znamya truda*, 12 November 2005, 2–5.

atheism in Central Asia.[4] In his introduction, al-Ṭarāzī describes his primary motivation as a deep concern for the local people about the lack of availability of Qur'anic teachings in their language, Uzbek, and positioned the work as a 'translation with commentaries' rather than a *tafsīr*. Its title, which employs an outdated term for the Uzbek language, was *Qurʾān karīm, mutarjam wa-muḥassuhā bi-l-lugha Turkistāniyya* ['The Qur'an, translation and commentary in the Turkistani language'].

The translation generally follows the premodern interlinear pattern. It comprises the Arabic text (reproduced from an unidentified Indian edition of the *muṣḥaf*) accompanied by a phrase-by-phrase translation into Uzbek using Arabic script, placed just below the lines of the original, and footnotes in the margins that provide short explanations. To date, no in-depth study of its content has been undertaken, but a few introductory findings make it possible to evaluate it from the perspective of twentieth-century Muslim translations. First of all, the translator notes that many 'translations and *tafsīr*s' already exist in Persian but that these are not accessible for the 'Turkistani' (meaning Central Asian, specifically Uzbek) reader.[5] Al-Ṭarāzī then explains that, at the request of numerous fellow Uzbeks and with the approval of a scholar named Ibn Yamīn, he embarked on his translation. Ibn Yamīn, also known as Muḥammad Amīn al-Andijānī, belonged to the same generation of migrants from Central Asia as al-Ṭarāzī and shared his Hanafi background.[6] From this, as well as names of the sponsors and distributors involved in the project, it is easy to determine that the primary target readership was members of Uzbek diaspora living outside Soviet Central Asia, for example, those living in living in India, Pakistan, or Arabic countries.The project was, then, not simply a devotional undertaking but also intended to partially compensate for the lack of education in the national language and identity available to members of this exiled community.

4 Khustuntdinov, 'Turkestani Muslim Communities', p. 86.

5 Uzbekistan is the most populous nationality of the region. Currently, half of the seventy-six million people living in the five countries that make up Central Asia, live in Uzbekistan.

6 On the term 'Turkestani/Turkistani' and Uzbek migration to the Hijaz, see Bayram Balci, 'Central Asian Refugees in Saudi Arabia: Religious Evolution and Contributing to the Reislamisation of Their Motherland', *Refugee Survey Quarterly*, 26.2 (2007), 2–21.

Another notable aspect of al-Ṭarāzī's introduction is the fact that he refers to previous efforts made in the field of Qur'an translation and interpretation, especially those by 'Indian' scholars. He does not mention any particular names but acknowledges their legacy as his *murshīd al-ṭarīq* ('guidance to the way') and *dustūr al-ʿamal* ('the basis for the work').[7] Al-Ṭarāzī may be referring here to Shāh Walī Allāh al-Dihlawī and his eighteenth-century translation into Persian or some later Qur'an commentators writing in the Indian subcontinent. Strictly from its introduction, however, the *Qurʾān karīm, mutarjam wa-muḥassuhā bi-l-lugha Turkistāniyya* seems to be a continuation of the Hanafi tradition of commenting on the Qur'an in other languages.

However, al-Ṭaraẓī's translation is not free from modern influences. A preface, written in 1954 by Shaykh Ibn Yamīn, describes the work as a 'literal translation' [*tarjama ḥarfiyya*]. It explains that such translations cannot be correct without the addition of interpretive commentary and that al-Ṭaraẓī's work is largely grounded in the *Tafsīr al-Jalālayn*.[8] Obviously, this accords with the 'translation of the meanings' paradigm, which was already well established in discussions of the translatability of the Qur'an at the time.

Although a comprehensive analysis of this translation is yet to be written, even a preliminary reading reveals some of the theological priorities of the text. For instance, in his commentary on Q. 1:3, al-Ṭarāzī says that this verse is the primary basis of the Islamic creed, as it highlights the concept of the 'Oneness of God in His essence and attributes'.[9] The translator had links to the official Saudi establishment and his works include an Uzbek translation of Muḥammad b. ʿAbd al-Wahhāb's *Kitāb al-Tawḥīd* (which was published and thus approved by the Saudi MOIA[10]). Nevertheless, his translation of the Qur'an appears to only partially reflect Salafi hermeneutics. It more fully accords with the Sunni mainstream Matūrīdī approach to Islamic theology, which does not problematise literal or metaphoric interpretations of the divine attributes, as happened later with the majority of Salafi translations.

7 Maḥmūd al-Ṭarāzī, *Qurʾān karīm, mutarjam wa-muḥassuhā bi-l-lugha al-Turkistāniyya* (Medina: Dār al-Imān, 1975), p. 6-7.

8 al-Ṭarāzī, *Qurʾān karīm*, p. 8.

9 al-Ṭarāzī, *Qurʾān karīm*, p. 2.

10 Maḥmūd al-Ṭarāzī, *Tawḥīd kitābī* (Riyadh: Ministry of Islamic Affairs, Call, and Guidance of the Kingdom of Saudi Arabia, [n. d.]).

Much of the extra-Qur'anic material in al-Ṭarāzī's commentaries touches on histories of the prophets and the meaning of rare Arabic words (*gharāʾib al-Qurʾān*), and it thus appears that he called upon classical *tafsīr* texts as his main sources. Al-Ṭarāzī's translation was initially quite popular among the Uzbek diaspora, and even in the first years of Uzbeki independence, but the modern generation of readers find it hard to read—primarily because the Arabic script is no longer used in Uzbekistan.

This case of Qur'an translation demonstrates some quite interesting connections between the classical Hanafi tradition of Qur'an interpretation in foreign languages using interlinear works, national revivalism in the Central Asian context, pre-Salafi Islamic education in Saudi Arabia, and, finally, the emerging interest in Qur'an translations inside the Kingdom. Al-Ṭarāzī's translation was widely published in a number of editions in India, Pakistan, Saudi Arabia, Qatar, and Uzbekistan, and it can be justly said to be a very successful project for its time. The reasons for its success can be attributed to the author's personal connections and his prestige as an Uzbek scholar both in the UzSR and the Uzbek diaspora, as well as his reputation as a fighter for the cause of religious revolution against Russio-Bolshevik imperialism. Al-Ṭarāzī sometimes signed off his writings with the title 'Grand Mufti of the People of Turkestan on behalf of al-Idāra al-Dīniyya li-Lajnat al-Waḥda al-Qawmiyya al-Turkistāniyya' (The Religious Administration of the Committee for the Liberation of Turkistan).[11] This organisation seems to be nothing other than the 'Nationales Turkistanisches Einheitskomitee' (NTE), which was created in 1942 in Nazi Germany to 'liberate' Central Asia under the leadership of the Uzbek Vali Qayumxon (1904–1993). After the fall of the Third Reich, it continued its efforts, mostly in cooperation with various US-supported anti-Soviet movements.[12] It is not yet clear how al-Ṭarāzī was connected to this movement, but it seems likely that his involvement may have begun in the early 1950s when Vali Qayumxon and his former NTE network joined the newly created

11 For some of al-Ṭarāzī's letters [in Arabic] in which he uses this title in his signature, see https://www.facebook.com/mahmudtarazi/photos/a.485055471545247/485056568211804/

12 See on this figure: Coşkun Kumru and Sevil Gözübüyük, 'Esir Türkistan Yargılanıyor: Veli Kayyum Hanᶜın Nürnberg Sorgulamalarına Dair Notlar', *Journal of Social and Humanities Sciences Research*, 7.58 (2020), 2424–33.

'Anti-Bolshevik Bloc of Nations' (ABN) and Qayumxon took up the post of vice-president under the leadership of the Ukrainian anti-Soviet freedom fighter Yaroslav Stetsko (1912–1986).[13] Although these links are not well-studied, they show that al-Ṭarāzī had some connections with Uzbek emigrants to the West as well. What is clear, however, is that al-Ṭarāzī's translation was the first contemporary interpretation of the Qur'an into Uzbek, the most widely spoken Central Asian language, and that the personality of the translator, who was famous in Uzbek circles, made a significant contribution to the popularity of this work.

The 'Saheeh International' Qur'an: A New 'Saudi' Team Translation into English

This translation, first published in 1997, has a few notable aspects that distinguish it from other works in the genre. First of all, it is the product of teamwork, rather than an individually-authored translation like most of the other interpretations that were printed in Saudi Arabia (and beyond) in the second half of the twentieth century. Secondly, it was produced by three Muslim converts, and, finally, all three translators are women, which is quite rare in this male-dominated field. For instance, until 2022 none of the translations published by the KFGQPC were authored by women; likewise, no women were employed to revise any of its Qur'an translations. The Saheeh International translation, despite these unusual aspects, has barely received any academic attention.

Recently, however, interviews conducted with the translation team have shed light on how this work came into being.[14] These interviews and also a further, personal interview with the principal member of the translation team,[15] Emily Assami (known as Umm Muhammad),

13 'Turkistan is not Alone', *ABN Correspondence*, III:5 (1952), 2–3.

14 See, in particular, 'Translators' Experiences I: Amatullah 'AJ' Bantley, Saheeh International', https://www.youtube.com/watch?v=k4JPZTHCnvo; 'EP 094—Atheism to Islam, Translating the Qur'an, Running a Publishing House—Amatullah Bantley', *Ilmfeed Podcast*, 10 April 2022, https://www.youtube.com/watch?v=4uPU4eM4sMo; 'First All-Female Team To Produce A Quran Translation', *Facebook*, 3 November 2021, https://www.facebook.com/watch/live/?ref=watch_permalink&v=957066955157664

15 Faraz Omar, 'Interview with Umm Muhammad of Saheeh International', *Musliminink*, 26 February 2015, https://www.muslimink.com/society/interview/interview-umm-muhammad-saheeh-intl/.

tell the story behind the Saheeh International translation, which can be summarised as follows.

From the 1980s onwards, the Saudi city of Jeddah had a growing community of foreigners, of both Muslim and non-Muslim religious backgrounds. Emily Assami (who was born in 1940 in California) moved there in 1981 from Damascus, where she had previously lived with her Syrian husband. The two other team members, Mary Kennedy and Amatullah 'AJ' Bantley, had similar backgrounds. Asam, however, taught Islam for foreigners at an Islamic Centre in Jeddah and was the only one to have studied Arabic and Islamic Studies on a level that would allow her to carry out translation projects. Thus, we have three American converts living in Jeddah at the beginning of 1990s who were dissatisfied with the availability of Islamic literature in English. According to Bantley, their original plan was to edit the Hilālī-Khān translation (which was known for its rather 'problematic' English). They later decided to undertake a completely new translation. The project began on a much smaller scale, as Asam explains:

> When I came to Jeddah, there were many English-speaking Muslims of various nationalities (something non-existent in Syria), and I was recruited to teach at an Islamic centre and became aware of the need to have printed material in understandable English for our students. I was also working with a charitable organisation that mailed whatever information they could find in English to individuals, organisations, and schools in several African countries.
>
> I often went to Abul-Qasim Bookstore looking for anything suitable to send to Africa and for our Islamic Centre. Since there was very little suitable material at that time, the owner asked me and two colleagues, a typesetter, and an English editor, to produce some booklets teaching prayer and other basic subjects, which he published. That was the beginning of Saheeh International. We continued to produce booklets for our Centre and others.[16]

The private initiative, registered as 'Abul-Qasim Publishing House and Bookstore', was the first printing press in Jeddah to concentrate on the production of Islamic books in English. Established at the end of the 1980s as a bookstore owned by Amatullah Bantley, it started actively publishing at the beginning of the 1990s. It printed a few books like *Hajj*

16 Omar, 'Interview with Umm Muhammad'.

and Umrah: according to the Qur'an and Sunnah by Abu Ameenah Bilaal Philips (1993), and *The Muslim at Prayer: A Comparison to Prayer in the Bible, with an Introduction to the Mosque in Islam* by Ahmed Deedat (1993), which appear to have been produced especially for *daᶜwa* purposes. The 'Saheeh International' translation of the Qur'an was similarly intended for promotion among English-speaking foreigners living in Saudi Arabia as well as abroad. Due to her academic qualifications in Arabic and Islam, Asam who took on the role of translator, while the two other team members were responsible for editing the target text. They were aware of the limitations of the most popular Muslim-authored Qur'an translations that were promoted by Islamic publishers in the early 1990s. The works by Abdullah Yusuf Ali (in both the KFGQPC and IIIT editions) and Muhammad Marmaduke Pickthall both used more or less archaic vocabulary and a Biblical style of writing. In contrast, the Saheeh International team adopted the innovative approach, like al-Hilālī and Khān, of opting to use modern English. Unlike them, however, the individuals behind this text were much more fluent in the target language.

A few things are immediately striking about the first edition of the Saheeh International translation (Jeddah, 1997).[17] The first is that the names of the people who actually worked on the project are not mentioned at all, perhaps due to the fact that they had no formal religious credentials. Secondly, the exact title of the work is *The Qur'an: Arabic Text with Corresponding English Meanings*. Thirdly, the cover references two new publishing institutions—the aforementioned Abulqasim Publishing House and al-Muntada al-Islami, a well-known Islamic charity based in London (est. 1986), also known as the Al-Muntada Trust. Due to the wide connections of the latter organisation, the Saheeh International translation quickly became known to readers outside Saudi Arabia.

The editorial preface to this first edition is very informative. It tells a story of a new translation, produced after thorough consideration of previous English translations of the Qur'an (by Yusuf Ali, Pickthall, and Hilālī-Khān), with a strong focus on the features of the target text:

17 Saheeh International, ed., *The Qur'an: Arabic Text with Corresponding English Meanings* (Jeddah: Abul-Qasim Publishing House, 1997).

> In spite of the amendments made by al-Hilālī and Khān in their translation of the Qur'an, certain drawbacks remain. They admittedly concentrated their efforts on corrections pertaining to *ᶜaqeedah* rather than perfecting the language, the English rendering leaves something to be desired [...] Consequently, many people have continued to prefer A. Yusuf Ali's translation because of its linguistic superiority and the fact that it is generally easier to follow without the numerous interruptions and insertions. The publisher concluded with a plea for a solution to such problems or an alternative. At length, we considered the possibility of editing the English text of The Noble Qur'an, but after some thought, decided that a thorough procedure involving systematic research would be more conducive to overall improvement.[18]

Other references in the prefatory material suggest the team's translatorial approach. This characterises the new text as 'presenting the core meanings, as far as possible, in accordance with the ᶜaqeedah of Ahl as-Sunnah wal-Jamiᶜah' [*sic*] and aligns itself, through mentions, with the teachings of Ibn Kathīr and Ibn Taymiyya.[19] These methodological aspects, as well as the special attention that is paid to the names and attributes of God,[20] generally accord with the modern Salafi hermeneutical tradition. Moreover, the prefatory texts contain justifications of Qur'an translation that cite an influential work called *Mabāḥith fī ᶜulūm al-Qurʾān* ['Studies in the Qur'anic Sciences'] by Shaykh Mannᶜā al-Qaṭṭān (1925–1999), an Egyptian-born scholar who spent most of his life working in Saudi universities. This book, first published in 1971, sanctions 'explanatory translation' of the Qur'an for use in *daᶜwa*, but also asserts that translation can provide a theologically correct vision of divine unity (*tawḥīd*) and worship (*ᶜibāda*) but really nothing more.[21] It is clear that this idea of 'approximate' translation, along with other milestones of Salafi exegesis, became main features of the Saheeh International translation. In contrast to many other translations (especially those produced in the Saudi context), the translators intended to translate almost every word in the text rather than loading it with Arabisms, as is the case in the newest editions of the Hilālī-Khān translation. This goes against the growing trend of adding to the English

18 Ibid., p. iii.
19 Ibid., p. viii.
20 Ibid., p. vi.
21 Mannᶜā al-Qaṭṭān, *Mabāḥith fī ᶜulūm al-Qurʾān* (Cairo: Dār Wahba, 2000), p. 309.

language by using newly introduced Arabic words, an idea expressed, for example, by the influential Palestinian-American thinker Ismail al-Faruqi (1921–1986), a leading figure in the International Institute of Islamic Thought. In his *Toward Islamic English* (1982, also republished later) al-Faruqi claimed that the English language, in terms of its use in the Islamic context, needs enrichment from Arabic; he also encouraged the use of Arabic vocabulary[22] and provided a list of transliterated terms and their explanations. The Saheeh International team, however, rejected this methodology, preserving only some basic terms, such as the divine name Allāh and *zakāt*.

A second edition of the Saheeh International translation was published in 2004 by the Al-Muntada al-Islami Trust, with a few corrections. This edition has been reprinted many times without any further changes. Comparison of the first edition of 1997 and a recent one from 2019 (both published in Saudi Arabia)[23] reveals some differences. Notably, the later edition demonstrates a further simplification of the text. For example, in Q. 1:7 ('who have evoked [Your] anger'), the word 'evoked' has been changed to 'earned', and a reference to al-Qurṭubī's *tafsīr* in the division between the divine names *al-Raḥmān* and *al-Raḥīm* has been erased. Some rephrasing can be observed in Q. 2:30, *nusabbiḥu bi-ḥamdika wa-nuqaddisu laka*, which is translated in the first edition as 'we declare Your praise and sanctify You', while in the recent version it reads as 'we exalt You with praise and declare Your sanctity', which seems to be a more precise rendition of the original. In other places, such as Q. 4:34, there are more significant changes, probably related to the purposes of justifying the Islamic position on the punishment a husband can inflict on his wife. The 1997 edition reads as follows:

> But those [wives] from whom you fear arrogance - [first] advise them; [then if they persist], forsake them in bed; and [finally], strike them.

and gives the following explanation in a footnote:

> As a last resort. It is unlawful to strike the face or to cause bodily injury.

22 Ismail Al-Faruqi, *Toward Islamic English* (Riyadh: IIPH, 1995), p. 15.
23 Saheeh International, ed., *The Qur'an: Arabic Text with English Meanings* (Riyadh: Dar Aljumuah, 2019).

In contrast, the 2019 edition contains a small but significant change, with the edition of 'lightly' in brackets:

> But those [wives] from whom you fear arrogance—[first] advise them; [then if they persist], forsake them in bed; and [finally], strike them [lightly].

The commentary is also completely changed. It reads:

> This final disciplinary measure is more psychological than physical. It may be resorted to only after failure of the first two measures and when it is expected to amend the situation and prevent family breakup; otherwise, it is not acceptable. The Prophet ﷺ (who never struck a woman or a servant) additionally stipulated that it must not be severe or damaging and that the face be avoided.

This shift may reflect that fact that, in the mid-1990s, the problem of 'wife-beating' was not yet widely discussed in Islamic scholarship. More recently, especially after 2001, the topic of violence in Islam has moved to centre stage in both academia and religious communities. The revised 2019 commentary, with its reference to Prophetic practice ('[he] never struck a woman or a servant'), is thus designed to be more dissuasive of domestic violence than the more or less literal translation from 1997.

There are some cases where the Saheeh International translation resembles a brief *tafsīr* rather than a translation. This result is common where the intention is to produce a widely accessible translation of the Qur'an, particularly through the use of modern plain language: such '*tafsīr*isation' is found in many Salafi interpretations of the Qur'an, which tend to produce a one-dimensional reading of the source text. This approach can be seen in the Shaheeh International text, where the literal translation of words relating to the divine attributes is accompanied by a footnote apology for it. For example, appended to Q. 2:19 is a note that reads 'Allah [...] has certain attributes [...] Islamic belief requires faith [...] without allegorical meanings or attempting to explain [...]'). It can also be seen in the work's translation of the phrase *ṣibghata-llāhi wa-man aḥsanu mina-llāhi ṣibghatan wa-naḥnu lahu ᶜābidūn* in Q. 2:138, especially when compared with other translations published in Saudi Arabia.

Since *ṣibgha* literally means 'colour' or 'hue',[24] a literal translation of the verse would be something like: 'The Colour of God! Who is better in colour than God alone? And we worship Him!' Some translations of the Qur'an do provide quite a literal reading of this verse, but these are still based on *tafsīr*. For example, Pickthall renders it as follows: '[We take our] colour from Allah, and who is better than Allah at colouring. We are His worshippers'. However, modern Salafi exegetes have tended to simplify the discussion by understanding *ṣibgha* as 'religion'. Al-Saᶜdī, for one, interprets the verse as meaning *ulzimū ṣibghat Allāh wa-huwa dīnuhu* ['accept the colouring of God, meaning His religion'].[25] This kind of interpretation is clearly given to avoid any anthropormphisation of God. English translations, produced and/or revised in Saudi Arabia, give the following picture (in chronological order):

Yusuf Ali (1965, reprint of 1946)
[Our religion is] the baptism of God; and who can baptise better than God? And it is He whom we worship.

Hilālī-Khān (1978)
[Our religion is] the Baptism of Allah and who can baptise better than Allah? And We are His worshippers?

Yusuf Ali (1991)
[Our religion] takes its hue from Allah, and who can give a better hue than Allah. It is He, Whom we worship.

Hilālī-Khān (KFGQPC, 1997)
[Our Sibghah (religion) is] the Sibghah [Religion] of Allah [Islam] and which Sibghah [religion] can be better than Allah's? And we are His worshippers [Tafsir ibn Kathir].

Saheeh International (1997)
[And say, 'Ours is] the religion of Allah. And who is better than Allah in [ordaining] religion? And we are worshippers of Him'.

---

24 *Ṣibgha* is sometimes used by Arabic Christians in their baptism rituals, during which a dye is added to the baptismal water, according to some exegetes and historians. For example, see al-Ṭabarī, *Jāmiᶜ al-bayān ᶜan tāʾwīl āy al-Qurʾān*, 16 vols (Cairo: Dār Hijr, 2001), II, p. 115.

25 Nāṣir b. ᶜAbd Allāh al-Saᶜdī, *Taysīr al-Karīm al-Raḥmān fī tafsīr kalām al-mannān* (Riyadh: Darussalam, 2002), p. 63. A similar interpretation can be found in *al-Tafsīr al-muyassar* and many of the KFGQPC translations.

This small example generally illustrates the way the meaning of *ṣibgha* has evolved and shifted in these English translations. While the first editions of Yusuf Ali and Hilālī-Khān mainly replicated the interpretation mentioned in classical *tafsīr* sources, which read the verse as referring to the Christian practice of baptism, later revisions and additions have eradicated this interpretation. It is also clear that the Saheeh International team rendered this verse in the same 'explanatory' *tafsīr*-based way as the revised Hilālī-Khān translation of 1997.

The Saheeh International translation has enjoyed growing popularity. This is due mainly to the simplicity and accessibility of both the core text and the accompanying commentary, which amounts to more than 2,000 footnotes (though many of these are brief). Although never published by any official institutions or with the official backing of any religious authorities in Saudi Arabia, it is widely used as a book for individual reading and as a source for quotations from the Qur'an. Indeed, in the UK, it is one of the most popular Muslim translations and is available in almost every Sunni mosque and Islamic centre in the country. Its success is partially due to the fact that it has been distributed gratis by the Al-Muntada al-Islami Trust and other Islamic networks. Recently, editions have also been published by Saudi publishing houses such as Aljumuah and Noor International, and these are distributed by Darussalam. Saudi ulema rarely discuss this work, but some 'pro-Salafi' literature on Qur'anic Studies evaluate it fairly positively. Abdur Raheem Kidwai, in his 2018 *God's Word, Man's Interpretations: A Critical Study of the 21st Century English Translations of the Quran*, for example, describes the Saheeh International translation as 'fairly good' for giving readers a 'clear and comprehensive picture of the articles of faith' but also 'somewhat vague and unspecific'.[26] This latter comment likely means that the authors are not always informative when it comes to commentary. Another reviewer has noted that 'What distinguishes the Saheeh International translation of the Qur'an from other female translations is that it does not reflect the feminist mindset. Instead, it enjoys widespread popularity with some of Islam's most conservative

26 Abdul Raheem Kidwai, *God's Word, Man's Interpretations: A Critical Study of the 21st Century English Translation of the Quran* (New Delhi: Viva Books, 2018), p. 92.

followers'.[27] This is an obvious jab against the feminist translation by Laleh Bakhtyar (2007), but the review nevertheless shows approval for the Saheeh International team's work. In 2017, the popular news website *Daily Beast* published a detailed article on this translation, claiming that it 'has become the main version used in English-language propaganda put out by ISIS'.[28] Overall, in comparison to the Hilālī-Khān translation, it has not received very much criticism. The interpretation of the Qur'an by the Saheeh International team is thus one of the most successful translation projects ever carried out in Saudi Arabia.

Private Publishers: Darussalam, the *Tafsīr al-ʿushr al-akhīr Project*, the Noor International Center, and Others

The history of Saudi book printing has its roots in the late nineteenth century, while the first Saudi law governing the activity of press and related resources was issued by royal decree in 1929.[29] Since its introduction, the originally strict law has been updated a few times to give more freedom to publishers while still protecting religious authorities from being criticised in any printed materials. For example, Article 3 of the Saudi 'Law on Printed Materials and Publication' (Royal decree No. M/32, enacted on 29 November 2000) currently says that 'The objectives of printed materials shall include the call to Islam, good moral standards, guidance to all that is right and good, and the dissemination of culture and knowledge'. Article 8, meanwhile, clearly states that 'Freedom of expression is guaranteed through all means of publication within the provisions of the Sharia and the law', and Article 9 says that 'Any person in charge of printed material shall observe [the highest standards of] objective and constructive criticism that serves the public interest, employing facts and true information'. As these

27 Neha Pasha, 'Translation of the Qurʾān: A Study of Saheeh International', *Aligarh Journal of Qur'anic Studies*, 3.2 (2020), 91–99 (p. 98).
28 Katie Zawadski, 'How Three American Women Translated One of the World's Most Popular Qurans', *Daily Beast*, 26 March 2017, https://www.thedailybeast.com/how-three-american-women-translated-one-of-the-worlds-most-popular-qurans.
29 Sulaymān al-ʿUnayzī, *Qirʾā fī niẓām al-maṭbūʿāt wa-l-nashr al-Saʿūdī* (Riyadh: al-Muntadā al-ʿĀlāmī al-Sanawī al-Awwal, 1424/2003), p. 1.

potentially contradictory articles do not apply to high-level religious institutions, the clearest directive come from Article 9, part 3:

> Any material impinging on the integrity or undermining the reputation or dignity of the Grand Mufti of the Kingdom, members of the Senior Ulema Council, state officials or employees, or any natural or corporate person [...] not be published by any means.

In the latest version of the law, Royal decree M/32 from 28 October 2003, the Grand Mufti's office has been removed.

The decree also sets out a number of criteria for publishers. To be a publisher, one must be a Saudi citizen, 'be well-known for good conduct', and obtain a licence for this activity (Article 5). Furthermore, 'any author, publisher, printer, or distributor who wants to print or distribute any printed material shall provide the Ministry with two copies for approval before printing or circulation' (Article 13). Thus, the publication industry within the country operates under quite strict regulations, although the practical application of the law might at times be more liberal. Certainly, when it comes to the publication of religious materials prior to the digital age (that is, until the early 2000s), it is hard to envisage that anything would be printed that was in explicit conflict with the Sunni-Salafi vision of Islam. This is why religious books were historically printed in Egypt and Lebanon in larger numbers than by any Saudi printing houses. One can hardly imagine, for example, any Shii books being published in Saudi Arabia.

The rapid changes and growth that took place in the Saudi publishing industry during the 1960s and 1970s reflected the age of modernisation but also the country's fight against illiteracy. In 1952, the United Nations reported that Saudi Arabia had 306 elementary schools but that illiteracy levels remained at between 92% and 95%.[30] Following the introduction of educational reforms in the 1960s and the propagation of mass education, the publishing market started to change rapidly, if not dramatically. A report published by the International Publishers Association in 2016 states that Saudi Arabia comprised the largest Arab

30 Tariq Elyas and Michelle Picard, 'A Brief History of English and English Teaching in Saudi Arabia', in *English as a Foreign Language in Saudi Arabia: New Insights into Teaching and Learning English*, ed. by Christo Moskovsky and Michelle Picard (London: Routledge, 2019), pp. 70–84.

book market that year, exporting $25m worth of books and related goods and importing $125m worth. The country published 2,387 different titles in 2014, primarily in the fields of religion and social sciences.[31] However, despite this rapid growth, Saudi Arabia still faces the same problem as many other Arab countries. As a study from 2017 points out,

> Arabs in two of the three countries with large expatriate populations—Saudi Arabia and the UAE—reported significantly lower levels of book reliance than Asian and Western expatriates. The study also found that Arabs rely less on books than on TV, interpersonal sources, or the Internet for information and entertainment.[32]

Darussalam

By the 1980s, the age of global Saudi missionary activities, carried out through organisations such as the Muslim World League and subsequently the King Fahd Complex, was in full swing. Demand for translations of Islamic materials into foreign languages such as English and French prompted the creation of commercial presses oriented towards the global Islamic book market.[33] One of the first such global publishers was Darussalam, which was established in Riyadh in 1986 and uses the tagline 'Global leader of Islamic books'. Now a multilingual international publishing house operating in twenty-eight countries, Darussalam remains a leading press in Islamic publishing at the global level, with large distribution networks in both the East and West. Its founder, Abdul Malik Mujahid, was a migrant from Pakistan who worked first in an advertising agency, then the Ministry of Education, and the Ministry of Defence before finally starting his own successful publishing business.[34] In 2016, Darussalam published more than 600 Islamic books

31 International Publishers Association, 'IPA Country Report on Saudi Arabia', 30 June 1916, https://www.internationalpublishers.org/copyright-news-blog/410-ipa-country-report-saudi-arabia.

32 Justin D. Martin, Ralph J. Martins, and S. Shageaa Naqvi, 'Do Arabs Really Read Less? "Cultural Tools" and "More Knowledgeable Others" as Determinants of Book Reliance in Six Arab Countries', *International Journal of Communication*, 11 (2017), 3374–93.

33 On state and non-state *daʿwa* publishing, see Matthew J. Kuiper, *Daʿwa: A Global History of Islamic Missionary Thought and Practice* (Edinburgh: Edinburgh University Pres, 2021), pp. 212–43, https://doi.org/10.1515/9781474451543

34 For a brief biography of Abdul Malik Mujahid, see his unofficial blog at https://abdulmalikmujahid.wordpress.com/2017/07/24/abdul-malik-mujahid-biography

in English ,[35] mostly on the Qur'an, Sunna, *tafsīr*, Islamic law, and history; it also published many textbooks, manuals, and children's books. As of 2023, Darussalam has published Qur'an translations in over twenty-five languages, the most prominent being English, French, Urdu, Spanish, Persian, Hindi, Pashto, Sinhala, Russian, Chinese, and Bengali. According to an article published in the *Daily Pakistan* in 2020, 'after launching the Punjabi translations by Prof. Roshan Khan Kakar and his assistant Rai Shahzad, Darussalam Publishers, is now the second largest publisher of translations of the Holy Quran in the world',[36] the largest being KFGQPC. But how true is this claim?

One of Darussalam's first Qur'an translation projects was (as mentioned in previous chapters) an edition of the Hilālī-Khān translation that appeared in 1994. Darussalam has since reprinted Hilālī-Khān ten times, and it is probably due to their endeavours that this work continues to be readily available in the West.[37] Darussalam still sells the Hilālī-Khān translation, but it has recently started to distribute other translations, including *The Clear Qura*n by Mustafa Khattab, sponsored by the US-based Al-Furqaan Foundation, and Adil Salahi's *The Quran: A Translation for the 21st Century* (both of these books are printed and distributed by other publishers in the UK and USA). In addition, Darussalam has produced a few textbooks designed for Qur'anic education in English, notably, *Methodical Interpretation of The Noble Qur'ān: Part 30* by Aḥmad Nawfal, which is a rather short explanatory Salafi *tafsīr* of the final juzʾ of the Qur'an, translated from the Arabic work *al-Tafsīr al-manhajī*.[38]

However, Darussalam has made a few original contributions to the Qur'an translation landscape. One is a translation into Sindhi (a language with thirty million speakers in Pakistan) by Amīr Buaksh

35 Talha Mujahid, 'Darussalam—the Global Leader in Islamic Publications', *Saudi Gazette*, 26 June 2023/8 Dhū-l-Hijja 1444, https://saudigazette.com.sa/article/161230

36 'Saudi-Based Publisher Introduces Punjabi Translation of Holy Quran', *Daily Pakistan*, 14 November 2020, https://en.dailypakistan.com.pk/14-Nov-2020/saudi-based-publisher-introduces-punjabi-translation-of-holy-quran

37 A further factor is that this translation is perceived as being 'approved' by the KFGQPC.

38 Ahmad Nawfal, *Methodical Interpretation of The Noble Quran* (*Part-30*) (Riyadh: Darussalam, 2020).

Channā, a scholar working in King Saud University.[39] Channā's *Qur'āni Karīm, Tarjami e Tafsīr* differs from the classic work published by KFGQPC (by Taj Maḥmūd Imrōtī, d. 1929)[40] in its use of modern language and incorporation of plenty of commentary. Darussalam has also produced original translations into Sinhala, Gurmukhi, Tamil, Marathi, Hindi, Pashto, Bengali, Malayam, Nepalese, and a few other languages, almost all of which are spoken in South Asia. Coupled with the aforementioned Punjabi translation, this list shows that this region is a particular priority for the company. Darussalam has also been more successful than the KFGQPC when it comes to Persian translations. In contrast to the KFGQPC's reliance on al-Dihlawī's classic translation from the eighteenth century, Darussalam have published an original work named *Tafsīr Aḥsan al-kalā*m (by Ḥusayn Tājī and ᶜAbd al-Ghafūr Ḥusayn), an explanatory translation that claims to be based on the Sunna corpus as well as the *tafsīr*s of Ibn Kathīr and al-Qurṭubī.[41] When it comes to African languages, Darussalam has produced two translations, the first into Somali (by the Salafi scholar Cabdicaziiz Xasan Yacquub)[42] and the second into Swahili (by ᶜAlī Muḥsin al-Barwānī [1919–2006], a scholar and politician from Zanzibar who spent most of his life in the UAE).[43] The Swahili translation was initially published in 1995 in Abu Dhabi,[44] but it looks as if Darussalam edited this text before publishing their edition, adding more commentary from the *ḥadīt*h corpus.

Interestingly, when it comes to Turkish and Albanian, Darussalam has chosen to translate the English Hilālī-Khān interpretation (1994 or

39 Amīr Buaksh Channā, *Qurʾāni Karīm, Tarjami e Tafsīr* (Riyadh: Darussalam, 2018).

40 For more on him, see Annemarie Schimmel, 'Translations and Commentaries of the Qurʾān in Sindhi Language', *Oriens*, 16 (1963), 233–35.

41 Ḥusayn Tājī and ᶜAbd al-Ghafūr Ḥusayn, *Tafsīr Aḥsan al-Kalām bi-zobān-Fārisī* (Riyadh: Darussalam, 2012).

42 Cabdicaziiz Xasan Yacquub, *Kuraanka Kariimka. y Waxaa Tarjumay C. Xasan Yacquub* (Riyadh: Darussalam, 2020), pp. i–ii.

43 ᶜAlī Muḥsin al-Barwānī, *Tafsiri ya maana ya Qur'an Tukufu kwa lugha ya Kiswahili* (Riyadh: Darussalam, 2012).

44 See Gerard C. van de Bruinhorst, 'Changing Criticism of Swahili Qur'an Translations: The Three "Rods of Moses"', *Journal of Qur'anic Studies*, 15.3 (2013), 206–31, (206), https://doi.org/10.3366/jqs.2013.0118. For more on the first edition of this translation, which was supported by al-Azhar University, see also: Faruk Topan, 'Polemics and Language in Swahili Translations of the Qur'an: Mubarak Ahmad (d. 2001), Abdullah Saleh al-Farsy (d. 1982) and Ali Muhsin al-Barwani (d. 2006)', in *The Qur'an and its Readers Worldwide*, ed. by Suha Taji-Farouki (New York: Oxford University Press in Association with the Institute of Ismaili Studies, London, 2015), pp. 491–501.

1996 edition) rather than the original Arabic. In the case of its Turkish translation, it even produced a trilingual edition in Arabic, English, and Turkish.[45] Darussalam has also printed a partial translation of Hilālī-Khān into Russian (comprising the last five parts of the Qur'an, *juz*ʾs 25–30), which looks like a word-for-word reconstruction of the English text with no influence from any other sources. This means it is effectively unable to compete with the numerous Russian translations available that are translated directly from the Arabic.[46]

Darussalam's Indonesian translation is a reprint of the KFGQPC's edition of *Al Quran Dan Terjemahnya*, the Qur'an translation produced by the Indonesian Ministry of Religious Affairs.[47] There are further cases of reprints from KFGQPC translations: for example, the Spanish translation published by Darussalam seems to be nothing more than a reproduction of Abdel-Ghani Melara Navío's translation which was published in 1997 by the KFGQPC. In this instance, Darussalam made the strange decision to use the Ḥafṣ reading for the Arabic text, despite the fact that the translation was based on the Warsh reading, which was (correctly) used in the original KFGQPC edition.[48]

Finally, the only original translation into a European language produced by Darussalam seems to be a work in French, *Le Sens Des Versets Du Saint Qouran*, which was printed in 1999 and later reprinted in 2000 and 2005.[49] The translator, Cheikh Boreima Abdou Daouda from Niger, is a graduate of IUM. In his introduction, Abdou Daouda says that his work depended on (or rather, was 'inspired by') the French translation published by the KFGQPC as well as the Hilālī-Khān English translation. The influence of the latter is quite evident not only from the core text but also from the commentary, which mentions the same *tafsīr* sources as are used in Hilālī-Khān. For example, in his rendition of Q. 1:7, Abdou Daouda refers explicitly to Jews ('juifs') and Christians ('chrétiens'), a feature that can be observed in the original version and earliest editions of the Hilālī-Khān translation. It is also apparent in his treatment of Q. 2:3, in which the wording of the verse is exactly the same

45 *İngilizce ve Türkçe Olarak Kur'an*ᶜ*ı Kerim*ᶜ*in Meali ve Tefsiri* (Riyadh: Darussalam, 2004).
46 *Perevod smyslov Blagorodnyi Kur*ʾ*an na russkom jazyke* (Riyadh: Darussalam, 2009).
47 *Al Quran Dan Terjemahnya* (Riyadh: Darussalam: 2010).
48 *Del Noble Coran* (Riyadh: Darussalam, 2003).
49 Cheikh Boreima Abdou Daouda, *Le sens des versets du Saint Qour'ân* (Riyadh: Darussalam, 1999).

as is found in the KFGQPC's version of Hamidullah, while the relevant explanation is exactly the same as in Hilālī-Khān:

> **Boreima Abdou Daouda (1999)**
> *Qui croient à l'Inconnaisable (ghayb), accomplisent la Çalât (Iqâmatouç-Çalât) et dépensent de ce que Nous leur avons attribute (c'est-à-dire donnent la Zakât, dépensent pour eux-mêmes, pour leurs parents, leurs enfants, leurs femmes et font charité aux pauvres et pour servir la cause d'Allah—Djihâd).*
>
> **Muhammad Hamidullah (1990/1991)**
> *Qui croient à l'invisible et accomplisent la Salat et dépensent [dans l'obéisance à Allah], de ce que Nous leur avons attributé.*
>
> **Hilālī-Khān (1997)**
> Who believe in the Ghaib and perform As-Salât (Iqâmat-as-Salât), and spend out of what We have provided for them [i.e., give Zakât, spend on themselves, their parents, their children, their wives, etc., and also give charity to the poor and also in Allâh's Cause—Jihâd].

A question that remains is how Darussalam's review processes work. Many of the editions contain absolutely no information about the names of any individuals or special committees that involved in any reviewing or editing activities prior to publication. What is known, however, is that one of Darussalam's co-founders, ᶜAbd Allāh al-Muᶜtāz, who was particularly involved in promoting the publication of Qur'an translations, is a student of Shaykh Ibn Bāz. He is an active member of many Saudi-run Islamic projects in the Middle East and Africa, including the authoring of some books on Qur'anic Studies, among them a popular *tafsīr* in Arabic.[50] It is also known that, for particular projects, Darussalam has historically invited external expert native speakers of specific languages with knowledge of Islam to join the board of their research committee [*al-lajna al-ᶜilmiyya*], on a similar basis as the KFGQPC.

The Hilālī-Khān translation exerts an enormous influence on Darussalam's translations. Not only has the company treated its new edition of this text as a kind of standard, producing 'versions' of this translation in multiple other languages, but many of its non-Hilālī-Khān-based Qur'an translations have clearly used it as a prototype when it comes to the issue of commentary and interpolations into the

50 ᶜAbd Allāh al-Muᶜtāz, *al-Fawāʾīd al-ḥisān min ayāt al-Qurʾān* (Riyadh: Darussalam, 2006).

text. The Hilālī-Khān translation is usually positioned in their literature as a 'summarising commentary' that offers a concise version of the opinions present in classical *tafsīr*. Beyond this, it should also be noted that, in contrast to the KFGQPC, Darussalam has relied on the authority of individual translators rather than its own institutional authority. This can be seen, for instance, in the fact that its translations never include any kind of preface or introduction written by religious scholars or established officials intended to endow the text with their stamp of approval.

Darussalam's reliance on the Hilālī-Khān translation has also contributed to the tone of Salafi *daᶜwa* activities. The company prioritises Asian languages primarily because of their large number of speakers and the high level of demand for Qur'an translations in them. Consequently, missionary activities in the corresponding areas follow the Hilālī-Khān in remaining loyal to the basic hermeneutical principles of the modern Wahhabi reading of the Qur'an.[51] Many of the translations Darussalam has printed for the rest of the world, however, have not fallen on fertile ground and so have remained relatively unsuccesful. Furthermore, in countries like the UK and USA in the West, and Pakistan in the East, Darussalam has developed very good networks for book distribution; in some other countries its translations have had little chance of reaching readers. Darussalam's commercial policy of pursuing copyright has also prevented many of its translations being reprinted by other publishers, and this has effectively limited the circulation of some of its texts. However, despite all this, having printed over twenty translations of the Qur'an, it is, indeed, the largest private Saudi publisher of Qur'an translations.

The *Tafsīr al-ʿushr al-akhīr* Project

In contrast to the other publishing projects discussed so far, the *Tafsīr al-ᶜushr al-akhīr* is dedicated solely to Qur'an interpretation in multiple languages and pursues a rather more 'centralised' exegetical approach. Its title translates as 'Commentary on the Last Tenth of the Qur'an', that

51 The theological bent of these translations can also be seen influencing other kinds of Islamic literature published by Darussalam, for example, through their use in quotation. Having said that, some books in English published by Darussalam instead use the KFGQPC edition of Yusuf Ali's translation.

is, *juz*ʾs 28–30, from sura 58 to the end of the Qur'an. It is a production of the Old Industrial City Communities Awareness Bureau [al-Maktab al-Taᶜāwunī li-Tawᶜiyyat al-Jāliyyāt], which is based near the Saudi capital, Riyadh. The organisation was set up in 1998 as a part of efforts by local ulema to work with fast-growing diaspora communities (both Muslim and non-Muslim) in the capital city. Later renamed *Jamᶜiyya* ['Society'], it is one of a few dozens of such 'awareness bureaus' established around the Kingdom. Their funding comes from both state and private sources in equal measure (and is coordinated by the MOIA),[52] and their network of offices has pursued many different projects, both local and global, including sending books abroad for missionary purposes. The bureaus' activities include the collection and distribution of charitable donations, the organisation of educational camps (especially during Ramadan), the provision of training in the basics of Islam, and the printing religious books. Websites of the *Jamᶜiyya* are usually filled with success stories of individuals' public conversion to Islam. Given the remit of the Communities Awareness Bureau, it is unsurprising that it has prioritised the production of Islamic texts in translation, particularly the most indispensable works.

In 2002, the Communities Awareness Bureau started to distribute its own book, *Tafsīr al-ᶜushr al-akhīr min al-Qurʾān al-karīm wa-ilayhi aḥkām tuhimmu al-musli*m ['An explanation of the last tenth of the noble Qur'an, also including critical matters in the life of a Muslim']. This volume contained a few statements on the virtues of the Qur'an in Islam, the Arabic text of the *tafsīr*, and a collection of traditions on various topics relating to Muslim life, the pillars of Islam, and basic Islamic rules for women. The last of these is imaginatively written, taking the form of a dialogue between two persons, one named ᶜAbd Allāh ['servant of God'], and the other named ᶜAbd al-Nabī [literally, 'servant of the Prophet']. Their conversations offer a simplified outline of Wahhabi/Salafi theological doctrine concerning the 'Oneness of God in divinity, attributes and dominion' and exhibits a strong anti-Sufi and anti-Shii bias, although neither of the contested groups are mentioned by name. The project's main website features letters of support for this

52 'Services and Statistics', *MOIA*, https://www.moia.gov.sa/AboutMinistry/Branches/Riyadh/Pages/Message.aspx

work from top-ranked Saudi scholars like Shaykh ʿAbd Allāh b. Jibrīn, a member of the Council of Senior Scholars, and many others.[53]

When it comes to the core text of the book, the *tafsīr* of suras 1 and 58–114, the project has changed a few times. Initially, the Communities Awareness Bureau used *Zubdat al-tafsīr* by ʿUmar b. Sulaymān al-ʿAshqar (1920–2012) but, by 2010, had started to promote the KFGQPC-published *al-Tafsīr al-muyassar*. Interestingly, just ten years later, the new (nineteenth) edition of the Arabic text was changed again, this time to *al-Mukhtaṣar fī tafsīr al-Qurʾān al-karīm*, which was originally published by the Tafsir Center for Qur'anic Studies. So, when the cover of the book and the relevant website says that it has been translated into sixty languages (!), it is not completely clear which version was the basis for these. However, it soon becomes apparent that most of the translations were carried out at the time when the Arabic text was drawn from *al-Tafsīr al-muyassar*, although apparently different editions were used. For example, a French version of *Tafsīr al-ʿushr al-akhīr* includes reference to Jews and Christians in Q. 1:7 (as is found in the first edition of *al-Muyassar*), while the English does not. Thus, the project remains the biggest promoter of this 'standard' exegesis as produced by the KFGQPC.

The translations of the Qur'anic verses that are provided before the *tafsīr* of each verse do not seem to have been guided by any coherent policy. The French translators used a quite rare recent work, published by Zeino Editorial House (Paris) called *Le Noble Coran*,[54] while the English translator used Saheeh International; the Russian translator used Abu Adel's translation; the Bosnian, Mehanovic's translation (which is said to be based on Ibn Kathīr); while the Spanish and German texts only provide a translation of the *tafsīr*, with no accompanying translation of the Qur'anic verses themselves. There is also variation in the popularity of the translations used. Despite this disparity, the translators demonstrate an overall orientation towards the use of distinctly Salafi interpretations in their respective languages.

Tafsīr al-ʿushr al-akhīr represents the final evolution of the Saudi translation movement, and illustrates how the vision of Qur'anic

53 See the promotional video at https://www.youtube.com/watch?v=rglM7ZCrPSs
54 *Le Noble Coran. Nouvelle traduction. Traduit par lʿéquipe des éditions Zeino* (Paris: Éditions Zeino, 2012).

interpretation as a kind of *tafsīr* has been subordinated to the promotion of Salafi doctrine. As a result, recourse to a somewhat authoritative but short and simplistic *tafsīr* (be it *al-Muyassar* or *al-Mukhtasar*) has become an inherent part of the multi-language *daᶜwa* strategy of Saudi organisations. With fifty million copies printed so far in such a large number of languages, this book has made its way around the world. It is available in at least seventy countries, according to the website, and can be found in mosques and Islamic centres in Europe, the UK, and the USA.[55]

Although none of the three *tafsīr*s used in the different editions of *Tafsīr al-ᶜushr al-akhīr* is particularly original, the project has made them so widely available globally that no other Qur'an commentaries can compete with them. Despite the diverse translation strategies and approaches, and taking into account the fact that some of the translations have not undergone any scrutiny or review process prior to publication, a kind of 'standardised' text has emerged. It is one and the same in every language and, as such, is now considered to be the basis for any 'authorised' translation that is 'correct' from the Salafi theological perspective. As a result, it is hard to find any systematic critique of this book, especially after the initial 'individual' *tafsīr* was replaced by collectively authored interpretations that are generally deemed to be 'more acceptable' (especially in the case of the KFGQPC's *al-Muyassar*). This seems to be a recent trend in Salafi circles, particularly since the rise of mass Islamic missionary activities in the 1980s. New works continue to be based on classical sources but reframe the tradition in a way that moves away from the encyclopedic nature of *tafsīr* towards more simplistic and linear ethical guidance, as Johanna Pink has shown in her analysis of translations of Ibn Kathīr's *tafsīr* into Indonesian.[56]

The Noor International Center

Around 2018, another publisher specialising in 'translating the meanings of the Holy Quran into international languages' emerged in

55 See their website at https://www.tafseer.info/en

56 Johanna Pink, 'Eight Shades of Ibn Kathīr: The Afterlives of a Premodern Qurʾānic Commentary in Contemporary Indonesian Translations' in *Malay-Indonesian Islamic Studies*, ed. by Majid Daneshgar and Ervan Nurtawab (Leiden: Brill, 2022), pp. 109–33.

Riyadh, registered as Noor International. This publishing house, during its first four years of operation, has printed English, French, Spanish, and Latin American Spanish translations of the Qur'an.[57] Their strategy is to rely on existing translations. In English, they have reprinted the most recent edition of Saheeh International, both the complete text and excerpts.[58] Their French translation is not new either. They have chosen to republish *Le sens des versets du Coran* by the Tunisian scholar Nebil Radhouane, first published in 2012 by the al-Muntadā al-Islamī Trust,[59] reproducing both the text of the translation and the accompanying commentary. According to the author's introduction to one of the latest editions (Noor International excluded this text, probably to make the text more practical in usage), he used *'les exegeses d'Ibn Kathîr, At-Tabarî, As-Sa 'dî et Al-Baghawî. Quant à la lecture, elle s'est toujours appuyée sur la version de Hafç'*.[60] This suggests that Noor International, like the KFGQPC, follows the 'standard' Salafi exegetical canon developed in established ulema circles. The use of the Ḥafṣ reading in this translation, however, has given it a more universal outlook than would the use of, for example, the Warsh reading.[61]

The most recent two texts published by Noor International, the Qur'an in European Spanish and in Latin American Spanish, are also reprints of existing translations. Both works were produced by the al-Muntada al-Islami foundation in association with Dār Qiraʾāt and share some features.[62] The introduction included in the first edition of each does not provide the names of the translators, instead referring to 'a team effort'. Hermeneutically, both translations contain a lot of interpolations and plenty of commentary, and they do not seem to be particularly dependent on popular pre-existing Spanish translations, such as those by Abdel-Ghani Melara Navío (also published by KFGQPC and Darussalam) or Isa Garcia. The introductions refer to the legacy of some 'exégetas' [exegetes], although no specific authority

57 See Noor International's online store at https://store.noorinternational.net/

58 *The Qur'an* (Riyadh: Noor International, 2019).

59 Nebil Radhouane, *Le Noble Coran—Sens traduits et annotés par les soins du Pr Nebil Radhouane* (Riyadh: IPC Al-Muntada Al-Islami, 2012).

60 Radhouane, *Le Noble Coran, p. 11.*

61 The Warsh reading is popular only in Tunisia, Algeria, Morocco, and some parts of West Africa.

62 *El Corán. Traducción en lengua española latinoamericana* (Riyadh: Al Muntada Al Islami, 2017).

is named. These works require further study, but, overall, they appear to be explanatory translations with a special accent on theological issues (for example, the divine attributes), simple commentary, and minimal use of Arabic terminology (such as *ghayb*). As the introduction clearly states, this kind of simplicity is used 'para que tanto el lector musulmán como el no musulmán se beneficien de dicho conocimiento' ['so that both the Muslim and non-Muslim reader can benefit from such knowledge'].[63] Although Noor International Center has only published four translations so far, only one of which is more or less original, it seems clear that their priority lies in distributing books outside the Muslim world for missionary purposes.

The three publishers of Qur'an translations discussed above are, of course, not the only ones. Although they are the biggest, some other, local publishers are active in the field as well. For example, a new translation of the last *juzʾ* of the Qur'an into Tigrinya (which is spoken in Eritrea) has recently been published by the Cooperative Office from Umm Hammam area in Riaydh. The translator, a Salafi preacher called Dr Bayan Salih, follows the trend we have already seen insofar as he applies the 'standard' exegetical canon, from al-Ṭabarī and al-Baghawī to al-Saᶜdī and al-Ashqar.[64]

Al-Mukhtaṣar fī tafsīr al-Qurʾān al-karīm: The Arabic Text and its Numerous Translations

The Tafsir Center for Qur'anic Studies (established in 2008) is another very active non-governmental institution that has generally toed the line when it comes to promoting the Salafi hermeneutical approach. Designed as a multipurpose think tank for Qur'an interpretation with generous funding (mostly from private Saudi nationals), the Center has managed to make its name in a very short time through one long-term project, *al-Mukhtaṣar fī tafsīr al-Qurʾān al-karīm*. Six editions of this work have come out in print since 2019.[65] Initially, it was a typical contemporary

63 Ibid., p. b.

64 Bayān Sāliḥ, *Tarjamat maᶜānī juzʾ ᶜamma. Al-Lugha al-Tijriniyā* (Riyadh: al-Maktab al-Taᶜāwunī li-l-Daᶜwa wa-l-Irshād wa-Taᶜwiyyat al-Jāliyāt bi-Umm Hammām, [n. d.]).

65 *al-Mukhtaṣar fī tafsīr al-Qurʾān al-karīm* (Riyadh: Markaz Tafsīr li-l-Dirāsāt al-Qurʾāniyya, 1441/2021).

Qur'an interpretation in Arabic (very similar to the KFGQPC's *al-Tafsīr al-muyassar* and obviously inspired by it). However, it has become available in fourteen languages, from Albanian to Spanish, over the last couple of years.[66] Not all of these translations have appeared in print as of 2022; many were instead designed for online use. Nevertheless, this breadth is quite impressive, exceeding the number of available languages of its main predecessor, *al-Tafsīr al-muyassar*. Who authored this work, what are its main features, and how it is being translated and promoted?

The cover page, somewhat similarly to *al-Tafsīr al-muyassar*, says the book is written by 'a group of *tafsīr* scholars', but the prefatory material gives a few specific names. The *matn* [core text of the work] was written by Shaykh Muḥammad b. Muḥammad al-Mukhtār al-Shinqīṭī[67] from Medina, a student of Ibn Bāz and a collaborator in the production of the *al-Tafsīr al-muyassar*. A number of other scholars involved in the project are also mentioned, including a well-known Saudi authority on *tafsīr*, Musāᶜid al-Ṭayyār from King Saud University, who performed the final edit.[68] Subject to an impressive number of revisions, their work was designed to provide: (i) a short outline of the meanings of the verses; (ii) explanation of unusual terms used in the Qur'an; (iii) guidance that accorded with the practice of the *salaf al-umma* (i.e., the first generation of Muslims); (iv) a selection of the meanings deemed most relevant and significant; and (v) an outline for the reader of the 'benefits' of every group of verses.[69]

The authors of *al-Mukhtaṣar* say they used the same style as al-Ṭabarī, and also comment that his interpretation was viewed as a decisive authority by the entire writing committee. In common with *al-Tafsīr al-muyassar*, again, the team behind this work made it 'accessible for translation into other languages',[70] thus we have a second modern *tafsīr* that is destined not only for the Arabic reader but also for a wider audience in other languages. The text keeps silent, however, on how this 'accessibility' was actually effected from a semantic perspective.

66 See 'Tarājim', https://mokhtasr.com/تصفح-المختصر-والتراجم/
67 *al-Mukhtaṣar*, p. 8.
68 Ibid.
69 Ibid., p. 6.
70 Ibid., p. 10.

The structure of the commentary in *al-Mukhtaṣar* differs a bit from that in *al-Tafsīr al-muyassar*. First of all, it provides a short introduction to every sura called 'aims of the sura' [*min maqāṣid al-suwar*] and additional explanations of (primarily moral) topics at the end of every page under the heading 'some benefits of the suras' [*min fawāʾid al-suwar*]. This makes the text more attractive for use as a kind of introductory textbook to the Qur'an, be it in Islamic schools or some other circle of learning. However, the work differs little from *al-Tafsīr al-muyassar*. It takes the same approach towards the divine attributes and their literal interpretation, mentions Jews and Christians in its discussion of Q. 1:7, uses many similar expressions, and is similar in size. Even its claim to explain unusual words is implemented in the same way. For example, for the word *ḥawwāriyūn*, which first occurs in Q. 3:52 and is used for the close followers of Jesus, both commentaries provide the synonym *aṣfiyāʾ* ['the chosen ones'].

Yet, *al-Mukhtaṣar* goes further than *al-Muyassar* on some levels—namely with regard to some legal rulings. Although both declare that they do not offer detailed commentary on Islamic legal issues, *al-Mukhtaṣar* includes the following explanation under Q. 9:12 to clarify the expression *ṭaʿanū fī dīnikum* ['revile your religion']: 'But if they break their oath after having made an agreement with you, if they revile your religion, then fight the leaders of disbelief—oaths mean nothing to them—so that they may stop'.[71] The Arabic *al-Mukhtaṣar* says, 'Some of the scholars argued that what is said by God as *ṭaʿanū fī dīnikum* is a proof of the necessity to kill anyone who reviles or mocks the religion intentionally, calling him to repentance before that'; however the relevant English translation rewords this to 'must be put to death'.[72] In contrast to al-Mukhtaṣar, al-Muyassar uses the more abstract word *qitāl* ['fight'] ffor the explanation of this verse without drawing any legal rulings.

It is interesting to trace how such an explicit, one-dimensional ruling, promoting death as the punishment for blasphemy,[73] has been interpreted in the various translations available on the project website (mokhtasr.

71 Translation by M. A. S. Abdel Haleem.

72 *al-Mukhtaṣar, p. 188.*

73 On the broader context for this issue, see John Tolan, 'Blasphemy and Protection of the Faith: Legal Perspectives from the Middle Ages', *Islam and Christian–Muslim Relations*, 27.1 (2016), 35–50.

com).[74] The Italian translation simply says: *'Alcuni degli studiosi citarono le Parole dell'Altisimo: "Hanno offeso la vostra religione" riguardo l'obbligo di uccidere chiunque offenda la religione di proposito, o la derida, dopo esere stato invitato a smettere'* ['Some scholars quoted the words of the Most High: "They have offended your religion" regarding the obligation to kill anyone who offends the religion on purpose, or mocks it, after being asked to stop'].

Conversely, the Russian translation seems to be less 'violent', using the vaguer word *'srazhenije'* ['fight']: *'Nekotoryje uchenyje schitajut obazatelnym srazhenije so vsemi, kto osoznanno porochit religiju'* ['Some scholars find it necessary to fight anyone who intentionally blames religion']. The French text, meanwhile, says: *'Certains savants se basent sur le verset 12 afin d'ᶜaffirmer que tout individu portant délibérément atteinte à la religion dans le desein de la railler doit obligatoirement être tué'* ['Some scholars base themselves on verse 12 in order to affirm that anyone who deliberately attacks religion with the intention of mocking it must be killed'].

This comparison of translations is hardly exhaustive, but it makes the general point that most of the translators have followed the wording of the Arabic original very strictly. It must be noted that, in contrast to some other translations like the *Last Tenth of the Qur'an*, none of the versions of *al-Mukhtaṣar* available in other languages provide the actual text of the Qur'an, so the reader cannot distinguish between the actual Qur'anic text and an interpretation written centuries later. In any case, in contrast to the rising popularity of the Arabic version of *al-Mukhtaṣar*, its translations have not really found a large readership, probably mainly because they are only available on the mokhtasr.com website, as well as a few other sites.

With its mostly anonymous literal translations, this *tafsīr* seems to be one more attempt to impose a 'standard' interpretation of the Qur'an that prioritises Salafi doctrinal readings over any other issues. *Al-Mukhtaṣar* shares the fate of its predecessor *al-Tafsīr al-muyassar*. As a work designed for an Arabic audience, it cannot compete in popularity with available translations of the Qur'an; rather, it fulfils a niche requirement as an auxiliary exegetical text with strong Salafi

74 Some of these versions has been already published in print (some even more than once, with minor revisions), while others are only available online.

tendencies, which essentially remains unchanged despite the fact that new editions are published almost every year or two. It does illustrate the latest development in the field of religious translations: by not even mentioning name of the translators, this type of translation makes the translator less visible, and because the final text completely opts out of engaging with any textual issues such as the rhetorical beauty of the Qur'an, or its linguistic features, the translation is reduced to a kind of mechanical enterprise that attempts to provide if not 'the only righteous' pragmatic text, at least 'the authoritative' one, based on the 'predominant' Muslim interpretation of the Qur'an.

Conclusion

Saudi Arabia was far from the area of the Muslim world where discussion of the translatability of the Qur'an began. Hanbali legal sources are generally quite silent on the issue, in contrast to the Hanafi sources, and an obvious reason for this, of course, is that the Hanbali school has never been predominant in any non-Arabic Muslim environment, which means it has not had to engage with the demand for interlinear or separate interpretation in foreign languages. Still, browsing the history of discussions on translatability in Saudi Arabia, it is clear that, over recent years, presentation of the Qur'an in non-Arabic languages has become an issue that is more debated and which has been subject to changing internal dynamics. While in the mid-twentieth century there were still questions over the permissibility of translating the Qur'an, by the 1960s and 1970s, the prevailing opinion had generally shifted to favour the idea of the 'translation of its meanings'. Just a few decades later, Saudi Arabian publishers, both official and non-governmental, have become the largest producers of Qur'an translations in the Muslim World.

In its first and earliest stage, this translation movement, which included many different actors (translators, religious authorities, state, publishers and, finally, readers), was not home grown. Most debates on whether and how to translate the Qur'an made their way to Saudi Arabia via scholars from Egypt, Turkey, and India. Despite tensions between al-Azhar scholars and Salafi circles, a huge network of these and other interested parties contributed to the discussions, despite their different intra-Sunni religious backgrounds. In the late 1920s and 1930s, before the rise of local education networks, al-Azhar dominated these discussions. This is not only because of scholarly mobility between Egypt and the Hijaz [the western region of modern-day Saudi Arabia that includes

©2024 Mykhaylo Yakubovych, CC BY-ND 4.0 https://doi.org/10.11647/OBP.0381.06

Mecca and Medina] but also because it was attended by Saudi students. At the same time, many Saudi scholars started to look at translation from the perspective of Salafi sources, above all, Ibn Taymiyya and later interpreters from the family of the *āl al-shaykh*, the descendants of Muḥammad b. ᶜAbd al-Wahhāb, the eponymous founder of the Wahhabi movement. The Wahhabi scholarly establishment began to reformulate its own views on translation, finding 'proofs' for its permissibility in new re-readings of Ibn Taymiyya and his followers. With the coming of a new generation of Western-educated Saudis, especially after the educational reforms implemented by King Faisal between 1964 and 1975, all of these discussions were finally contextualised within modernity. Increased levels of migration of foreign workers to Saudi Arabia also catalysed an interest in translation. This also had the effect of facilitating translation projects that were carried out by non-Saudi expats, such as the globally popular Saheeh International translation by three American female converts.

These groups, united by the developing Salafi canon, reached a consensus about the 'permissibility' of translating the Qur'an by conceptualising translation as a kind of 'interpretation' (*tafsīr*) that could be used as a powerful missionary tool. They agreed that such translations could be used, firstly, to 'correct' the creed of non-Arabic speaking Muslims and, secondly, to promote the 'correct' version of Islam to non-Muslims. The core values of the Qur'an promoted by this approach as 'universal meanings' include Islam's two most important theological issues, namely, *tawḥīd* ('Divine Oneness') and *ᶜibāda* ('Worship of God'). The Salafi approach to translation generally prioritises theology over all other issues. In most of the translations produced in or for Saudi Arabian publishers, as well as those published by Saudi sponsors abroad, the foremost concern is how to interpret references to God's divine attributes. Many other issues are relegated to the periphery, to the extent that the reader is usually directed to consult other sources for information about them. It is only recently, during the 1990s and 2000s, that Saudi scholarship has started to contextualise issues such as the relationship between Islam and science, religious violence, interreligious relations, women rights, and so on. This process has also been subject to changing dynamics, broadly moving from more conservative (even 'radical') readings to more liberal interpretations in recent years. A good example of this, which has been reused throughout this volume, is the treatment of Q. 1:7—whether or not a translation names Jews and Christians in a rather negative context.

The majority of these theological shifts have mainly taken place following the establishment of a number of specific institutions in the 1960s, and, especially, the 1980s. The first Qur'an translations published in Saudi Arabia (into Uzbek and English) had nothing to do with Salafi scholarship, and even those works published by the Muslim World League still adhered to mainstream Sunni exegetical trends. It was only with the appearance of the KFGQPC that a new approach was implemented, one that prioritised a Salafi reading over all other interpretations. Sanctioned by state authorities, the translation movement in Saudi Arabia reached its highest point with the establishment of the KFGQPC. It was only then that 'authorised' versions of the translations of the Qur'an were published and the idea that an institutional effort produced a kind of 'theology of correct translation' entered the field. This emphasised that translation should not be (or even could not be) an individual undertaking but, instead, must be a communal expression of *ijmāᶜ* [scholarly consensus]. The model of the KFGQPC, with its numerous boards that 'approve' every work at various stages, has since been followed by many other publishers. Henceforth, the act of translation is only one part of a collective effort, and translators are sometimes rendered invisible to shift focus onto the numerous commissions and committees that revise and approve the text. This institutionalisation is exemplified by the many editions that are known as 'King Fahd Complex translations' rather than by the name of their translator/author.

However, not all of the complete and partial translations into one hundred different languages that have been published in Saudi Arabia, can be labelled as having 'Salafi/Wahhabi' hermeneutical features—and, of course, this raises the issue of how to contextualise this term at all. For example, if it comes to the 'literal' [*ẓāhir*] interpretation of divine attributes such as God's 'hand' [*yad*], which is mentioned in Q. 67:1, almost all existing translations, from late-medieval interlinear translations to so-called 'Orientalist' renditions, provide the same reading.[1] Those interpretations, especially once republished for a

1 For example, among more than twenty translations into Russian, there is only one that interprets *yad* as 'power' ['vlast'], see *Kalyam Sharif* (Kazan: Huzur, 2020).

second time after being first issued by institutions such as the KFGQPC, have made their way to readers in a broader Sunni or generally Muslim context, and are not limited to especially 'Salafi' religious circles.

It is also true that the Saudi translation networks were not the first to use *tafsīr* as their primary translation tool (albeit normally conceptualised as a kind of exegesis), and the question of which exegetical sources should be used to guide translation choices was always of paramount importance. From the early twentieth century onwards, Salafi scholarship developed its own canon of exegetes, starting from al-Ṭabarī and finishing with Ibn Kathīr. Another crucial set of questions has been how those interpretations are used, which opinions are selected and why, how reliable are printed editions grounded in the manuscript tradition, and what is the impact of the numerous 'abridgements' (*mukhtaṣar*s) on the transmission of information. It was partly because of these issues that publishers and revising committees (primarily the KFGQPC) started to recommend the use of contemporary interpretations with a one-dimensional hermeneutic. Relying on the modern tafsīr by the Saudi scholar ᶜAbd al-Raḥmān b. Nāṣir al-Saᶜdī, for example, is much easier than using classical works because it usually only gives one interpretation per verse. This simplification of meaning accords well with a strategy that aims to provide a clear-cut core text in translation.

Most of the key features of the modern Salafi approach are represented by one of the earliest and probably the most influential Saudi translations of the Qur'an, that by Hilālī and Khān. Even keeping in mind the fact that its later incarnations are much more influenced by Salafi hermeneutics than the earlier ones, the work was revolutionary in terms of both its language and approach. First, it used modern English (though neither al-Hilālī nor Khān were native speakers) and, secondly, it used plenty of *tafsīr* sources, mostly drawn from the classical Sunni corpus and the exegetical legacy of al-Ṭabarī, al-Qurṭubī, and Ibn Kathīr. This is probably the main reason why this translation has been so popular: it is not merely an English translation but is viewed as a

---

According to its introduction, this translation is designed to avoid any kind of 'literality', especially in the verses dealing with the divine attributes (labelled by the translators as 'ambiguous' ['nejasnyje']). From this point of view, it proposes its Sunni theological interpretation (in its Ashᶜarī/Māturīdī manifestation) as comprising a kind of 'correct' non-Arabic *tafsīr*, rather than an actual 'translation' of the text.

'trustworthy' interpretation. The authority of the Hilālī-Khān translation was further solidified by Darussalam's and other publishers' decision to retranslate it into a number of other languages because of its broad use of classical exegetical sources.

Another recent example of the Salafi approach can be seen in a partial translation of the Qur'an into English by Waleed Bleyhesh al-Amri, a Saudi scholar affiliated with Taibah University, who spent long time working in various research and administrative positions for the KFGQPC. Published in 2019 under the title *The Luminous Qur'an*, this comprises the first three suras of the Qur'an. Al-Amri includes plenty of commentary, in which he almost always mentions his exegetical sources, since, according to the introduction, 'the aim must be to overcome, as much as possible, the intermediary rule of the exegetical corpus—whose importance in understanding the Original is undeniable—in the actual representation available in the product of translation'.[2]

The recent trend of writing *tafsīr* specifically for translation, either as a whole or to be partially used in Qur'an translations (be it the KFGQPC-produced *al-Muyassar* or its recent alternative, *al-Mukhtaṣar*) also continues the classical trend of conceptualising translations as a kind of commentary. Such commentary, both then and now, prioritises the provision of a 'correct' perspective of religious creed and treats as secondary anything related to other aspects of the text such as literary style, historical background, and legal rules. This theological stance is the main reason that Salafi scholarship has generally remained critical of so-called Bucaillism, an attempt to harmonise modern science with Islamic belief. Even though numerous booklets talking about the compatibility of the Qur'an, Islam, and science are published in Saudi Arabia for missionary purposes, this trend has been less present in exegetical literature and, subsequently, in translations of the Qur'an. As Muḥammad b. Ṣāliḥ al-ᶜUthaymīn, a very popular Salafi religious authority, wrote in his commentary on Q. 35:13:[3]

2 Waleed Bleyhesh al-Amri, *The Luminous Qur'an. A Faithful Rendition, Annotated Translation of the First Three Suras of the Message of God by Waleed Bleyhesh al-Amri* (Medina: Endowment for Cherishing the Two Glorious Revelations, 1440/2019), p. 38.

3 'He makes the night merge into the day and the day into the night; He has subjected the sun and the moon—each runs for an appointed term' (Abdel Haleem).

> We do not agree nor disagree with the question of whether the Earth is revolving around the Sun or not: maybe it revolves, maybe the sun also revolves [...] What is the benefit of this kind of knowledge? Glory to Allah, who made Earth firm, revolves it or not.[4]

First and foremost, he suggests, readers' focus should be on belief and worship rather than scientific understanding.

When it comes to the promotion of these Qur'an translations, many digital projects realised in Saudi Arabia are playing a critical role. Texts are available on KFGQPC websites or via multilanguage resources like IslamHouse.com, and newer projects are being developed for use in specialised apps. Processes of digitisation contribute to the 'standardisation' of Qur'an interpretations in order to expedite their dissemination in many languages. The result is an even further simplification of the text, as can be illustrated by the recent example of *al-Tafsīr al-mukhtaṣar* and its translation. Another case in point is the Saudi-based Rowwad Translation Center, the main caretaker of QuranEnc.com, probably the biggest (in terms of the number of translations uploaded) online source for Qur'anic interpretations. This project was initiated in 2019 with the help of IslamHouse, through the efforts of their director Shaykh Ibrāhīm b. ᶜAbd al-ᶜAzīz al-ᶜUlī. Financed by donations from the Awqaf Mohammed Abdelaziz al-Rajhi Foundation, the Rowwad Translation Center now curates material on QuranEnc.Com in over sixty languages (which includes around a hundred complete translations of the Quran), many of which have been 'corrected'. The 'corrections' implemented by the Rowwad Translation Center mostly relate to Salafi theological issues such as their stance on God's divine attributes. As of the beginning of 2023, this emerging network has produced five more or less 'new' translations in just three years: into Fulani, English, Bosnian, Tamil, and Serbian. The last of these is obviously based on their Bosnian translation, while the Bosnian translation itself looks somewhat like an edited version of the Besim Korkut translation (also published by the KFGQPC). It is not entirely clear whether these have already been distributed in printed form, but the digital versions contain King Fahd National Library cataloguing numbers, ISBNs, and a publishing

4 Muḥammad al-ᶜUthaymīn, *Tafsīr al-Qurʾān al-karīm*, 36 vols (Qasim: Muʾassasat Muḥammad b. Ṣāliḥ al-ᶜUthaymīn al-Khayriyya, 1436/2014), xxxvi, p. 117.

date, so some copies at least must exist in print as well. Their format is very similar to the translations printed by KFGQPC—a short formal introduction followed by a translation with parallel Arabic text in verse-by-verse style.[5] What is noteworthy about these works is that they make no mention of the names of any translators or editors at all, listing just the name of the Rowwad Translation Center.

Innovative in the production of both printed and digital versions, Saudi Arabia continues to demonstrate more support for and promotion of Qur'an translations, both at official and private levels, than any other country. Huge investment in this field in the 1960s and 1970s led to the growth of a flourishing Qur'an translation industry, and it is hard to believe that its supremacy will be challenged by any other state or institution in the near feature. Whether the works themselves are accepted or criticised, popularised or neglected, Qur'an translations published in Saudi Arabia or with Saudi support abroad now undoubtedly constitute the biggest contribution to the contemporary Muslim understanding of the sacred text of Islam at a global level.

5 See *Plemeniti Kur'an Prijevod značenja na bosanski jezik* (Riyadh: Jamaᶜat al-Daᶜwa wa-l-Irshād al-Taᶜwiyya al-Jāliyāt bi-l-Rabwa, 1444/2022).

Bibliography

A Kegyes Korán értelmi és tartalmi fordítása magyar nyelvre (Medina: King Fahd Glorious Qur'an Printing Complex, 2009)

Abay, Muhammet, 'Türkçedeki Kur'an Meâllerinin Tarihi ve Kronolojik Bibliyografyası', *Türkiye Araştırmaları Literatür Dergisi, 10.19–20 (2012), 232–303*

ᶜAbd al-Raḥīm, F., *Iqsām al-aymān fī aqsām al-Qurᵓān* (Damascus: Dār al-Qalām, 2016)

Abdel Haleem, M.A.S., *The Qur'an: English Translation and Parallel Arabic Text* (Oxford: Oxford University Press, 2010)

Abdou Daouda, Cheikh Boreima, *Le sens des versets du Saint Qour'ân* (Riyadh: Darussalam, 1999)

Abdul-Raof, Hussein, *Qur'an Translation: Discourse, Texture and Exegesis* (London–New York: Routledge, 2001), https://doi.org/10.4324/9780203036990

Afandī, Ismāᶜīl Ḥaqqī, *Rūḥ al-bayān*, 10 vols (Beirut: Dār Iḥyāᵓ al-Turāth al-ᶜArabī, 1985)

Ahmeti, Sherif, *Kur'an-i përkthim me komentim në gjuhën shqipe* (Medina: King Fahd Glorious Qur'an Printing Complex, 1992)

Āl al-Shaykh, Abd al-Raḥmān, *al-Muḥajja* (Riyadh: Maktabat Dār al-Hidāya, [n. d.])

—— *Mashāhir ᶜulamāᵓ al-Najd* (Riyadh: Dār al-Yamama, 1974)

Al-Faruqi, Ismail, *Toward Islamic English* (Riyadh: International Islamic Publishing House, 1995)

Ali, Syed Nazim, Wijdan Tariq, and Bahnaz Al Quradaghi, eds, *The Edinburgh Companion to Shariᶜah Governance in Islamic Finance* (Edinburgh: Edinburgh University Press, 2020)

Al-Kur'ani mai girma. Da Kuma Tarjaman Maᶜanōninsa Zuwa Ga Harshen Hausa (Beirut: Dār al-ᶜArabiyya, 1979)

Al-Kurani ti a tumo si ede Yorub (Beirut: Dār al-ᶜArabiyya, 1973)

Allan, J. A., and Kaoru Sugihara, *Japan and the Contemporary Middle East* (London: Taylor and Francis, 2005), [first, 1993 edn:] https://doi.org/10.4324/9780203975060

Al Quran Dan Terjemahnya (Riyadh: Darussalam, 2010)

Al Saud, Abdulmohsen, 'The Development of Saudi Arabia in King Fahd's Era', *Asian Culture and History*, 10.1 (2018), 48–57, http://doi.org.10.5539/ach.v10n1p48

Altay, Halifa, *Kälam-Şarïf: tüzetip, tolıqtırıp bastırwsı X. Altay* (Istanbul: Elïf-ofset baspası, 1989)

—— *Quran Kärim: qazaqsa mağına jäne tüsinigi* (Medina: King Fahd Glorious Qur'an Printing Complex, 1991)

—— *Quran Şarïf* (Almatı: Jazwşı: Sözstan, 1991)

al-Alūsī, Shihāb al-Dīn, *Rūḥ al-maᶜānī fī tafsīr al-Qurʾān al-ᶜaẓīm wa-l-sabᶜa al-mathānī*, 11 vols (Beirut: Dār al-Kutub al-ᶜIlmiyya, 2014)

Amghar, Samir, 'The Muslim World League in Europe: An Islamic Organization to Serve the Saudi Strategic Interests?', *Journal of Muslims in Europe*, 1.2 (2012), 127–41

al-Amri, Waleed Bleyhesh, *The Luminous Qur'an. A Faithful Rendition, Annotated Translation of the First Three Suras of the Message of God by Waleed Bleyhesh al-Amri* (Medina: Endowment for Cherishing the Two Glorious Revelations, 1440/2019)

Asad, Muḥammad, 'al-Muqaddima fī tarjamat al-Qurʾān', *The Muslim World League Journal*, 11 (1964), 42–54.

—— *The Message of the Qurʾān (Suras 1–9)* (Mecca: Muslim World League, 1964).

—— *The Message of the Qurʾān, Translated and Explained by Muhammad Asad* (Gibraltar: Dar al-Andalus, 1980)

'Asım ve Sabri Ülker kardeşlerin 43 yıllık ortaklığını, yönetimdeki uyuşmazlık bitiriyor', http://sabriulkerinhayathikayesi.com/hikaye/asim-ve-sabri-ulker-kardeslerin-43-yillik-ortakligini-yonetimdeki-uyusmazlik-bitiriyor

Ateş, Süleyman, *Kur'an-ı Kerim Meali* (Istanbul: Yüksel Matbaası, 1974)

—— *Kur'an-ı Kerim ve Yüce Meali* (Ankara: Kılıç Kitabevi, 1977)

Aṭfayyash, Muḥammad, *Taysīr al-tafsīr* (Muscat: Wizārat al-Turāth wa-l-Thaqāfa, 2004)

Balci, Bayram, 'Central Asian Refugees in Saudi Arabia: Religious Evolution and Contributing to the Reislamisation of Their Motherland', *Refugee Survey Quarterly*, 26.2 (2007), 2–21

Baltabayeva, K. N., S. E. Azhigali, S. S. Korabay, G. Gabbasuly, R. S. Kozhakhmetov, K. M. Konyrbayeva, and Abd. H. Altay, eds, *Altay Halifa Gaqypuly: Biobibliographic Index* (Almaty: [n. pub.], 2017).

al-Barwānī, ᶜAlī Muḥsin, *Tafsiri ya maana ya Qur'an Tukufu kwa lugha ya Kiswahili* (Riyadh: Darussalam, 2012)

al-Bayṭār, Muḥammad Bahja, 'Naqḍ al-manṭiq', *Majallat mujammaᶜ al-ᶜilmī al-ᶜArabī*, 27 (1952), 300–02

Bint Mohamed, Aicha, 'Une traduction mauritanienne du Saint Coran', *al-Mutarǧim*, 10.1 (2010), 27–36

Binark, İsmet, Halit Eren, and Ekmeleddin İhsanoğlu, *World Bibliography of Translations of the Meanings of the Holy Qurʾān: Printed Translations, 1515–1980* (Istanbul: Research Centre for Islamic History, Art, and Culture, 1986)

al-Birmāwī, Ilyās, *Imtāᶜa al-fuḍalāʾ bi-tarājim al-qurāʾa fīmā baᶜd al-qarn al-thāmin al-hijrī*, 2 vols (Riyadh: Dār al-Nadwa al-ᶜĀlamiyya, 2000)

Bodley, R. V. C., *The Messenger: The Life of Mohammad* (New York: Doubleday & Company, Inc., 1966)

Brigaglia, Andrea, 'Two Published Hausa Translations of the Qurʾân and Their Doctrinal Background', *Journal of Religion in Africa*, 35.4 (2005), 424–49

Būdlī, R. F., *al-Rasūl: hayāt Muḥammad*, trans. by ᶜAbd al-Ḥamīd al-Saḥḥār and Muḥammad Faraj (Cairo: Maktabat Miṣr, 1946)

al-Bukhārī, *al-Jāmiᶜ al-ṣaḥīḥ*, trans. by Muhammad Muhsin Khan (Ghakkhar: Sethi Straw Board Mills Ltd, 1971)

al-Bulūshī, ᶜAbd al-Gafūr, 'Tārīkh taṭwīr tarjamāt maᶜānī al-Qurʾān ilā al-Fārisiyya', in *Abḥāth al-nadwa tarjamat maᶜānī al-Qurʾān: taqwīm li-l-māḍī wa-takhṭīṭ li-l-mustaqbal*, 2 vols (Medina: King Fahd Glorious Qur'an Printing Complex, 2002)

—— *Tafsīr Qurʾāni karīm* (Lahore: Dawᶜatu l-Ḥaqq, 1433/2011)

Campanini, Massimo, *The Qur'an: Modern Muslim Interpretations*, trans. by Caroline Higgitt (London—New York: Routledge, 2010)

de Carbonnel, Alissa, 'Russian Muslim Clerics Warn of Unrest over Ban of Translation of Koran', 20 September 2013, https://www.reuters.com/article/us-russia-koran-idUSBRE98J0YW20130920

Channā, Amīr Buaksh, *Qur'āni Karīm, Tarjami e Tafsīr* (Riyadh: Darussalam, 2018)

Dar-us-Salam Publications, 'Muhammad Muhsin Khan', https://dar-us-salam.com/authors/muhsin-khan.htm

'Al-Ḍawᶜ ᶜalā tarjmāt al-Qurʾān', *The Muslim World League Journal*, 10 (1964), 42–44

Del Noble Coran (Riyadh: Darussalam, 2003)

Dobrev, Ivan, *Svescheniyat Koran, prevod od Ivan Dobrev* (Sofia: BMK, 2008)

'Dr. Muhammad Muhsin Khan Passes Away', *Muslim Mirror*, https://muslimmirror.com/eng/dr-muhammad-muhsin-khan-passes-away/

'Dr Wajih Abderrahman, Major Linguistics Scholar Passes Away', *Muslim World Journal*, https://www.muslimworldjournal.com/dr-wajih-abderrahman-major-linguistics-scholar-passes-away/

al-Ḍubayb, Aḥmad, *Bawākīr al-ṭibāʿa wa-l-maṭbūʿāt fī bilād al-ḥaramayn al-sharifayn* (Riyadh: KFNL, 1408/1987)

Eden, Anthony, and Moustapha el-Nahas, 'Anglo-Egyptian Treaty of Alliance, 1936', *Current History*, 22.128 (1952), 231–39

El Corán. Traducción en lengua española latinoamericana (Riyadh: Al Muntada Al Islami, 2017)

el-Hilâlî, Muhammed Takıyüddin, see al-Hilālī, Taqī al-Dīn

El Noble Coran y Su Traduccion Comentario En Lengua Española (Medina: King Fahd Glorious Qur'an Printing Complex, 1997)

Elma Ruth Harder, 'Muhammad Asad and the Road to Mecca: Text of Muhammad Asad's Interview with Karl Günter Simon', *Islamic Studies*, 37.4 (1998), 533–44

Elnemr, M. I. R., 'The Ideological Impact on the English Translations of the Qur'an: A Case Study of Muhammad Asad's Translation', *International Journal of Linguistics, Literature, and Translation*, 3.7 (2020), 30–41

Elyas, Tariq, and Michelle Picard, 'A Brief History of English and English Teaching in Saudi Arabia', in *English as a Foreign Language in Saudi Arabia: New Insights into Teaching and Learning English*, ed. by Christo Moskovsky and Michelle Picard (London: Routledge, 2019), pp. 70–84

Emer, Emin, *Kurani Me perkthim ne gjuhen shqipe* (Istanbul: Çağrı Yayınları, 2007)

'EP 094—Atheism to Islam, Translating the Qur'an, Running a Publishing House—Amatullah Bantley', *Ilmfeed Podcast*, 10 April 2022, https://www.youtube.com/watch?v=4uPU4eM4sMo

Faruk, Usman, *The Life and Times of Sheikh Abubakar Mahmud Gumi: Lessons for the Muslim Ummah* (Zaria: Ahmadu Bello University Press Limited, 2013)

Fatāwā al-lajna al-dāʾima li-l-buḥūth al-ʿilmiyya wa-l-iftāʾ, 4 vols (Riyadh: Maktabat al-ʿUbaykān / Riʾāsat Idārat al-Buḥūth al-ʿIlmiyya wa-l-Iftāʾ, 1412/1992)

al-Fawzān, Ṣāliḥ b. Fawzān, *Sharḥ ʿaqīdat al-Imām Muḥammad b. ʿAbd al-Wahhāb* (Riyadh: Maktabat al-Minhāj, 1436/2011)

Fremantle, Anne, *Loyal Enemy* (London: Hutchinson & Co, 1938)

Garcia, Isa, *El Corán. Traducción Comentada. Traducción Isa Garcia* (Bogota: [n. pub.], 2013).

Gardet, L., 'Karāma', in *Encyclopaedia of Islam, Second Edition*, ed. by P. Bearman, Th. Bianquis, C. E. Bosworth, E. van Donzel, and W. P. Heinrichs (Leiden: Brill, 2006) http://dx.doi.org/10.1163/1573-3912_islam_COM_0445

Ḥabīb, Aḥmad, *al-Sayyid Ḥabīb b. Maḥmūd Aḥmad: lamaḥāt min sīra ḥayāt wa-masīra injāz* (Medina: [n. pub.], 1434/2013)

al-Ḥajjawī, Muḥammad, 'al-Wahhābiyyūn Sunniyyūn Ḥanābila', *al-Sirāt al-Sawī*, 1.3 (1352/1933), 45–47

—— *Ḥukm tarjamat al-Qurʾān al-ʿaẓīm* (Tétouan: [n. pub.], 2011)

Ḥāmid, ʿAbd Allāh b. Muḥammad, *al-Jihād fī al-Qurʾān wa-l-sunna* (Qasim–Burayda: Dār al-Bukhārī, [n. d.])

Hamidi, Shaikhalislam, *al-Itqān fī tarjamat al-Qurʾān* (Doha: [n. pub.], 1987)

Hamidullah, Muhammad, *Le Coran : Texte original en arabe et traduction française par M. Hamidullah* (Ankara: Hilal Yayinlari; Beyrouth: Salih Ozcan, 1973)

—— *Le Saint Coran* (Paris: Club Français du Livre, 1959)

—— *Le Saint Coran et la traduction en langue française de ses sens* (Medina: King Fahd Glorious Qur'an Printing Complex, 1989)

—— 'Lettre ouverte du Pr. M. Hamidullah au Roi Fahd de l'Arabie Saoudite', *Le Musulman*, 5.6 (1989), 13–15

Hanania, Aida, and Jean Lauand, *O diplomata da língua e cultura árabes—estudos em homenagem a Helmi Nasr* (São Paulo: Factash Editora, 2015)

Ḥaqqī, Ismaʿīl, *Rūḥ al-bayān*, 10 vols (Beirut: Dār Iḥyāʾ al-Turāth al-ʿArabī, 1985)

Harder, Elma Ruth, 'Muhammad Asad and the Road to Mecca: Text of Muhammad Asad's Interview with Karl Günter Simon', *Islamic Studies*, 37.4 (1998), 533–44

Hasan, Muhammad Haniff, 'Mobilization of Muslims for Jihad: Insights from the Past and Their Relevance Today', *Counter Terrorist Trends and Analyses*, 5.8 (2013), 10–15

Hawamdeh, Mohammad, and Kais Kadhim, 'Parenthetical Cohesive Explicitness: A Linguistic Approach for a Modified Translation of the Quranic Text', *International Journal of Applied Linguistics & English Literature*, 4.5 (2015), 161–69, http://dx.doi.org/10.7575/aiac.ijalel.v.4n.5p.161

Henning, Max, *Der Gnadenreiche Koran* (Ankara: DITIB, 1991)

al-Hilālī, Taqī al-Dīn (Taki Ed Din Al Hilali), *Die Einleitung zu al-Bīrūnīs Steinbuch. Mit Erläuterungen übersetzt.* Dissertation unter Aufsicht von Richard Hartmann und Hans Heinrich Schaeder. Mit einer Widmung an Herbert W. Duda (Leipzig: Harrassowitz, 1941)

—— 'Taᶜlīm al-lugāt: ḥukmuhu wa-fīᶜīdatahu', *Lisān al-dīn*, 3.10 (1949), 7–10

—— 'al-Taqaddum wa-l-rajaᵓiyya', *Majallat al-jāmiᶜa al-Islāmiyya* 1.2 (1969), 8–10

—— (Muhammed Takıyüddin el-Hilâlî), 'Misyoner ve Müsteşriklerin İslam Düşmanlığı', *İslam'ın İlk Emri Oku*, 10.120 (1972), 16

—— (Muhammed Takıyüddin el-Hilâlî), 'Misyoner ve Müsteşriklerin İslam Düşmanlığı', *İslam'ın İlk Emri Oku*, 11.12 (1972), 12

—— (Muhammed Takıyüddin el-Hilâlî), 'Hz. İsa'nın İnsan Olduğuna ve İlahlıkla İlgisinin Bulunmadığına Dair İncil'den Kesin Deliller', *Diyanet İlmi Dergi Yazı*, 16.2 (1977), 101–16

—— *Taqwīm al-lisānayn* (Cairo: Maktabat al-Maᶜārif, 1978)

—— *al-Daᶜwa ilā Allāh fī aqṭār mukhtalifa* (al-Shārqa: Maktabat al-Ṣaḥāba, 2003)

—— *Sabīl al-rashād fī hudā khayr al-ᶜabbād*, 4 vols (Amman: al-Dār al-Athriyya, 2006)

al-Hilālī, Taqī al-Dīn, and Muḥammad Muḥsin Khān, *Explanatory English Translation of the Holy Qur'an, by Taqī al-Dīn al-Hilālī, Muḥammad Muḥsin Khān* (Chicago: Kazi Publications, 1977)

—— *Explanatory English Translation of the Holy Qur'an, by Taqī al-Dīn al-Hilālī, Muḥammad Muḥsin Khān* (Ankara: Hilal Yayınları, 1978)

—— *Explanatory English Translation of the Holy Qur'an, by Taqī al-Dīn al-Hilālī, Muḥammad Muḥsin Khān* (Riyadh: Maktab al-Rāᵓīs al-ᶜĀmm, 1985)

—— *Interpretation of The Meaning of The Noble Quran* (Istanbul: Hilal Yayınları, 2018)

—— *The Noble Qur'an*, tr. by Taqī al-Dīn al-Hilālī and Muḥammad Muḥsin Khān (Riyadh: Darussalam, 1997)

—— *The Noble Qur'an: Translation of the Meanings and Commentary* (Medina: King Fahd Glorious Qur'an Printing Complex, 1997)

—— *The Noble Qur'an: Translation of the Meanings and Commentary* (Medina: King Fahd Glorious Qur'an Printing Complex, 2019)

Hoxha, Salih Ferhat, *Kur'ani me përkthim në gjuhën shqipe nga Ferhat Hoxha* (Skopje: Logos—A, 2016)

Ibn Ḥasan, ᶜAbd al-Raḥmān, *Bayān kalimat al-tawḥīd wa-l-radd ᶜalā al-Kashmīrī ᶜAbd al-Maḥmūd*, in *Majmūᶜ al-rasāᵓil wa-l-masāᵓil al-Najdiyya*, 4 vols (Cairo: al-Manār, 1926)

Ibn Qudāma, *Kitāb al*-Mughnī, 15 vols (Riyadh: Dār ᶜAlām al-Kutub, 1997)

Ibn Taymiyya, *Naqḍ al-manṭiq* (Cairo: Dār al-Maᶜrifa, 1951)

—— *al-Tisᶜīyniyya* (Riyadh: Maktabat al-Maᶜārif, 1999)

—— *al-Radd ʿalā-l-manṭiqiyyīn* (Beirut: al-Rayān, 2005)

—— *Naqḍ al-manṭiq* (Riyadh: Dār ʿAlām al-Fawāʾīd, 1435/2013)

Ibrahim, Hassan Ahmed, 'Shaykh Muḥammad ibn ʿAbd al-Wahhāb and Shāh Walī Allāh: A Preliminary Comparison, Some Aspects of their Lives and Careers', *Asian Journal of Social Science,* 34.1 (2006), 103–19

Ichwan, Moch Nur, 'Differing Responses to an Ahmadi Translation and Exegesis: The Holy Qurʾân in Egypt and Indonesia', *Archipel,* 62 (2001), 143–61

İngilizce ve Türkçe Olarak Kur'anʿı Kerimʿin Meali ve Tefsiri (Riyadh: Darussalam, 2004)

International Publishers Association, 'IPA Country Report on Saudi Arabia', 30 June 1916, https://www.internationalpublishers.org/copyright-news-blog/410-ipa-country-report-saudi-arabia

Ismail, Raihan, *Saudi Clerics and Shia Islam* (Oxford: Oxford University Press, 2019), https://doi.org/10.1093/acprof:oso/9780190233310.001.0001

Jabo, Sahabi Maidamma, and Umar Ubandawaki, 'Nigeria-Saudi Arabia: Socio-Cultural and Educational Relations', *RIMA International Journal of Historical Studies (RIJHIS),* 4.1 (2019), 29–37

Jassem, Zaidan Ali, '*The Noble Quran*: A Critical Evaluation of Al-Hilali and Khan's Translation', *International Journal of English and Education,* 3.2 (2014), 237–73

Jawad, Haifaa A., 'Pan-Islamism and Pan-Arabism: Solution or Obstacle to Political Reconstruction in the Middle East?', in *The Middle East in the New World Order*, ed. by H. A. Jawad (London: Palgrave Macmillan, 1997), 140–61

al-Jawālīqī, Abū Manṣūr Mawhūb, *al-Muʿarrab,* ed. by F. ʿAbd al-Raḥīm (Damascus: Dār al-Qalām, 1990)

al-Jazāʾirī, Abū Bakr, *Aysar al-tafāsir li-l-kalām al-ʿalī al-kabīr,* 2 vols (Jeddah: Rāsim, 1990)

Joseph, Abdul-Haleem, *Den Ädla Koranens fem första delar* (Medina: King Fahd Glorious Qur'an Printing Complex, 2011)

Kalyam Sharif (Kazan: Huzur, 2020)

Karamustafa, Ahmet T., 'Islamic Dīn as an Alternative to Western Models of "Religion"', in *Religion, Theory, Critique,* ed. by Richard King (New York: New York Columbia University Pres, 2017), pp. 163–72

Khan, Abdul Majid, 'A Critical Study of Muhammad Asad's The Message of the Qur'an' (unpublished doctoral thesis, Aligarh Muslim University, 1980

Khan, Mofakhkhar Husain, 'Translation of the Holy Qurʾān in the African Languages', *The Muslim World,* 77.3–4 (1987), 250–58

Khiyāṭ, ᶜAbd Allāh, *al-Tafsīr al-muyassar: khulāṣat muqtabasa min ashhār al-tafāsīr al-muᶜtabara* (Jeddah: Maktabat al-Najāḥ, 1377/1958)

Khurramshāhī, Bahāᵓ al-Dīn, 'Terjume Shāh Weli Allāh Dehlawi', *Terjuman e-Wahy*, 9 (Shahriyār 1380), 61–71.

Khustuntdinov, Fillip, '"Turkestani Muslim Communities ... Have Been Deprived of this Happiness": The Dissemination of Tarazi's Qur'an Translation and Exegesis in Soviet Uzbekistan', *Islamology*, 11.1 (2021), 84–103, http://dx.doi.org/10.24848/islmlg.11.1.07

Kidwai, Abdul Raheem, 'Review on Hilali's and Khan's *Noble Quran*', *Muslim World Book Review*, 15 (1995), 3–5

—— *Bibliography of The Translations of The Meanings of The Glorious Quran into English: 1649–2002* (Medina: King Fahd Glorious Qur'an Printing Complex, 2007)

—— 'Muhammad Marmaduke Pickthall's English Translation of the Quran (1930): An Assessment', in *Marmaduke Pickthall: Islam and the Modern World*, ed. by Geoffrey P. Nash (Leiden: Brill, 2017), pp. 230–47, https://doi.org/10.1163/9789004327597_013

—— *God's Word, Man's Interpretations: A Critical Study of the 21st Century English Translation of the Quran* (New Delhi: Viva Books, 2018)

Korkut, Besim, *Kur'an: prevod Besim Korkut* (Sarajevo: Orijentalni institut, 1977)

—— *Kur'an s prevodom* (Medina: King Fahd Glorious Qur'an Printing Complex, 1991)

Koutlaki, Sofia, and Hekmatollah Salehi, 'Quranic Translation in Greek: Challenges and Opportunities', in *International Conference for Quranic Translation* (Tehran: Allameh TIbataba'i University, 2014), pp. 125–34

Kramer, Martin, 'The Road from Mecca: Muhammad Asad (born Leopold Weis)', in *The Jewish Discovery of Islam: Studies in Honor of Bernard Lewis*, ed. by Martin Kramer (Tel Aviv: The Moshe Dayan Center for Middle Eastern and African Studies, 1999), pp. 225–47

—— 'Pan-Asianism's Religious Undercurrents: The Reception of Islam and Translation of the Qur'ān in Twentieth-Century Japan', *The Journal of Asian Studies*, 73.3 (2014), 632–35, https://doi.org/10.1017/S0021911814000989

Kryms'kyi, Agatangel, and Ol. Bogolybskyi, *Do istorii wyschoi osvity u arabiv* (Kyiv: Vseukrainska Akademiya Nauk, 1928)

Kuiper, Matthew J., *Daᶜwa: A Global History of Islamic Missionary Thought and Practice* (Edinburgh: Edinburgh University Press, 2021), https://doi.org/10.1515/9781474451543

Kumru, Coşkun, and Sevil Gözübüyük, 'Esir Türkistan Yargılanıyor: Veli Kayyum Hanᶜın Nürnberg Sorgulamalarına Dair Notlar', *Journal of Social and Humanities Sciences Research*, 7.58 (2020), 2424–433

Kur'an so Prevod (Medina: King Fahd Glorious Qur'an Printing Complex, 1997)

Kur'an-ı Kerim ve Açıklamalı Meali (Istanbul: Ayyıldız Matbaası, 1982)

Kur'an-ı Kerim ve Yüce Meali (Ankara: Kılıç Kitabevi, 1977)

Kurani Me perkthim ne gjuhen shqipe, Përktheu Emin İmre (Istanbul: Çağrı Yayınları, 2007)

al-Kūsūfī, Rajab, *al-Ittijāh al-ᶜaqdī li-l-Shaykh Sharīf Aḥmadī min khilāl muʾllafātihi wa-atharihi ᶜalā al-wāqiᶜ* (Baghdad: Dār al-Māʾmūn li-l-Nashr wa-l-Tawzīᶜ, 2010)

Lauzière, Henri, 'The Evolution of the Salafiyya in the Twentieth Century Through the Life and Thought of Taqi al-Din al-Hilali' (unpublished doctoral dissertation, Georgetown University, 2008)

—— 'Islamic Nationalism through the Airwaves: Taqī al-Dīn al-Hilālī's Encounter with Shortwave Radio 1937–39', *Die Welt des Islams*, 56.1 (2016), 6–33, https://doi.org/10.1163/15700607-00561p03

Lawal, A. I., 'Sheikh Aminuddeen Abubakar: A Scholar per excellent', *The Pen*, 2.8 (1987), 7

Lawrence, Bruce B., *The Koran in English: A Biography* (Princeton: Princeton University Press, 2017)

Le Noble Coran et la traduction en langue française de ses sen (Medina : King Fahd Glorious Qur'an Printing Complex, 2007)

Le Noble Coran. Nouvelle traduction. Traduit par l'équipe des éditions Zeino (Paris : Éditions Zeino, 2012)

Lepeska, David, 'Islamic Publishing House Flourishes in US', *The National News*, https://www.thenationalnews.com/world/the-americas/islamic-publishing-house-flourishes-in-us-1.436788

'Liqāʾ ṣuḥufī maᶜa al-duktūr', *Majallat al-jāmiᶜa al-Islāmiyya*, 12 (1971), 4–6

Lukman, Fadhli, *The Official Indonesian Qurʾān Translation* (Cambridge: Open Book Publishers, 2022), https://doi.org/10.11647/OBP.0289

al-Maʾāyrigī, Ḥasan, *al-Hayʾa al-ᶜalamiyya li-l-Qurʾān al-karīm: ḍarūrahu li-l-daᶜwa wa-l-tablīgh* (Doha: [n. pub]., 1991)

—— (Ma'ayergi, Hasan), 'Translations of the Meanings of the Holy Qur'an into Minority Languages: The Case of Africa', *Institute of Muslim Minority Affairs Journal*, 14.1-2 (1993), 156–80

'al-Madrasa al-layliyya li-taᶜlīm al-luga al-Injliziyya al-Fārisiyya wa-l-Urdiyya', *Ṣawt al-Ḥijāz*, 28 April 1936, p. 4

al-Makkī, Majd, 'Rāḥil al-ᶜAllāma al-Duktūr ᶜAbd al-Azīz Ismāᶜīl', https://islamsyria.com/ar/التراجم/المترجمين/جمع-وترتيب-مجد-مكي

al-Makkī, Muḥammad b. Ṭāhir al-Kurdī, *Tārīkh al-Qurʾān wa-garāʾīb rasmihi wa-ḥukmihi* (Jeddah: al-Fatḥ, 1946)

—— *Tārīkh al-Qurʾān wa-garāʾīb rasmihi wa-ḥukmihi* (Cairo: Maṭbaᶜat Muṣṭafā al-Bābī al-Ḥalabī, 1953)

—— *Irshād al-zumra li-manāsik al-ḥajj wa-l-ᶜumra ᶜalā madhhab al-Imām al-Shāfiᶜī* (Cairo: Maṭbaᶜat Muṣṭafā al-Bābī al-Ḥalabī, 1955)

—— *Tabarruk al-saḥāba* (Cairo: Maktabat al-Qāhira, 1987)

—— *Tārīkh al-Qurʾān wa-garāʾīb rasmihi wa-ḥukmihi* (Riyadh: Dār Aḍwāʾ al-Salaf li-l-Nashr wa-l-Tawzīᶜ, 2008)

al-Marāghī, *Baḥth fī tarjamat al-Qurʾān al-karīm wa-aḥkāmuhā* (Cairo: Maṭbaᶜat al-Raghāʾib, 1936)

—— *Tafsīr al-Marāghī*, 30 vols (Cairo: Sharikat al-Ḥalabbī, 1946)

Martin, Justin D., Ralph J. Martins, and Shageaa Naqvi, 'Do Arabs Really Read Less? "Cultural Tools" and "More Knowledgeable Others" as Determinants of Book Reliance in Six Arab Countries', *International Journal of Communication*, 11 (2017), 3374–393

Massimo Campanini, *The Qur'an: Modern Muslim Interpretations*, trans. by Caroline Higgitt (London and New York: Routledge, 2010)

Mirza, Younus Y., 'Tafsīr Ibn Kathīr: A Window onto Medieval Islam and a Guide to the Development of Modern Islamic Orthodoxy', in *The Routledge Companion to the Qur'an*, ed. by George Archer, Maria Dakake, and Daniel Madigan (London: Routledge, 2022) pp. 245–52, http://doi.org/10.4324/9781315885360-26

al-Miṣrī, Muḥammad Amīn, *Min hudā Sūrat al-Anfāl* (Kuwait: Dār al-Arqam, [n. d.])

Mohamed, Aicha Bint, 'Une Traduction Mauritanienne Du Saint Coran', *Al-Mutargim*, 10.1 (2010), 27–36

Mohammed, Khaleel, 'Assessing English Translations of the Qur'an', *Middle East Quarterly*, 12.2 (2005), 58–71

Motadel, David, *Islam and Nazi Germany's War* (Cambridge: The Belknap Press of Harvard University Press, 2014)

Mujahid, Talha, 'Darussalam—the Global Leader in Islamic Publications', *Saudi Gazette*, 26 June 2023, https://saudigazette.com.sa/article/161230

'Mujammaᶜ al-Maliki Fahd', *Fayṣal Magazine*, 13 (1990), 51–57

al-Mukhtaṣar fī tafsīr al-Qurʾān (Riyadh: Markaz al-Tafsīr li-l-Dirāsāt al-Qurʾāniyya, 1436/2014)

al-Mukhtaṣar fī tafsīr al-Qurʾān al-karīm (Riyadh: Markaz Tafsīr li-l-Dirāsāt al-Qurʾāniyya, 1441/2021)

Muminov, Vahrom, and Valihan Alihanov, 'Prosvetitel iz Taraza', *Znamya truda*, 12 November 2005, pp. 2–5

al-Muntakhab fī tafsīr al-Qurʾān al-karīm (Cairo: al-Majlis al-Aᶜlā li-l-Shuᶜūn al-Islāmiyya, 1381/1961)

Muqaddimat tarjamāt al-Qurʾān al-karīm (Medina: King Fahd Glorious Qur'an Printing Complex, 2019)

Musa, Mohd Faizal, 'The Riyal and Ringgit of Petro-Islam: Investing Salafism in Education', in *Islam in Southeast Asia: Negotiating Modernity*, ed. by Norshahril Saat (Singapore: ISEAS Publishing, 2018)

Muṣḥaf al-Madīna al-sharīf wa-iqtirāḥ al-amīr Nāṣir al-Shaghār http://www.otaibah.net/m/archive/index.php/t-117246.html

Mustafa, Abdul Rahman, 'Ibn Taymiyya & Wittgenstein on Language', *The Muslim World*, 108.3 (2018), 465–91

al-Muᶜtāz, ᶜAbd Allāh, *al-Fawāʾīd al-ḥisān min ayāt al-Qurʾān* (Riyadh: Darussalam, 2006)

al-Nadwī, ᶜAbd Allāh ᶜAbbās, *Vocabulary of the Holy Qur'an* (Jeddah: Dār al-Shurūq, 1983)

—— *Tarjamāt maᶜānī al-Qurʾān al-karīm wa-taṭwīr fahmihi ᶜind al-gharb* (Mecca: Muslim World League, 1996)

Nadwi, Abul Hasan Ali, 'Education and Society in Saudi Arabia', in *Education and Society in the Muslim World*, ed. by M. W. Khan (Jeddah: King Abdulaziz University, 1981), 89–99

Nafi, Basheer M., 'A Teacher of Ibn ᶜAbd al-Wahhāb: Muḥammad Ḥayāt al-Sindī and the Revival of *Ashāb al-Hadīth*'s Methodology', *Islamic Law and Society*, 1.2 (2006), 103–18, http://doi.org/10.1163/156851906776917552

al-Nāṣir, Muḥammad Ḥāmid, *Ulamāʾ al-Shām fī qarn al-ᶜashrīn* (Kuwait: Dār al-Maᶜālī, [n. d.])

Naṣr, Ḥilmī, 'Tārīkh taṭwīr tarjamāt maᶜānī al-Qurʾān ilā al-Burtugāliya', in *Abḥāth al-nadwa tarjamat maᶜānī al-Qurʾān: taqwīm li-l-māḍī wa-takhṭīṭ li-l-mustaqbal*, 3 vols (Medina: King Fahd Glorious Qur'an Printing Complex, 2002)

—— *Nobre Alcorão: para a língua portuguesa* (Medina: King Fahd Glorious Qur'an Printing Complex, 2006)

Nawfal, Ahmad, *Methodical Interpretation of The Noble Qur'ān: Part 30* (Riyadh: Darussalam, 2020)

Nazifoff, Natanail, 'The Bulgarian Koran', *The Muslim World*, 23.2 (1933), 187–90

Nimer, Mohamed, *The North American Muslim Resource Guide: Muslim Community Life* (London–New York: Taylor & Francis Ltd, 2002)

Nöldeke, Theodor, *Geschichte des Qorâns* (Göttingen: Verlag der Dieterichschen Buchhandlung, 1860)

—— *Geschichte des Qorāns* (Leipzig: Dieterich, 1909)

Nursî, Bedîüzzaman Said, *Tevafukat i-Kuraniye Dair*, https://hizmetvakfi.org/ekitap/TEVAFUK-kitapcigi.pdf

Ochsenwald, William, 'The Transformation of Education in the Hijaz, 1925–1945', *Arabian Humanities Journal*, 12 (2019), 1–25, https://doi.org/10.4000/cy.4917

Omar, Faraz, 'Interview with Umm Muhammad of Saheeh International', *Muslimink*, 26 February 2015, https://www.muslimink.com/society/interview/interview-umm-muhammad-saheeh-intl/

O Sagrado Alcorao (Tilford: Islam International Publications, 1988)

Ould Bah, Mohamed El-Moktar, *Le Saint Coran, tr. par Mohamed El-Moktar Ould Bah* (Casablanca: Maktabat al-Najah, 2001)

—— (Walad Abbāh, Muḥammad al-Mukhtār), *Tārīkh al-qirāʾāt fī al-mashriq wa-l-maghrib* (Sale: ISESCO, 2001)

—— *Le Noble Coran et la traduction en langue française de ses sens* (Medina: King Fahd Glorious Qur'an Printing Complex, 2007)

Özek, Ali, Hayrettin Karaman, Ali Turgut, Mustafa Çağrıcı, İbrahim Kafi, Dönmez, and Sadrettin Gümüş, *Kur'an-ı Kerim ve Açıklamalı Meali* (Istanbul: Ayyıldız Matbaası, 1982)

Ozkan, Behlul, 'Cold War Era Relations Between West Germany and Turkish Political Islam', in *Islam, Populism and Regime Change in Turkey: Making and Re-making the AKP*, ed. by M. Hakan Yavuz and Ahmet Erdi Öztürk (London—New York: Routledge, 2020), pp. 31–54

Pasha, Neha, 'Translation of the Qurʾān: A Study of Saheeh International', *Aligarh Journal of Qur'anic Studies*, 3.2 (2020), 91–99

Pazarbaşı, Erdoğan, 'Kur'an'ın Azerbaycan'da Yaygın Tefsir ve Tercümeleri', *Bilig*, 25 (2003), 73–97

Peres de Oliveira, Vitória, 'Islam in Brazil or the Islam of Brazil?', *Religião & Sociedade*, 2 (2006), 1–20

Perevod smyslov Blagorodnyi Kur'an na ruskom jazyke (Riyadh: Darussalam, 2009).

Piccardo, Hamza Roberto, *Il Corano* ([n. p.]: Newton & Compton, 1994)

—— Pino Blasone, and Grandi tascabili economici Newton, *Il Corano* (Rome: Grandi tascabili economici Newton, 1996)

—— *Il Nobile Corano e la tradizione dei suoi significati in lingua Italiana* (Medina: King Fahd Glorious Qur'an Printing Complex, 2011)

—— *Il Sacro Corano: traduzione interpretativa in italiano* (Ankara: TDRA, 2015)

Pickthall, Muhammad Marmaduke, *The Meaning of the Glorious Qur'an* (Hyderabad-Deccan: Government Central Press, 1938)

—— *The Meaning of the Glorious Qur'an. Text and Explanatory Translation by Muhammad Marmaduke Pickthall* (Mecca: Muslim World League, 1977)

Pillars of Islam: Shahadah & Salah (Riyadh: Darussalam, 1995)

Pink, Johanna, *Muslim Qur'anic Interpretation Today: Media, Genealogies and Interpretive Communities* (Bristol: Equinox, 2019), https://doi.org/10.1558/isbn.9781781797051

—— 'Eight Shades of Ibn Kathīr: The Afterlives of a Premodern Qurʾānic Commentary in Contemporary Indonesian Translations', in *Malay-Indonesian Islamic Studies*, ed. by Majid Daneshgar and Ervan Nurtawab (Leiden: Brill, 2022), pp. 109–33, https://doi.org/10.1163/9789004529397_006

—— 'Translation', in *The Routledge Companion to the Qur'an*, ed. by George Archer, Maria Dakake, and Daniel Madigan (London: Routledge, 2022), pp. 364–76, http://doi.org/10.4324/9781315885360-36

—— 'Qur'an Translation of the Week #152: Between Mauritius and Saudi Arabia: The Trilingual Qur'an Translations of Houssein Nahaboo', 14 April 2023, https://gloqur.de/quran-translation-of-the-week-152-between-mauritius-and-saudi-arabia-the-trilingual-quran-translations-of-houssein-nahaboo/

—— Riḍā, Rashīd', in *Encyclopaedia of the Qurʾān*, https://referenceworks.brillonline.com/entries/encyclopaedia-of-the-quran/*-EQCOM_050503#d110807225e792

Plemeniti Kur'an Prijevod značenja na bosanski jezik (Riyadh: Jamāᶜat al-Daᶜwa wa-l-Irshād al-Taʾwiyya al-Jāliyāt bi-l-Rabwa, 1444/2022)

al-Qaṭṭān, Mannᶜā, *Mabāḥith fī ᶜulūm al-Qurʾān* (Cairo: Dār Wahba, 2000)

Quliyev, Elmir, *Sviashchennyĭ Koran: Smyslovoi perevod na ruskij jazyk* (Medina: King Fahd Glorious Qur'an Printing Complex, 1422/2002)

Qur'anEnc.com, *The Noble Qur'an Encyclopedia*, https://quranenc.com/en/home

Qur'ānī Pīrūz (Medina: King Fahd Glorious Qur'an Printing Complex, 1443/2020)

Qurani kerim ve Azerbaycan dilinde manaca tercümesi (Medina: King Fahd Glorious Qur'an Printing Complex, 1434/2013)

al-Qurṭubī, Abū ᶜAbd Allāh, *al-Jāmiᶜ li-aḥkām al-Qurʾān*, 11 vols (Beirut: Dār al-Kutub al-ᶜIlmiyya, 2013)

Radhouane, Nebil, *Le Noble Coran—Sens traduits et annotés par les soins du Pr Nebil Radhouane* (Riyadh: al-Muntada al-Islami, 2012)

Rahayul, Ely Triasih, and Ahmad Fauzan, 'The Language Choice as a Reflection of Islamic Communication in the Quran-Japanese Translation', *Madania*, 24.1 (2020), 73–82, http://dx.doi.org/10.29300/madania.v24i1.3073

'Rāḥil al-ʿAllāma ʿAbd al-ʿAzīz Ismāʿīl, ṣāḥib *al-Tafsīr al-muyassar*', https://al-maktaba.org/book/31617/71606

Ramadani, Zymer, 'Tarihte Yapılmış Arnavutça Kur'an Mealleri', *Marife*, 6.2 (2006), 241–47, https://doi.org/10.5281/zenodo.3343729

al-Rasheed, Madawi, 'God, the King and the Nation: Political Rhetoric in Saudi Arabia in the 1990s', *Middle East Journal*, 50.3 (1996), 359–71

Riyad, Umar, 'A Salafi Student, Orientalist Scholarship, and Radio Berlin in Nazi Germany: Taqi al-Din al-Hilali and His Experiences in the West', in *Transnational Islam in Interwar Europe*, ed. by G. Nordbruch and U. Ryad (New York: Palgrave Macmillan, 2014), pp. 107–55, https://doi.org/10.1057/9781137387042_6

Sabjan, Muhammad Azizan, 'The Al-Sābiʾūn (the Sabians) in the Quran: An Overview from the Quranic Commentators, Theologians, and Jurists', *Journal of Religious & Theological Information*, 13 (2014), 79–87

al-Saʿdī, Nāṣir b. ʿAbd Allāh, *Taysīr al-Karīm al-Raḥmān fī tafsīr kalām al-mannān* (Riyadh: Darussalam, 2002)

Saheeh International, ed., *The Qur'an: Arabic Text with Corresponding English Meanings* (Jeddah: Abul-Qasim Publishing House, 1997)

—— *The Qur'an: Arabic Text with English Meanings* (Riyadh: Dar Aljumuah, 2019)

Sajjadi, Seyyed Jaʿfar, 'Abū ʿAbd Allāh al-Zanjānī', trans. by Nacim Pak, in *Encyclopaedia Islamica*, ed. by Farhad Daftary and Wilferd Madelung, http://dx.doi.org/10.1163/1875-9831_isla_COM_0034

Saleh, Walid A., 'Ibn Taymiyya and the Rise of Radical Hermeneutics: An Analysis of an Introduction to the Foundations of Qur'anic Exegesis', in *Ibn Taymiyya and His Times*, ed. by S. Ahmed and Y. Rapoport (Oxford: Oxford University Press, 2010), 123–62

—— 'Preliminary Remarks on the Historiography of *tafsīr* in Arabic: A History of the Book Approach', *Journal of Qur'anic Studies* 12 (2010), 6–40, http://doi.org/10.3366/jqs.2010.0103

Sāliḥ, Bayān, *Tarjamat maʿānī juzʾ ʿamma. Al-Lugha al-Tijriniyā* (Riyadh: al-Maktab al-Taʿāwunī li-l-Daʿwa wa-l-Irshād wa-Tawʿiyyat al-Jāliyāt bi-Umm Hammām, [n. d.])

Saudi Arabian Cultural Mission to the U.S., 'SACM History', http://www.sacm.org/about/history

'Saudi-Based Publisher Introduces Punjabi Translation of Holy Quran', *Daily Pakistan*, 14 November 2020, https://en.dailypakistan.com.pk/14-Nov-2020/saudi-based-publisher-introduces-punjabi-translation-of-holy-quran

'al-Saᶜūdiyya wazaᶜat 270 milyūn nuskhat al-Qurᵓān al-karīm mundhu 1985', *al-Iqtiṣādiyya*, 27 December 2013. https://www.aleqt.com/2013/12/27/article_810812.html

Schimmel, Annemarie, 'Translations and Commentaries of the Qurᵓān in Sindhi Language', *Oriens*, 16 (1963), 233–35

Schulze, Reinhard, *Islamischer Internationalismus im 20. Jahrhundert: Untersuchungen zur Geschichte der Islamischen Weltliga* (Leiden: Brill, 1990)

Shaybūb, al-Ḥabīb, *al-Ṣiḥāfī al-adīb Nūr al-Dīn b. Maḥmūd: ḥayātuhu wa-mukhtārāt min kitābihi* (Tunis: Wizārat al-Thaqāfa, 2000)

al-Shibaylī, ᶜAbd al-Raḥman, 'Risālat al-Qurᵓān: tarjamat Muḥammad Asad li-l-muṣḥaf al-sharīf', *al-Sharq al-awsaṭ*, 15 June 2017, p. 7

Solihu, Abdul Kabir Hussain, 'The Earliest Yoruba Translation of the Qur'an: Missionary Engagement with Islam in Yorubaland', *Journal of Qur'anic Studies*, 17.3 (2015), 10–37

al-Ṣubḥī, Yūsuf, *Wisām al-kiram fī tarājim aᵓima wa-khuṭabāᵓ al-haram* (Beirut: Dār al-Bashāᵓīr, 2004)

Sveschen Koran. Prevod Nedim Gendzhyjev (Sofia: Kral Fahd bin Abdul Aliz, 1993)

Svyachennyi Koran. Smyslovoi perevod s kommentariyami, red. Damir Mukhetdinov (Moscow: ID Medina, 2015)

al-Ṭabarī, *Jāmiᶜ al-bayān ᶜan tāᵓwīl āy al-Qurᵓān*, 16 vols (Cairo: Dār Hijr, 2001)

al-Tafsīr al-mawḍūᶜī li-l-suwar al-Qurᵓān al-karīm (Sharjah: Jāmiᶜa al-Shāriqa, 2010)

al-Tafsīr al-muyassar (Medina: King Fahd Glorious Qur'an Printing Complex, 2019)

Tājī, Ḥusayn, and ᶜAbd al-Ghafūr Ḥusayn, *Tafsīr aḥsan al-kalām bi-zobān-Fārisī* (Riyadh: Darussalam, 2012)

Ṭāhir, Aḥmad, *Jamāᶜat anṣār al-sunna al-Muḥammadiyya: nashātuhā, ahdāfuhā, minhajuhā wa-juhūduhā* (Algiers: Dār al-Faḍīla, 2004)

al-Ṭāᶜī, Kamāl al-Dīn, *Muᶜjiz al-bayān fī al-mabāḥith takhtaṣṣu bi-l-Qurᵓān* (Baghdad: Maṭbaᶜat al-Tafayyiḍ al-Ahliyya, 1940)

Taqrīr al-mujammaᶜ (Medina: King Fahd Glorious Qur'an Printing Complex, 2003) al-Ṭarāzī, Maḥmūd, *Qurʾān karīm, mutarjam wa-muḥassuhā bi-l-lugha al-Turkistāniyya* (Medina: Dār al-Imān, 1975)

—— *Tawḥīd kitābī* (Riyadh: Ministry of Islamic Affairs, Call, and Guidance of the Kingdom of Saudi Arabia, [n. d.])

'Tarjamat maᶜānī al-Qurʾān al-karīm ilā al-Iṭāliyya', *Alfaisal Magazine*, 128 (1987), 113–14

'Tarjamat maᶜānī al-Qurʾān bayn al-taᶜāyid wa-l-taḥrim', *Majallat al-buḥūth al-Islamiyya*, 12 (1405/1985), 311–25

'Tarjamat al-Qurʾān shabīha bi-baᶜḍ ᶜamaliyyāt zaraᶜa al-aᶜḍāʾ', *al-Quds al-ᶜArabī*, 14 June 2006, https://www.alquds.co.uk/ترجمة-القرآن-شبيهة-ببعض-عمليات-زرع-ال/

Telci, Ismail, and Aydzhan Peneva, 'Turkey and Saudi Arabia as Theo-Political Actors in the Balkans', *Insight Turkey*, 21.2 (2019), 249–52

Teofanov, Tsvetan, *Prevod na Sveschenija Koran. Prevede Tsvetan Teofanov* (Sofia: Tayba, 1997)

Terem, Etty, 'Muslim Men, European Hats: A *fatwā* on Cultural Appropriation in a Global Age', *The Journal of North African Studies*, 28.3 (2023), 563–88, https://doi.org/10.1080/13629387.2021.1973246

The Lebanese National Library, 'Viscount Philippe de Tarrazi', http://bnl.gov.lb/english/Tarrazi.html

The Noble Qur'an: Translation of the Meanings and Commentary (Medina: King Fahd Glorious Qur'an Printing Complex, 1997)

The Qur'an (Riyadh: Noor International, 2019)

The Qur'an in Bulgarian (Tilford: International Islamic Publishing House, 1989)

Tolan, John, 'Blasphemy and Protection of the Faith: Legal Perspectives from the Middle Ages', *Islam and Christian–Muslim Relations*, 27.1 (2016), 35–50

Topan, Faruk, 'Polemics and Language in Swahili Translations of the Qur'an: Mubarak Ahmad (d. 2001), Abdullah Saleh al-Farsy (d. 1982) and Ali Muhsin al-Barwani (d. 2006)', in *The Qur'an and its Readers Worldwide*, ed. by Suha Taji-Farouki (New York: Oxford University Press in Association with the Institute of Ismaili Studies, London, 2015), pp. 491–501

al-Traif, Hamad bin Ibrahim, 'Révision de la Traduction Coranique de Hamidullah par le Complexe du Roi Fahd (CRF): (Sourate Al-Hajj en tant que modèle)', *Altralang Journal*, 3.1 (2021), 26–50.

'Translators' Experiences I: Amatullah "AJ" Bantley, Saheeh International', *YouTube*, https://www.youtube.com/watch?v=k4JPZTHCnvo

'Turkistan is not Alone', *Anti-Bolshevik Bloc of Nations Correspondence*, III.5 (1952), 2–3

Tūtūnjī, Aḥmad, *Sittūn ʿāmman bayn al-sharq wa-l-gharb: al-takhṭīṭ wa-l-muthābara wa-l-tanfīdh* (Amman: Dār Fan, 2022)

al-ʿUnayzī, Sulaymān, *Qirʾa fī niẓām al-maṭbūʿāt wa-l-nashr al-Saʿūdī* (Riyadh: al-Muntadā al-ʿAlāmī al-Sanawī al-Awwal, 1424/2003)

al-ʿUtaybī, Ibrāhīm, 'Bidāyat tārīkh al-maṭābiʿ wa-l-nashr fī al-mamlaka', *Majallat al-fayṣal*, 247 (1997), 60–64

al-ʿUthaymīn, Muḥammad, *Tafsīr al-Qurʾān al-karīm*, 36 vols (Qasim: Muʾassasat Muḥammad b. Ṣāliḥ al-ʿUthaymīn al-Khayriyya, 1436/2014)

van de Bruinhorst, Gerard C., 'Changing Criticism of Swahili Qur'an Translations: The Three "Rods of Moses"', *Journal of Qur'anic Studies*, 15.3 (2013), 206–31, https://doi.org/10.3366/jqs.2013.0118

Vidino, Lorenzo, 'The Muslim Brotherhood's Conquest of Europe', *Middle East Quarterly*, (2005), 25–34

Wajdī, Muḥammad Farīd, *al-Adilla al-ʿilmiyya ʿalā jawāz tarjamat maʿānī al-Qurʾān ilā al-lughāt al-ajnabiyya* (Cairo: Maṭbaʿat al-Maʿāhid al-Dīniyya, 1936)

Wild, Stefan, 'Muslim Translators and Translations of the Qur'an into English', *Journal of Qur'anic Studies*, 17.3 (2015), 158–82, https://doi.org/10.3366/jqs.2015.0215

Wilson, M. Brett, *Translating the Qur'an in an Age of Nationalism: Print Culture and Modern Islam in Turkey* (Oxford: Oxford University Press, 2014)

Yacquub, Cabdicaziiz Xasan, *Kuraanka Kariimka. Y Waxaa Tarjumay C. Xasan Yacquub*, 2 vols (Riyadh: Darussalam, 2020)

Yakubovych, Mykhaylo, *Preslavnyi Koran. Pereklad smysliv Ukrainskoju movoju* (Medina: King Fahd Glorious Qur'an Printing Complex, 2013)

——'Qur'an Translations into Central Asian Languages: Exegetical Standards and Translation Processes', *Journal of Qur'anic Studies*, 24.1 (2022), 89–115, https://doi.org/10.3366/jqs.2022.0491

—— 'The First Vernacular Tafsir in the Caucasus: The Legacy of Two 20th Century Azerbaijani Qurʾān Commentaries', *Australian Journal of Islamic Studies*, 7.1 (2022), 72–95, https://doi.org/10.55831/ajis.v7i1.457

—— 'Nieznane tłumaczenie Koranu', *Przegląd Tatarski*, 1 (2023), 23–25

Yusuf Ali, Abdullah, *The Holy Qur'an. An Interpretation in English, with the Original Arabic Text in Parallel Columns, a Running Rhythmic Commentary in English, and Full Explanatory Notes, by Allamah Abdullah Yusuf Ali* (Lahore: Shaikh Muhammad Ashraf, 1934)

—— *The Holy Qurʾān: English Translation of the Meanings, and Commentary by Abdullah Yusuf Ali* (Medina: King Fahd Glorious Qur'an Printing Complex, 1985)

—— *The Holy Quran: Text, Translation and Commentary by A. Y. Ali* (New York: Hafner Publishing Company, 1946)

—— *The Holy Qur'an: Text, Translation and Commentary by A. Y. Ali* (Mecca: Muslim World League, 1965)

—— *The Holy Qur'an. Tr. By Abdullah Yusuf Ali* (Ankara: TDRA, 2018)

Zadeh, Travis, 'The *Fātiḥa* of Salmān al-Fārisī and the Modern Controversy over Translating the Qurʾān', in *The Meaning of the Word: Lexicology and Qur'anic Exegesis*, ed. by Stephen Burge (Oxford: Institute of Ismaili Studies–Oxford University Press, 2015), pp. 375–420

Zaman, Muhammad Qasim, 'Shāh Walī Allāh of Delhi, His Successors, and the Qurʾān', in *Ways of Knowing Muslim Cultures and Societies*, ed. by Bettina Gräf, Birgit Krawietz, and Schirin Amir-Moazami (Leiden: Brill, 2019), pp. 280-297

al-Zanjānī, Abū ᶜAbd Allāh, *Tārīkh al-Qurʾān* (Cairo: Lajnat al-Tāʾlīf wa-l-Tarjama wa-l-Nashr, 1935)

Zawadski, Katie, 'How Three American Women Translated One of the World's Most Popular Qurans', *Daily Beast*, 26 March 2017, https://www.thedailybeast.com/how-three-american-women-translated-one-of-the-worlds-most-popular-qurans.

Ziyādah, Mayy, *al-Musāwwāh* (Cairo: Hindāwī, 2013)

al-Zurqānī, Muḥammad, *Manāhil al-ᶜirfān fī ᶜulūm al-Qurʾān*, 4 vols (Beirut: Dār al-Kitāb al-ᶜArabī, 1995)

Index

ᶜAbduh, Muḥammad 40
Aberdeen 69
Abu Adel 169
Abu Bakr, Amin al-Din 78
Abū Suᶜūd, Muḥammad 48
Aḥmad, Aḥsan Shāh 12
Ahmadiyya 96, 141
Ahmeti, Sherif 104–106
Akanni, Tijani A. 50
Āl al-Shaykh, ᶜAbd al-Raḥman b. Ḥasan 27–28, 178
al-Alūsī, Shihāb al-Dīn 48
al-Amri, Waleed Bleyhesh 181
al-Andijānī, Muḥammad Amīn 149
Al-Azhar 10, 12–14, 16–17, 19, 21, 26–27, 29–32, 69, 96, 110, 112, 124, 131–133, 177
al-Azhar 15–16
al-Baghawī, al-Ḥusayn b. Masᶜūd 27, 114, 124, 172
Albanian 54, 104–106, 116, 136, 164, 173
al-Bannā, Ḥasan 59, 69
al-Barwānī, ᶜAlī Muḥsin 164
al-Bayṭār, Muḥammad Bahja 25–26
al-Bulūshī, ᶜAbd al-Gafūr 118
Al-Chinquity, Ahmad 101
Al-Faruqi, Ismail 156
al-Fawzān, Ṣāliḥ b. Fawzān 127–128
al-Fiqī, ᶜAbd al-Muhaymin 23, 132
al-Ghāzalī, Abu Ḥāmid 21, 29
al-Ḥajjawī, Muḥammad b. al-Ḥasan 94–96
al-Ḥasanayn, ᶜAlī al-Fātiḥ 51–52
al-Hilālī, Muḥammad Taqī al-Dīn 32, 40, 55–63, 67–72, 79, 83, 86–87, 148, 154–155, 180
Ali, Abdullah Yusuf 29, 41–43, 45, 54, 63, 65, 77, 81–84, 94, 96–101, 117–118, 126, 142, 154–155, 158–159, 167
Ali, Liaquat 64
Ali, Muhammad 11, 40
al-Jazaʾīrī, Abū Bakr 121
al-Karmī, Ḥāzim Ḥaydar 124
al-Makkī, Muḥammad b. Ṭāhir al-Kurdī 29, 31
al-Marāghī, Muḥammad 12–14, 16, 31, 39
al-Maṣrī, M. Amīn 68–69
al-Maʾāyrigī, Ḥasan 93, 107
al-Nadwī, ᶜAbd Allāh ᶜAbbās 44–46
al-Nafīsī, Khālid 92
al-Qannawjī, Ṣiddīq Ḥasan Khān 105
al-Qāsimī, Jamāl al-Dīn 25
al-Qaṭṭān, Mannᶜā 155
al-Rāzī, Fakhr al-Dīn 105
al-Ṣabbān, Muḥammad Sarūr 39
al-Saᶜdī, ᶜAbd al-Raḥmān b. Nāṣir 114, 119, 121, 127, 130, 158, 172, 180
Āl Saᶜūd, Fayṣal b. ᶜAbd al-ᶜAzīz 35, 59
al-Shaghār, Nāṣir 91
al-Shāṭibī, Abu Isḥāq 21
al-Shilbī, ᶜAbd al-Jalīl 132
al-Shinqīṭī, Muḥammad al-Mukhtār 102, 124, 173
al-Shinqīṭī, ᶜAbd Allāh 102, 124
al-Sindī, Muḥammad Ḥayyāt 11
al-Suyūṭī, Jalāl al-Dīn 29
al-Ṭabarī, Abū Jaᶜfar 27, 70, 75, 114, 124, 126, 135, 172–173, 180
al-Ṭarāzī, Maḥmūd 148–152
Altay, Halifa 106–109
al-Ṭayyār, Musāᶜid 173
al-Ṭāᶜī, Kamāl al-Dīn 26
al-Vaniyāmbādī,ᶜAbd al-Raḥīm (V. Abdur Rahim) 112
al-Wajdī, Muḥammad Farīd 16–17, 31
al-Zanjānī, Abū ᶜAbd Allāh 18–19

al-Ẓawāhirī, Muḥammad al-Aḥmadī 12–13
al-Zurqānī, Muḥammad 17–21, 23
al-ᶜAshqar, ᶜUmar b. Sulaymān 169
al-ᶜAẓmī, Muḥī ad-Dīn 68–69
al-ᶜUlī, Ibrāhīm b. ᶜAbd al-ᶜAzīz 182
al-ᶜUthaymīn, Muḥammad b. Ṣāliḥ 181
Ankara 65, 80, 100
Arabic 1–2, 5, 9–11, 14–15, 18–19, 22, 24–26, 29–31, 35, 38, 44–47, 50, 52, 56–57, 59, 63, 65, 67–68, 70, 72–74, 78, 90–93, 95, 97, 100–101, 105–108, 110, 112–114, 116–119, 122–123, 125–127, 130–142, 144–147, 149, 151, 153–154, 156, 158, 163, 165–166, 168–169, 172–175, 177–178, 180, 183
Assami, Emily (Umm Muhammad) 152–153
Ateş, Süleyman 46
Aṭfayyash, Muḥammad 121
Augusto, Muhammadul-Awwal 50
Azerbaijanian 117, 138–140

Bāballī, Maḥmūd 102
Baghdad 59
Bakhtyar, Laleh 160
Baku 138–140
Bantley, Amatullah ('AJ') 153
Beirut 65
Bello, Ahmadu Ibrahim 49–50, 103
Berlin 56, 59
Bilāl, Khalīl Jihād 117, 132
Bilaloğlu, Tariyel 138
Bodley, R. V. C. 31
Bosnian 42, 105, 109–111, 116, 136, 138, 169, 182
Bucaillism 181
Buddhism 45, 113
Bukhara 148
Bulgarian 51–54, 138
Bunyadov, Ziya 138

Çağrıcı, Mustafa 47
Cairo 29–30, 69, 91, 100, 132
Cambridge 69
Čaušević, Džemaludin 105
Channā, Amīr Buaksh 163–164
Chicago 64, 80
Chinese 36, 54, 115, 163
Christianity 9, 17–18, 45, 52, 67, 75–77, 84, 100–101, 110, 113, 129–131, 133, 135–137, 141–142, 158–159, 165, 169, 174, 179
colonialism 57, 59
commentary 6, 9, 22, 28, 30, 48, 70, 72–73, 77–79, 97–101, 103, 105, 108, 113, 119, 121–130, 132, 134, 137, 139, 141–143, 149–150, 157, 159, 164–167, 171–172, 174, 181
communism 54, 66, 105
Communities Awareness Bureau 125, 168–169
conservatism 49, 55, 60–61, 89, 159, 178
Crimean Tatar 49

Damascus 18, 153
Daouda, Boreima Abdou 165–166
Darussalam 6–7, 61, 71–80, 84, 86, 159–160, 162–167, 171, 181
Deedat, Ahmed 154
digitisation 7, 109, 111, 120, 128, 138, 143, 182–183
Dihlawī, Shāh Walī Allāh 10–11, 150, 164
Dindey, Hasani Yusau 50
Dobrev, Ivan 52
Doha 107
Dönmez, İbrahim Kafi 47
Dzanaltay, Dalilkhān 107
Dzilo, Hasan 117, 136–138

education 5, 16–17, 33
Elmalılı, Muhammed Hamdi Efendi 46–47
English 3, 6–7, 11, 14, 21, 29, 31–32, 36–38, 40, 42–45, 52, 54–59, 62–70, 72–73, 77–78, 83–84, 86–87, 94, 96–97, 99, 102, 111–112, 115, 118, 121, 125–126, 128, 130, 148, 152–156, 158–160, 162–165, 167, 169, 171, 174, 179–182
exegesis. *See* commentary

Fazıl, Riza 49
Feti Mehdiu 106
French 16, 36–37, 43, 59, 63, 66, 99–102, 111, 115, 121, 141, 162–163, 165, 169, 171, 175

Ganioğlu, Memmedhasan 138
Garcia, Isa 117, 171
Gasimzade, Nariman 138
Gendzev, Nedim 52
Geneva 38, 77
German 18, 21, 38, 42, 63, 66, 92, 96, 143, 169
Greek 95, 116–117, 131–134
Gumi, Abu Bakr Mahmud 50–51
Gümüş, Sadrettin 47

Hakimov, Shamsuddin 144
Hamidullah, Muhammad 3, 37, 43, 65–66, 99–104, 118, 166
Ḥāmid, ᶜAbd Allāh b. Muḥammad 70, 79
Hanafism 10, 21, 26, 68, 96, 129, 149–151, 177
Hanbalism 22, 26, 129, 177
Ḥaqqī Afandī, Ismāᶜīl 128
Hausa 50–51, 54
Hungarian 37, 53, 116
Ḥusayn, ᶜAbd al-Ghafūr 164

Ibn Bāz, ᶜAbd Allāh 41, 44, 60–61, 63, 71, 94, 166, 173
Ibn Jibrīn, ᶜAbd Allāh 169
Ibn Kathīr, al-ᶜImād Ismāᶜīl 27–28, 67, 70, 74, 77, 86, 105, 114, 124, 130, 155, 164, 169–170, 180
Ibn Qudāma 22
Ibn Taymiyya 5, 22–28, 32, 85, 120, 155, 178
Ibn ᶜAbd al-Wahhāb, Muḥammad 5, 11, 27, 127, 150, 178
Ibn ᶜAbd al-ᶜAzīz, Fahd b. 29, 35, 37–38, 51, 59, 89, 182
Indonesian 21, 109–111, 120, 165, 170
International Institute of Islamic Thought, IIIT 41, 99, 154, 156
Iqbal, Muhammad 65
IslamHouse 182
Islamic University of Madinah, IUM 5–6, 54–55, 59–61, 68–69, 92, 101, 105, 112, 115, 117, 124, 139, 165
Ismaᶜīl, ᶜAbd al-Azīz 124
Istanbul 5, 47, 67, 80, 107
Italian 53, 134–136, 175
Izetbegović, Alija 51

Japanese 36, 44–46, 51, 54
Jeddah 148, 153–154

Kaddoura, Omar 117
Karaman, Hayrettin 47
Karaoğlu, Fazıl 49
Kazakh 106–109, 111
Kazan 12, 30, 107
Kemalism 12
Kemal Pasha, Mustafa 13
Kennedy, Mary 153
Khān, Mīrzā ᶜAbd al-Karīm 148
Khān, Muḥammad Muḥsin 40, 55, 58–59, 61–64, 67–68, 71–72, 80, 83, 86–87, 148, 154–155, 180
Khattab, Mustafa 163
Khiyāṭ, ᶜAbd Allāh 121
Kidwai, Abdur Raheem 3, 159
King Fahd Glorious Qur'an Printing Complex, KFGQPC 5–6, 43, 46, 49–50, 52–54, 58, 68–72, 75, 77–80, 84, 86, 90–94, 96–103, 105, 107–125, 129, 131–136, 139–146, 152, 154, 158, 163–167, 169–171, 173, 179–183
Kirimal, Edige Mustafa 66
Korkut, Bessim 105, 110–111, 182
Kurdish 120
Kyrgyz 106, 115, 144

Lahore 61, 80, 96
Latsis, Marianna 132
Latsis, Yiannis 132
Leturmy, Michel 100
Libya. *See* Tripoli (Libya)
literacy 161
literality 13–14, 19, 25, 30, 48, 74, 77, 98, 103–104, 109, 113, 119, 125, 128–130, 137, 142–143, 150, 157–158, 174–175, 179–180

London 154
Lviv 37

Macedonian 53, 111, 116–117, 136–138
Madinah. *See* Islamic University of Madinah, IUM; *See* Medina
Malikism 21, 96, 129
Mammadaliyev, Vasim 138
Maududi, Abul A'la 65
Mecca 25, 29–30, 35, 38, 41–42, 70, 89, 91, 115, 117, 120, 138, 178
Medina 24, 63, 78, 80, 91–93, 120, 122, 138, 148, 173, 178
Ministry of Islamic Affairs, Call, and Guidance of the Kingdom of Saudi Arabia, MOIA 92, 115–116, 119–120, 124, 145, 150, 168
Mita, Umar (Ryoichi) 44–46
modernity 12, 17, 21, 26, 31, 35–36, 89, 97, 137, 161, 178
Monavar, Mohammad 73
Mujahid, Abdul Malik 72, 162
Musayev, Alikhan 138–140
Muslim World League, MWL 5, 33, 35–39, 41–54, 62, 64, 66, 70, 77, 93, 102, 105, 107, 109, 115, 141, 145–146, 162, 179

Nahaboo, Houssein 102
Nahi, Hasan 106
Nasr, Helmi 140–142
nationalism 12, 17
Navio, Abdel Ghani Melara 117
New Delhi 80
Nöldeke, Theodor 18–19
Noor International 159–160, 170–172

Old Industrial City Communities Awareness Bureau 168
Orientalism 31, 103, 132
Ottoman Empire 10, 12, 29–30
Ould Bah, Mohamed El-Moktar 99, 102–104
Özcan, Salih 65–68
Özek, Ali 47, 52, 108

Pandža, Muhammed 105
Paris 100, 169
Permanent Committee for Scholarly Research and Ifta, PCSRI 40–41, 44
Persian 9–11, 32, 46, 95–96, 118, 149–150, 163–164
Philips, Ameenah Bilaal 154
Piccardo, Hamza Roberto 134–136
Pickthall, Muhammad Marmaduke 14, 19, 43, 45, 64–65, 154, 158
Polish 66, 113
Portuguese 54, 121, 140–142, 145
Prishtina 104
Protestantism 55

Qāḍī, Yāsir 63
Qayumxon, Vali 151–152
Quevedo, Isa Amer 117
Quliyev, Elmir 115, 143

Rabat 59
Radhouane, Nebil 171
rationalism 24, 49, 74
Riḍā, Rashīd 12, 59
Riyadh 71, 80, 115, 123, 125, 132, 162, 168, 171
Rowwad Translation Center 182–183
Russian 12, 21, 49, 52–53, 70, 99, 107, 115, 117, 134, 139, 143, 163, 165, 169, 175, 179

Ṣabrī, Muṣtafā 12
Saheeh International 7, 87, 126, 130, 152–160, 169, 171, 178
Salafism 1–3, 6–7, 11, 21–26, 28, 30–32, 35, 40, 42–43, 48–51, 53, 56, 58–59, 61, 68–69, 74, 76–77, 79–80, 84–87, 90, 96, 98–99, 101, 104, 109, 111, 114–115, 121–122, 124, 127–128, 130–131, 134, 140, 143–145, 147, 150–151, 155, 157–159, 161, 163–164, 167–172, 175, 177–182
Salahi, Adil 163
Salih, Bayan 172
Schmiede, Hulusi Achmed 66

scientism 15, 49, 74, 85, 111, 178, 181–182
secularism 12, 35, 60, 94–95, 104
Sethi, Muhammad Yusuf 62
Shafiism 21, 30, 129
Shākir, Muḥammad Ḥabīb 12
Shiism 16, 18–19, 118, 139, 161, 168
Spanish 21, 42, 115, 117, 121, 163, 165, 169, 171, 173
Stetsko, Yaroslav 152
Sufism 28, 50, 127–128, 168
Sultanov, Aladdin 138, 140
Sunnism 1–2, 6–7, 10–11, 16, 18–19, 28–29, 40–42, 49, 56–57, 68, 84, 87, 90, 105, 111, 118–119, 128, 135, 137, 139–140, 143, 147, 150, 159, 161, 177, 179–180
Swahili 125, 128, 130, 164
Swedish 42, 116, 139
Szynkiewicz, Jakub 66

Tafsīr Centre for Qur'anic Studies, The 123
Taha, Ali Ismail 120
Ṭāhā, ᶜUthmān 93
Tājī, Ḥusayn 164
Tajik 115, 125–126, 128–130
Tamazight 139
de Tarrazi, Viscount Philippe 18
Tashkent 148
traditionalism 17, 26, 96, 99, 121
translatability 3, 5, 9–10, 12–13, 17, 21, 23, 29, 31, 58, 108, 113, 150, 177
Tripoli (Libya) 95, 105, 144
Tunis 100
Turgut, Ali 47
Turkish 12, 42, 46–49, 51–52, 54, 65–68, 70, 80, 99, 105, 107–109, 111, 132, 136–137, 139, 144, 164–165
Turkish Directorate of Religious Affairs, TDRA 67, 99, 109, 135–136, 144
Turkish-Islamic Union for Religious Affairs, DITIB 66
Turkish Religious Foundation, TDV 49

Ukrainian vii, 53, 100, 125, 128, 143–144, 152
Ülker, Sabri 67
United Nations 43, 64, 161
Urdu 32, 96, 163
Uzbek 70, 79, 108, 115, 148–152, 179

Wahhabism 1, 11, 21, 24, 27–28, 32, 51, 55, 86, 167–168, 178–179
Wajīh, ᶜAbd al-Raḥman 78
World Assembly of Muslim Youth, WAMY 52
World Islamic Call Society, WICS 91, 105, 144

Yacquub, Cabdicaziiz Xasan 164
Yoruba 36, 49–51, 54

Zahir, Fazal Elahi 78
Ziyādah, Mayy 16

About the Team

Alessandra Tosi was the managing editor for this book.

Jennifer Moriarty and Cecilia Thon copy-edited this book.

Jennifer Moriarty created the index for this book.

Jeevanjot Kaur Nagpal designed the cover. The cover was produced in InDesign using the Fontin font.

Cameron Craig typeset the book in InDesign and produced the paperback and hardback editions. The text font is Tex Gyre Pagella and the heading font is Californian FB.

Cameron also produced the PDF, EPUB, XML and HTML editions. The conversion was performed with open-source software and other tools freely available on our GitHub page at https://github.com/OpenBookPublishers.

This book has been anonymously peer-reviewed by experts in their field. We thank them for their invaluable help.

This book need not end here...

Share

All our books — including the one you have just read — are free to access online so that students, researchers and members of the public who can't afford a printed edition will have access to the same ideas. This title will be accessed online by hundreds of readers each month across the globe: why not share the link so that someone you know is one of them?

This book and additional content is available at:
https://doi.org/10.11647/OBP.0381

Donate

Open Book Publishers is an award-winning, scholar-led, not-for-profit press making knowledge freely available one book at a time. We don't charge authors to publish with us: instead, our work is supported by our library members and by donations from people who believe that research shouldn't be locked behind paywalls.

Why not join them in freeing knowledge by supporting us:
https://www.openbookpublishers.com/support-us

Follow @OpenBookPublish

Read more at the Open Book Publishers BLOG

You may also be interested in:

The Official Indonesian Qurʾān Translation

The History and Politics of Al-Qur'an dan Terjemahnya

Fadhli Lukman

https://doi.org/10.11647/obp.0289

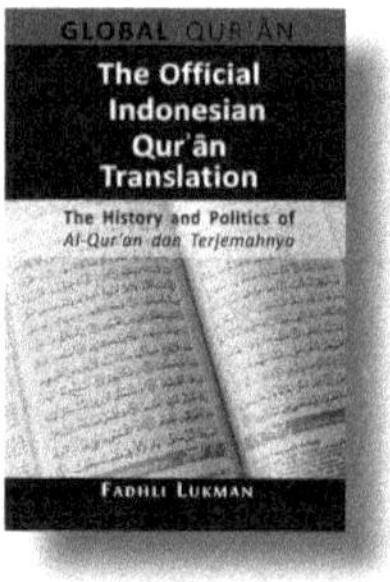

Jewish-Muslim Intellectual History Entangled

Textual Materials from the Firkovitch Collection, Saint Petersburg

Camilla Adan, Bruno Chiesa, Omar Hamdan, Wilferd Madelung, Sabine Schmidtke, and Jan Thiele(editors)

https://doi.org/10.11647/obp.0214

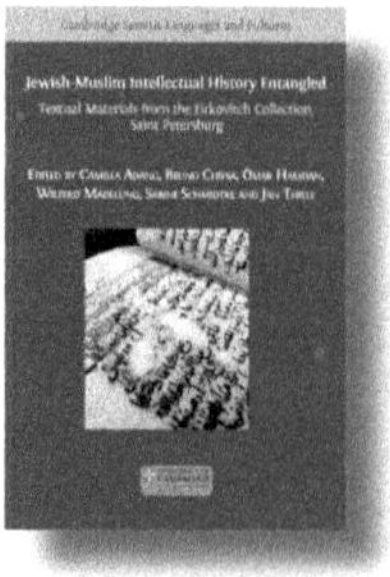

Points of Contact

The Shared Intellectual History of Vocalisation in Syriac, Arabic, and Hebrew

Nick Posegay

https://doi.org/10.11647/obp.0271

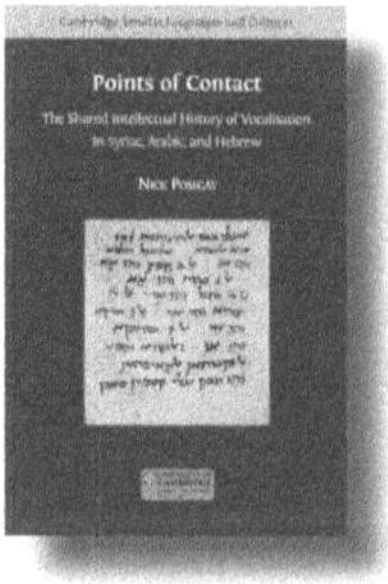

www.ingramcontent.com/pod-product-compliance
Lightning Source LLC
Chambersburg PA
CBHW050524170426
43201CB00013B/2076